AF658093

GENETICS AND BIOENGINEERING

CONCEPTS AND ISSUES

ENV BOOKS SERIES

GENETICS AND BIOENGINEERING

CONCEPTS AND ISSUES

Editors

Dr. Ashok K. Rathoure

GM-Consultancy

Eco Group of Companies

New Civil Road

Surat (GJ) (India)

&

Dr. Pawan Kumar 'Bharti'

Society for Environment, Health

Awareness of Nutrition & Toxicology (SEHAT)

B-225/5D, Top Floor, Subhash Gali, Road No. 7, Block B

Ashok Nagar, Shahdara

Delhi-110093

(India)

DPH

DISCOVERY PUBLISHING HOUSE PVT. LTD.

INDIA

Published by:
Namit Wasan

DISCOVERY PUBLISHING HOUSE PVT. LTD.
4383/4B, Ansari Road, Darya Ganj
New Delhi-110 002 (India)
Phone : +91-11-23279245; 23253475; 43596065
E-mail : discoverybooksindia@gmail.com
discoverypublishinghouse@gmail.com
namitwasan9@gmail.com
web : www.discoverypublishinggroup.com

***First Edition:* 2019**

ISBN: 978-93-86841-92-6

Genetics and Bioengineering: ***Concepts and Issues***

© Editors

All rights reserved. No part of this publication should be reproduced, stored in a retrieval system, or transmitted in any form or by any means: electronic, mechanical, photocopying, recording or otherwise, without the prior written permission of the author and the publisher.

This book has been published in good faith that the material provided by authors/editors is original. Every effort is made to ensure accuracy of material, but the publisher and printer will not be held responsible for any inadvertent error(s). In case of any dispute, all legal matters are to be settled under Delhi jurisdiction only.

Printed at:
Infinity Imaging Systems
Delhi

PREFACE

Genetics is the study of genes, genetic variation, and heredity in living organisms. It is generally considered a field of biology, but intersects frequently with many other life sciences and is strongly linked with the study of information systems. The discoverer of genetics is Gregor Mendel, a late 19th-century scientist and Augustinian friar. Mendel studied "trait inheritance", patterns in the way traits are handed down from parents to offspring. He observed that organisms (pea plants) inherit traits by way of discrete "units of inheritance". This term, still used today, is a somewhat ambiguous definition of what is referred to as a gene. Trait inheritance and molecular inheritance mechanisms of genes are still primary principles of genetics in the 21st century, but modern genetics has expanded beyond inheritance to studying the function and behavior of genes. Gene structure and function, variation, and distribution are studied within the context of the cell, the organism (e.g. dominance), and within the context of a population. Genetics has given rise to a number of subfields, including epigenetics and population genetics. Organisms studied within the broad field span the domains of life..

Genetic processes work in combination with an organism's environment and experiences to influence development and behavior, often referred to as nature versus nurture. The intracellular or extracellular environment of a cell or organism may switch gene transcription on or off. A classic example is two seeds of genetically identical corn, one placed in a temperate climate and one in an arid climate. While the average height of the two corn stalks may be genetically determined to be equal, the one in the arid climate only grows to half the height of the one in the temperate climate due to lack of water and nutrients in its environment.

The present book updates the subject content of genetic variation, heredity, next generation sequencing, modern molecular techniques, genetically improved organisms, RNA binding, assessment of genetic diversity, screening for protein content, bioinformatics, and tools for recombinant antibody production.

Thanks are due to publisher and contributors from various institutions and universities.

The book will be helpful for the researchers, academia working in the field of genetic variation, heredity, next generation sequencing, modern molecular techniques, genetically improved organisms, RNA binding, assessment of genetic diversity, screening for protein content and bioinformatics.

Editors
(envbooks@gmail.com)

CONTENTS

Genetics and Bioengineering : *Concepts and Issues* **Pages 1-6**
Edited by: **Dr. Ashok K. Rathoure and Dr. Pawan Kumar 'Bharti'**
ISBN: 978-93-86841-92-6
Edition: **2019**
Published by: **Discovery Publishing House Pvt. Ltd., New Delhi (India)**

1 Introduction

Genetics is the study of heredity and variations. Heredity and variations are controlled by genes—what they are, what they do, and how they work. Genes inside the nucleus of a cell are strung together in such a way that the sequence carries information: that information determines how living organisms inherit various features (phenotypic traits). For example, offspring produced by sexual reproduction usually look similar to each of their parents because they have inherited some of each of their parents' genes. Genetics identifies which features are inherited, and explains how these features pass from generation to generation. In addition to inheritance, genetics studies how genes are turned on and off to control what substances are made in a cell—gene expression; and how a cell divides—mitosis or meiosis.

Some phenotypic traits can be seen, such as eye color while others can only be detected, such as blood type or intelligence. Traits determined by genes can be modified by the animal's surroundings (environment): for example, the general design of a tiger's stripes is inherited, but the specific stripe pattern is determined by the tiger's surroundings. Another example is a person's height: it is determined by both genetics and nutrition.

Chromosomes are tiny packages which contain one DNA molecule and its associated proteins. Humans have 46 chromosomes (23 pairs). This number varies between species—for example, many primates have 24 pairs. Meiosis creates special cells, sperm in males and eggs in females, which only have 23 chromosomes. These two cells merge into one during the fertilization stage of sexual reproduction, creating a zygote. In a zygote, a nucleic acid double helix divides, with each single helix occupying one of the daughter cells, resulting in half the normal number of genes. By the time the zygote divides again, genetic recombination has created a new embryo with 23 pairs of chromosomes, half from each parent. Mating and resultant mate choice result in sexual selection. In normal cell division (mitosis) is possible when the double helix separates, and a complement of each separated half is made, resulting in two identical double helices in one cell, with each occupying one of the two new daughter cells created when the cell divides.

Chromosomes all contain DNA made up of four nucleotides, abbreviated C (cytosine), G (guanine), A (adenine), or T (thymine), which line up in a particular sequence and make a long string. There are two strings of nucleotides coiled around one another in each chromosome: a double helix. C on one string is always opposite from G on the other string; A is always opposite T. There are about 3.2 billion nucleotide pairs on all the human chromosomes: this is the human genome. The order of the nucleotides carries genetic information, whose rules are defined by the genetic code, similar to how the order of letters on a page of text carries information. Three nucleotides in a row—a triplet—carry one unit of information: a codon.

The genetic code not only controls inheritance: it also controls gene expression, which occurs when a portion of the double helix is uncoiled, exposing a series of the nucleotides, which are within the interior of the DNA. This series of exposed triplets (codons) carries the information to allow machinery in the cell to "read" the codons on the exposed DNA, which results in the making of RNA molecules. RNA in turn makes either amino acids or micro RNA, which are responsible for all of the structure and function of a living organism; i.e. they determine all the features of the cell and thus the entire individual. Closing the uncoiled segment turns off the gene.

The heritability of a trait (like height) in a population essentially conveys what percentage of the observed variation comes from differences in genes vs. differences in environment. Each unique form of a single gene is called an allele; different forms are collectively called polymorphisms. As an example, one allele for the gene for hair color and skin cell pigmentation could instruct the body to produce black pigment, producing black hair and pigmented skin; while a different allele of the same gene in a different individual could give garbled instructions that would result in a failure to produce any pigment, giving white hair and no pigmented skin: albinism. Mutations are random changes in genes creating new alleles, which in turn produce new traits, which could help, harm, or have no new effect on the individual's likelihood of survival; thus, mutations are the basis for evolution.

Genetics is the study of genes, genetic variation, and heredity in living organisms. It is generally considered a field of biology, but intersects frequently with many other life sciences and is strongly linked with the study of information systems. The discoverer of genetics is Gregor Mendel, a late 19th-century scientist and Augustinian friar. Mendel studied "trait inheritance", patterns in the way traits are handed down from parents to offspring. He observed that organisms (pea plants) inherit traits by way of discrete "units of inheritance". This term, still used today, is a somewhat ambiguous definition of what is referred to as a gene.

Trait inheritance and molecular inheritance mechanisms of genes are still primary principles of genetics in the 21st century, but modern genetics has expanded beyond inheritance to studying the function and behavior of genes. Gene structure and function, variation, and distribution are studied within the context of the cell, the organism (e.g. dominance), and within the context of a population. Genetics has given rise to a number of subfields, including epigenetics and population genetics. Organisms studied within the broad field span the domains of life (archaea, bacteria, and eukarya).

Genetic processes work in combination with an organism's environment and experiences to influence development and behavior, often referred to as nature versus nurture. The intracellular or extracellular environment of a cell or organism may switch gene transcription on or off. A classic example is two seeds of genetically identical corn, one placed in a temperate climate and one in an arid climate. While the average height of the two corn stalks may be genetically determined to be equal, the one in the arid climate only grows to half the height of the one in the temperate climate due to lack of water and nutrients in its environment.

History

The observation that living things inherit traits from their parents has been used since prehistoric times to improve crop plants and animals through selective breeding. The modern science of genetics, seeking to understand this process, began with the work of the Augustinian friar Gregor Mendel in the mid-19th century.

Prior to Mendel, Imre Festetics, a Hungarian noble, who lived in Kőszeg before Mendel, was the first who used the word "genetics." He described several rules of genetic inheritance in his work The genetic law of the Nature (Die genetische Gesätze der Natur, 1819). His second law is the same as what Mendel published. In his third law, he developed the basic principles of mutation (he can be considered a forerunner of Hugo de Vries).

Other theories of inheritance preceded Mendel's work. A popular theory during the 19th century, and implied by Charles Darwin's 1859 On the Origin of Species, was blending inheritance: the idea that individuals inherit a smooth blend of traits from their parents. Mendel's work provided examples where traits were definitely not blended after hybridization, showing that traits are produced by combinations of distinct genes rather than a continuous blend. Blending of traits in the progeny is now explained by the action of multiple genes with quantitative effects. Another theory that had some support at that time was the inheritance of acquired characteristics: the belief that individuals inherit traits strengthened by their parents. This theory (commonly associated with Jean-Baptiste Lamarck) is now known to be wrong—the experiences of individuals do not affect the genes they pass to their children, although evidence in the field of epigenetics has revived some aspects of Lamarck's theory. Other theories included the pangenesis of Charles Darwin (which had both acquired and inherited aspects) and Francis Galton's reformulation of pangenesis as both particulate and inherited.

Mendelian and Classical Genetics

Modern genetics started with Mendel's studies of the nature of inheritance in plants. In his paper "Versuche über Pflanzenhybriden" ("Experiments on Plant Hybridization"), presented in 1865 to the Naturforschender Verein (Society for Research in Nature) in Brünn, Mendel traced the inheritance patterns of certain traits in pea plants and described them mathematically. Although this pattern of inheritance could only be observed for a few traits, Mendel's work suggested that heredity was particulate, not acquired, and that the inheritance patterns of many traits could be explained through simple rules and ratios.

The importance of Mendel's work did not gain wide understanding until 1900, after his death, when Hugo de Vries and other scientists rediscovered his research. William Bateson, a proponent of Mendel's work, coined the word genetics in 1905 (the adjective genetic, derived from the Greek word genesis—γένεσις, "origin", predates the noun and was first used in a biological sense in 1860). Bateson both acted as a mentor and was aided significantly by the work of female scientists from Newnham College at Cambridge, specifically the work of Becky Saunders, Nora Darwin Barlow, and Muriel Wheldale Onslow. Bateson popularized the usage of the word genetics to describe the study of inheritance in his inaugural address to the Third International Conference on Plant Hybridization in London in 1906.

After the rediscovery of Mendel's work, scientists tried to determine which molecules in the cell were responsible for inheritance. In 1911, Thomas Hunt Morgan argued that genes are on chromosomes, based on observations of a sex-linked white eye mutation in fruit flies.[19] In 1913, his student Alfred Sturtevant used the phenomenon of genetic linkage to show that genes are arranged linearly on the chromosome.

Molecular Genetics

Although genes were known to exist on chromosomes, chromosomes are composed of both protein and DNA, and scientists did not know which of the two is responsible for inheritance. In 1928, Frederick Griffith discovered the phenomenon of transformation (see Griffith's experiment): dead bacteria could transfer genetic material to "transform" other still-living bacteria. Sixteen years later, in 1944, the Avery–MacLeod–McCarty experiment identified DNA as the molecule responsible for transformation. The role of the nucleus as the repository of genetic information in eukaryotes had been established by Hämmerling in 1943 in his work on the single celled alga Acetabularia. The Hershey–Chase experiment in 1952 confirmed that DNA (rather than protein) is the genetic material of the viruses that infect bacteria, providing further evidence that DNA is the molecule responsible for inheritance.

James Watson and Francis Crick determined the structure of DNA in 1953, using the X-ray crystallography work of Rosalind Franklin and Maurice Wilkins that indicated DNA has a helical structure (i.e., shaped like a corkscrew). Their double-helix model had two strands of DNA with the nucleotides pointing inward, each matching a complementary nucleotide on the other strand to form what look like rungs on a twisted ladder. This structure showed that genetic information exists in the sequence of nucleotides on each strand of DNA. The structure also suggested a simple method for replication: if the strands are separated, new partner strands can be reconstructed for each based on the sequence of the old strand. This property is what gives DNA its semi-conservative nature where one strand of new DNA is from an original parent strand.

Although the structure of DNA showed how inheritance works, it was still not known how DNA influences the behavior of cells. In the following years, scientists tried to understand how DNA controls the process of protein production. It was discovered that the cell uses DNA as a template to create matching messenger RNA, molecules with nucleotides very similar to DNA. The nucleotide sequence of a messenger RNA is used to create an amino acid sequence in protein; this translation between nucleotide sequences and amino acid sequences is known as the genetic code.

With the newfound molecular understanding of inheritance came an explosion of research. A notable theory arose from Tomoko Ohta in 1973 with her amendment to the neutral theory of molecular evolution through publishing the nearly neutral theory of molecular evolution. In this theory, Ohta stressed the importance of natural selection and the environment to the rate at which genetic evolution occurs. One important development was chain-termination DNA sequencing in 1977 by Frederick Sanger. This technology allows scientists to read the nucleotide sequence of a DNA molecule. In 1983, Kary Banks Mullis developed the polymerase chain reaction, providing a quick way to isolate and amplify a specific section of DNA from a mixture. The efforts of the Human Genome Project, Department of Energy, NIH, and parallel private efforts by Celera Genomics led to the sequencing of the human genome in 2003.

Genes and Evolution

A population of organisms evolves when an inherited trait becomes more common or less common over time. For instance, all the mice living on an island would be a single population of mice: some with white fur, some gray. If over generations, white mice became more frequent and gray mice less frequent, then the color of the fur in this population of mice would be evolving. In terms of genetics, this is called an increase in allele frequency.

Alleles become more or less common either by chance in a process called genetic drift, or by natural selection. In natural selection, if an allele makes it more likely for an organism to survive and reproduce, then over time this allele becomes more common. But if an allele is harmful, natural selection makes it less common. In the above example, if the island were getting colder each year and snow became present for much of the time, then the allele for white fur would favor survival, since predators would be less likely to see them against the snow, and more likely to see the gray mice. Over time white mice would become more and more frequent, while gray mice less and less.

Mutations create new alleles. These alleles have new DNA sequences and can produce proteins with new properties. So if an island was populated entirely by black mice, mutations could happen creating alleles for white fur. The combination of mutations creating new alleles at random, and natural selection picking out those that are useful, causes adaptation. This is when organisms change in ways that help them to survive and reproduce. Many such changes, studied in evolutionary developmental biology, affect the way the embryo develops into an adult body.

Genetic Engineering

Since traits come from the genes in a cell, putting a new piece of DNA into a cell can produce a new trait. This is how genetic engineering works. For example, rice can be given genes from a maize and a soil bacteria so the rice produces beta-carotene, which the body converts to Vitamin A. This can help children suffering from Vitamin A deficiency. Another gene being put into some crops comes from the bacterium Bacillus thuringiensis; the gene makes a protein that is an insecticide. The insecticide kills insects that eat the plants, but is harmless to people. In these plants, the new genes are put into the plant before it is grown, so the genes are in every part of the plant, including its seeds. The plant's offspring inherit the new genes, which has led to concern about the spread of new traits into wild plants.

The kind of technology used in genetic engineering is also being developed to treat people with genetic disorders in an experimental medical technique called gene therapy. However, here the new gene is put in after the person has grown up and become ill, so any new gene is not inherited by their children. Gene therapy works by trying to replace the allele that causes the disease with an allele that works properly.

REFERENCES

https://en.wikipedia.org/wiki/Genetics

https://en.wikipedia.org/wiki/Introduction_to_genetics

Genetics and Bioengineering : *Concepts and Issues* **Pages 7-27**
Edited by: Dr. Ashok K. Rathoure and Dr. Pawan Kumar 'Bharti'
ISBN: 978-93-86841-92-6
Edition: 2019
Published by: Discovery Publishing House Pvt. Ltd., New Delhi (India)

2

Bioinformatics and Next Generation Sequencing

[1]Prasann Kumar and [2]Shweta Pathak

GRAPHICAL ABSTRACT

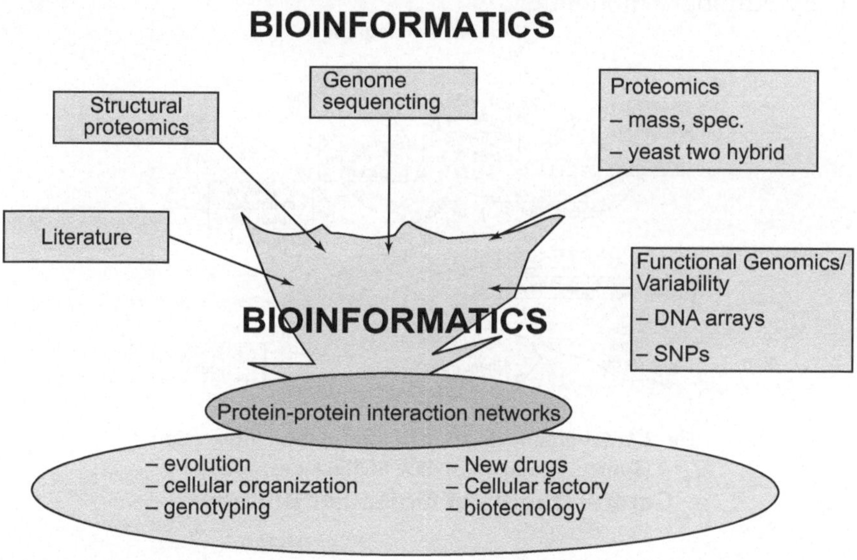

Keywords: Bioinformatics, Crop, Dose, Energy, Generation, Sequencing

INTRODUCTION

Genome annotation is the process of finding and designating locations of individual genes and other features on raw DNA sequences, called assemblies.

Steps of Genome Analysis

1. Genome sequence assembled
2. Identify repetitive sequences – mask out
3. Gene prediction – train a model for each genome

[1] Department of Agronomy, School of Agriculture, Lovely Professional University, Jalandhar, Punjab, 144411, India
[2] Department of Plant Physiology, I.Ag. Sci., BHU., Varanasi, 221005, U.P., India

4. Look for EST and cDNA sequences
5. Genome annotation
6. Microarray analysis
7. Metabolic pathways and regulation
8. Protein 2D gel electrophoresis
9. Functional genomics
10. Gene location/gene map
11. Self-comparison of proteome
12. Comparative genomics
13. Identify clusters of functionally related genes
14. Evolutionary modeling

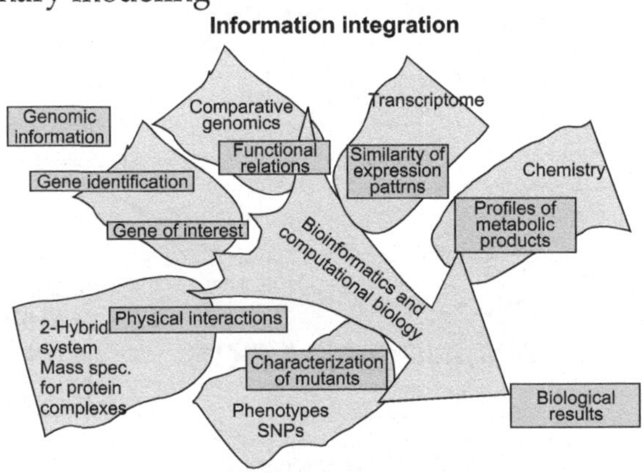

Fig. 2.1: Schematic diagram of information integration (Source: Based on review of literature, 2018)

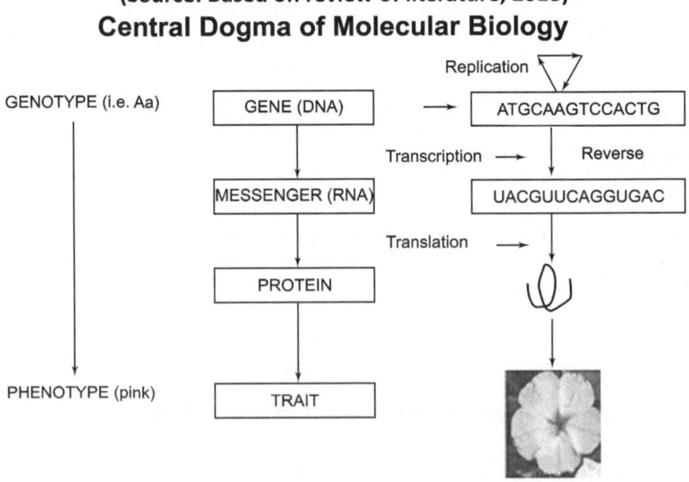

Fig. 2.2: Central dogma of molecular biology (Source: Based on review of literature, 2018)

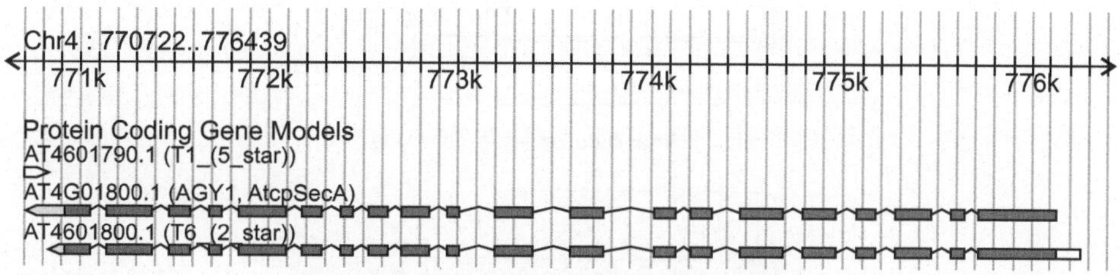

Fig. 2.3: Gene annotation for a target gene
(Source: Based on review of literature, 2018)

Annotation of Genomic Sequence

Given the sequence of an organism's genome, we would like to be able to identify:

- Genes and gene functions
- Exon boundaries & splice sites
- Beginning and end of translation
- Alternative splicing
- Regulatory elements (e.g. promoters)

The only certain way to do this is experimentally, but it is time consuming and expensive. Computational methods can achieve reasonable accuracy quickly, and help direct experimental approaches.

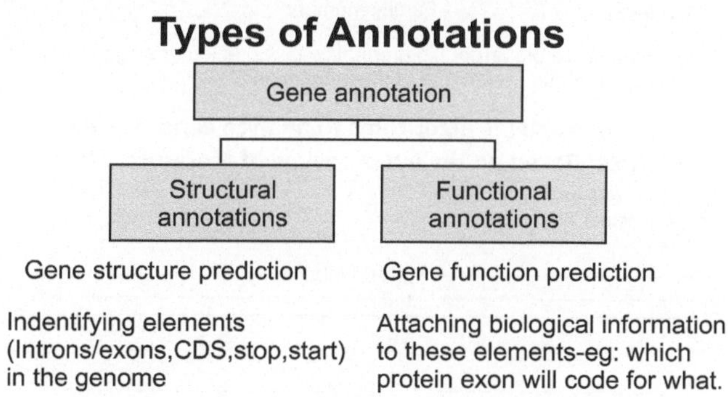

Fig. 2.4: Types of Annotation
(Source: Based on Review of Literature, 2018)

Prokaryotic Gene Structure

- Most bacterial ***promoters*** contain the Shine-Delgarno signal, at about -10 that has the consensus sequence: 5′-TATAAT-3′.
- The ***terminator***: a signal at the end of the coding sequence that terminates the transcription of RNA.
- The ***coding sequence*** is composed of nucleotide triplets. Each triplet codes for an amino acid. The AAs are the building blocks of proteins.

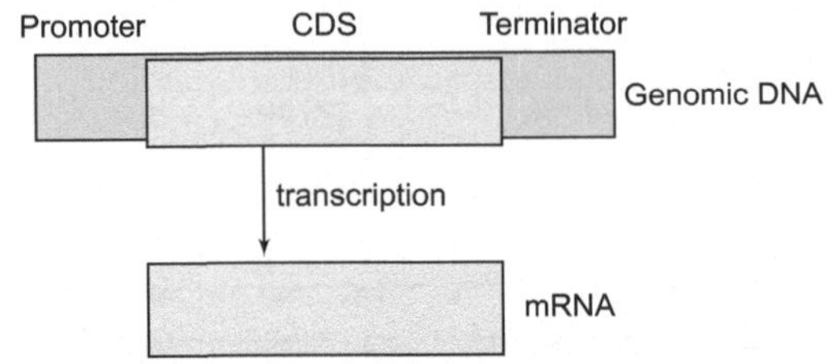

Fig. 2.5: Prokaryotic gene structure (Source: Based on review of Literature 2018)

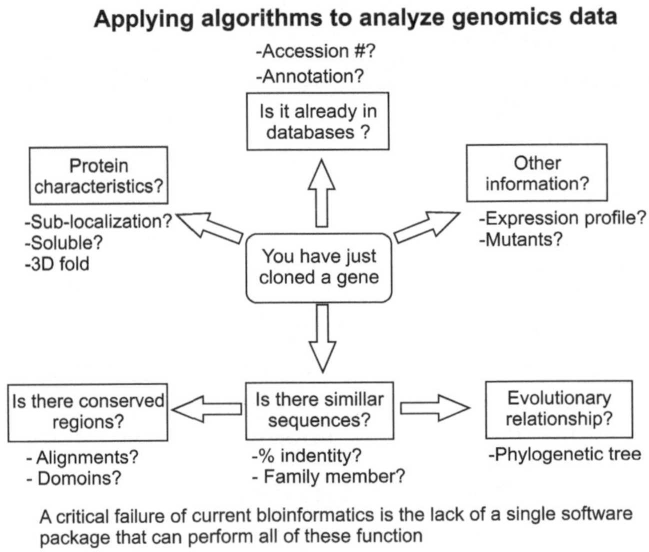

Fig. 2.6: Applying algorithms to analyze genomics data (Source: Based on review of review of literature, 2018)

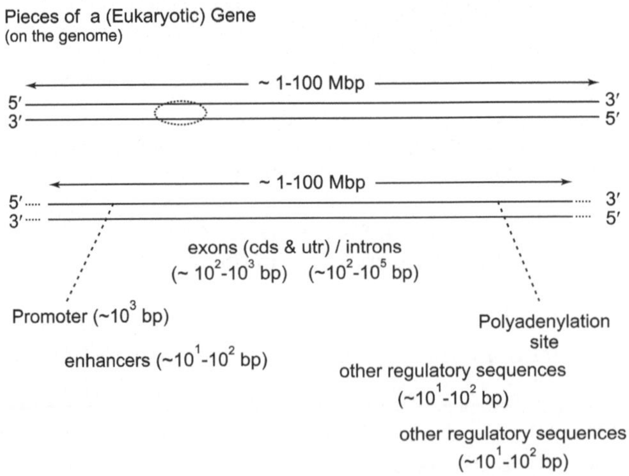

Fig. 2.7: Pieces of a (Eukaryotic) Gene(on the genome) (Source: Based on review of literature, 2018)

STRUCTURAL ANNOTATION

Identification of genomic elements

- Open reading frame and their localization
- Coding regions
- Location of regulatory motifs
- Start/Stop
- Splice Sites
- Non coding Regions/RNA's

METHODS FOR STRUCTURAL ANNOTATION

- Homology based methods- (Using pairwise sequence alignment)
- Ab-initio methods- (codon usage table)

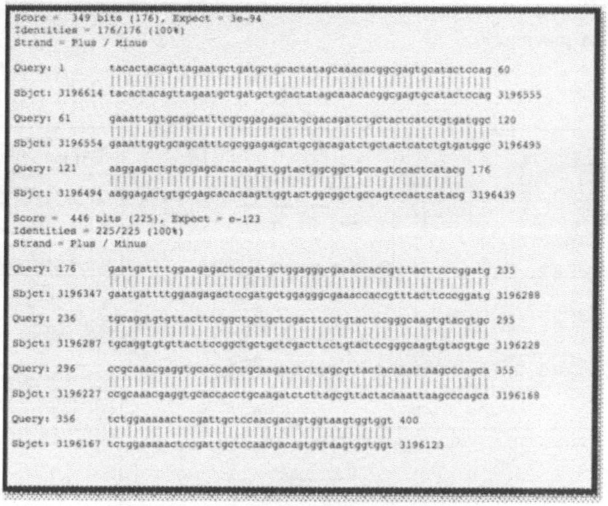

```
Score =  349 bits (176), Expect = 3e-94
Identities = 176/176 (100%)
Strand = Plus / Minus

Query: 1       tacactacagttagaatgctgatgctgcactatagcaaacacggcgagtgcatactccag 60
               ||||||||||||||||||||||||||||||||||||||||||||||||||||||||||||
Sbjct: 3196614 tacactacagttagaatgctgatgctgcactatagcaaacacggcgagtgcatactccag 3196555

Query: 61      gaaattggtgcagcatttcgcggagagcatgcgacagatctgctactcatctgtgatggc 120
               ||||||||||||||||||||||||||||||||||||||||||||||||||||||||||||
Sbjct: 3196554 gaaattggtgcagcatttcgcggagagcatgcgacagatctgctactcatctgtgatggc 3196495

Query: 121     aaggagactgtgcgagcacacaagttggtactggcggctgccagtccactcatacg 176
               ||||||||||||||||||||||||||||||||||||||||||||||||||||||||
Sbjct: 3196494 aaggagactgtgcgagcacacaagttggtactggcggctgccagtccactcatacg 3196439

Score =  446 bits (225), Expect = e-123
Identities = 225/225 (100%)
Strand = Plus / Minus

Query: 176     gaatgatttggaagagactccgatgctggagggcgaaaccaccgtttacttcccggatg 235
               |||||||||||||||||||||||||||||||||||||||||||||||||||||||||||
Sbjct: 3196347 gaatgatttggaagagactccgatgctggagggcgaaaccaccgtttacttcccggatg 3196288

Query: 236     tgcaggtgtgttacttccggctgctgctcgacttcctgtactccgggcaagtgtacgtgc 295
               ||||||||||||||||||||||||||||||||||||||||||||||||||||||||||||
Sbjct: 3196287 tgcaggtgtgttacttccggctgctgctcgacttcctgtactccgggcaagtgtacgtgc 3196228

Query: 296     ccgcaaacgaggtgcaccacctgcaagatctcttagcgttactacaaattaagcccagca 355
               ||||||||||||||||||||||||||||||||||||||||||||||||||||||||||||
Sbjct: 3196227 ccgcaaacgaggtgcaccacctgcaagatctcttagcgttactacaaattaagcccagca 3196168

Query: 356     tctggaaaaactccgattgctccaacgacagtggtaagtggtggt 400
               |||||||||||||||||||||||||||||||||||||||||||||
Sbjct: 3196167 tctggaaaaactccgattgctccaacgacagtggtaagtggtggt 3196123
```

Second letter

First letter	U	C	A	G	Third letter
U	UUU Phe UUC Phe UUA Leu UUG Leu	UCU Ser UCC Ser UCA Ser UCG Ser	UAU Tyr UAC Tyr UAA Stop UAG Stop	UGU Cys UGC Cys UGA Stop UGG Trp	U C A G
C	CUU Leu CUC Leu CUA Leu CUG Leu	CCU Pro CCC Pro CCA Pro CCG Pro	CAU His CAC His CAA Gln CAG Gln	CGU Arg CGC Arg CGA Arg CGG Arg	U C A G
A	AUU Ile AUC Ile AUA Ile AUG Met	ACU Thr ACC Thr ACA Thr ACG Thr	AAU Asn AAC Asn AAA Lys AAG Lys	AGU Ser AGC Ser AGA Arg AGG Arg	U C A G
G	GUU Val GUC Val GUA Val GUG Val	GCU Ala GCC Ala GCA Ala GCG Ala	GAU Asp GAC Asp GAA Glu GAG Glu	GGU Gly GGC Gly GGA Gly GGG Gly	U C A G

Fig. 2.8: Methods for structural annotation (Source: Based on review of literature, 2018)

FUNCTIONAL ANNOTATION

Attaching biological information to genomic elements

- Biochemical function
- Biological function
- Involved regulation and interactions
- Expression
- Utilize known sequence information to predicted protein sequence from the gene
- Is based on the idea that some sequence similarity detected between two proteins means they are homologous.
- Homologous proteins share same ancestry and hence similar biochemical functions.

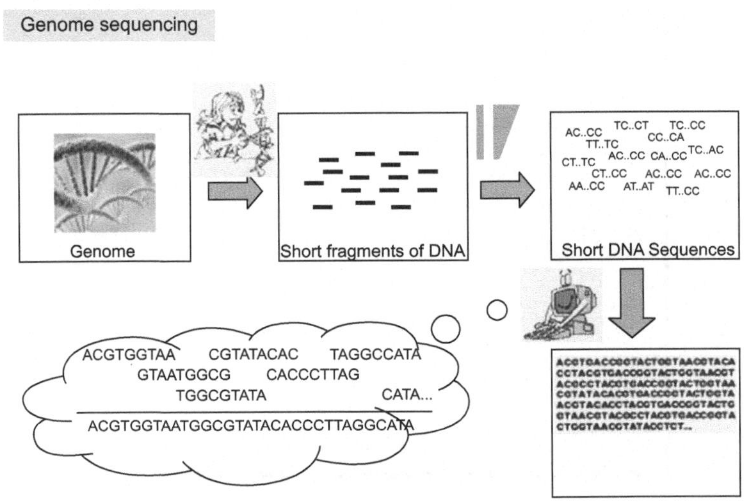

Fig. 2.9: Genome sequencing
(Source: Based on review of literature, 2018)

EVALUATION OF SEQUENCING TECHNOLOGY

1st Gen: Gel based sequencing and capillary electrophoresis

- Sanger sequencing
- Gels
- Cycle sequencing
- Fluorescence
- Capillary electrophoresis

2nd Gen: Next-Generation Sequencers:

- "Sequencing by synthesis"

- Pyrosequencing (Roche/454)
- Cluster sequencing (Illumina/Solexa)
- Sequencing by ligation (ABI/SOLiD)

3rd Generation Sequencers:

- Single molecule sequencing (ABI SMS, PacBio SMRT, Helicos), nanopore sequencing.

Library Preparation for Sequencing

In general, the core steps in preparing RNA or DNA for NGS analysis are:

(*i*) fragmenting and/or sizing the target sequences to a desired length,
(*ii*) converting target to double-stranded DNA,
(*iii*) attaching oligonucleotide adapters to the ends of target fragments, and
(*iv*) quantitating the final library product for sequencing

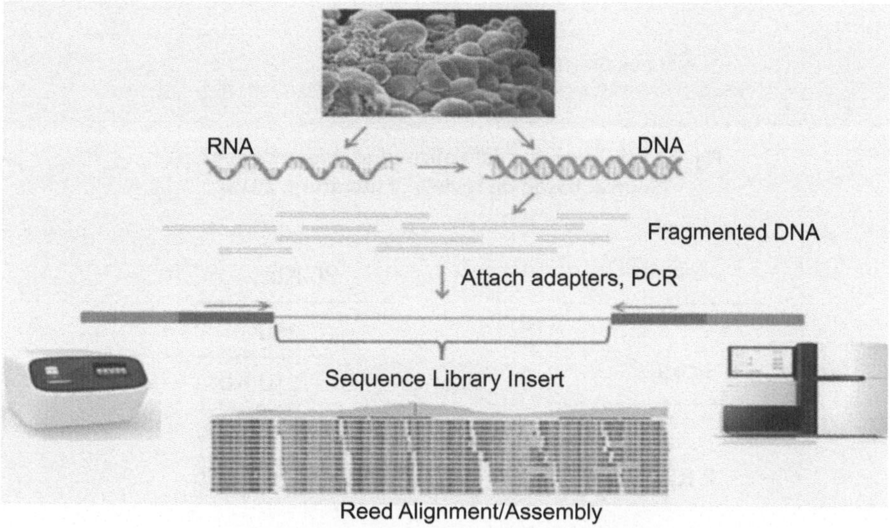

Fig. 2.10: Library preparation for sequencing (Source: based on review of literature, 2018)

DEPTH AND COVERAGE OF SEQUENCING

- Sequencing depth represents the number of nucleotides contributing to a portion of an assembly.
- On a genome basis, it means that, on average, each base has been sequenced a certain number of times (10X, 20X...).
- Coverage describes the average number of reads that align to, or "cover," known reference bases.

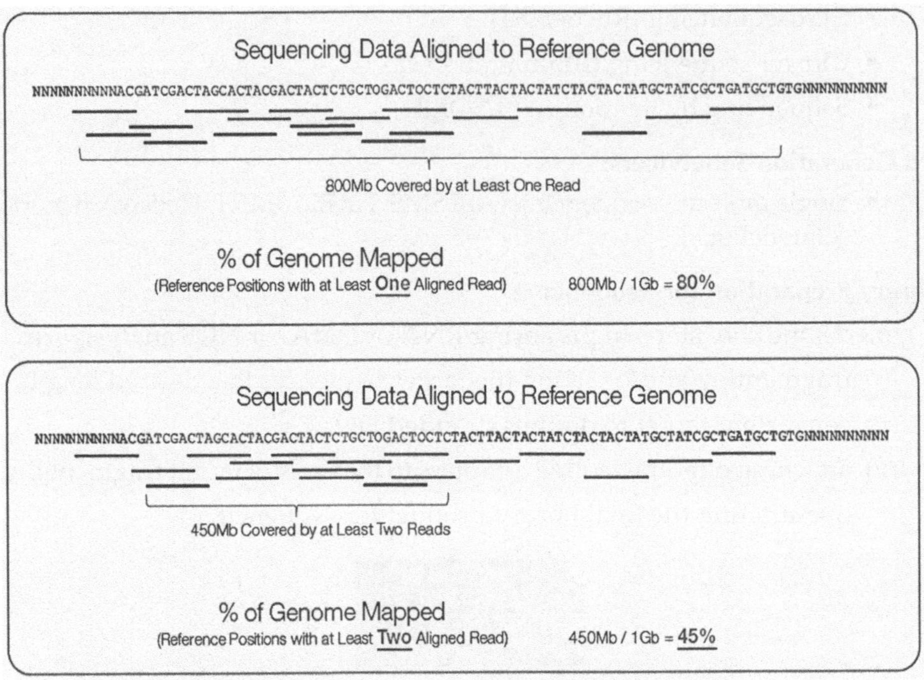

Fig. 2.11: Sequencing data aligned to reference genome
(Source: based on review of literature, 2018)

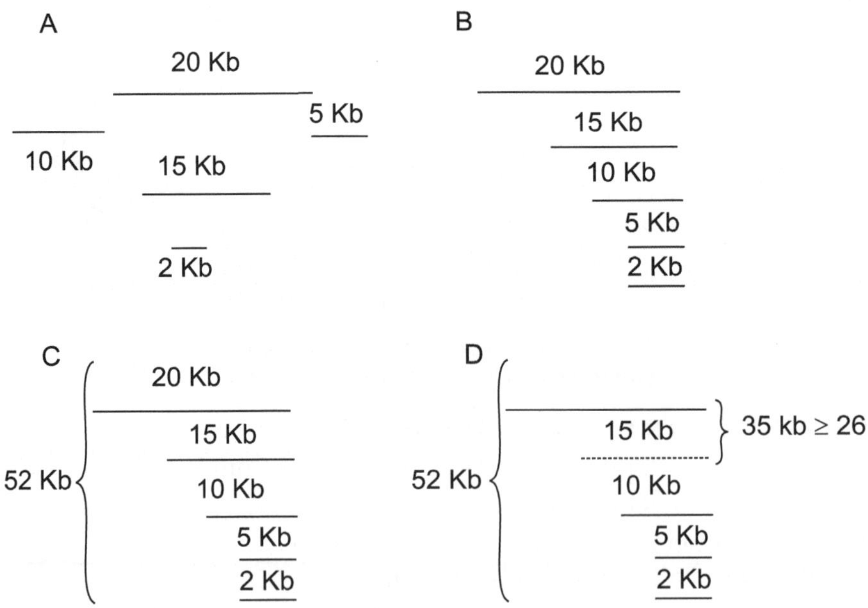

Fig. 2.12: N50 calculation
(Source: Based on review of literature, 2018)

CONTIGS AND SCAFFOLDS

- A scaffold is a portion of the genome sequence reconstructed from end-sequenced whole-genome shotgun clones.
- Scaffolds are composed of contigs and gaps.
- A contig is a contiguous length of genomic sequence in which the order of bases is known to a high confidence level.

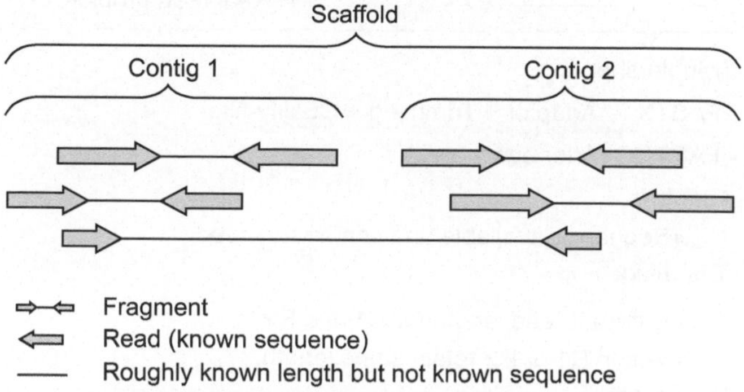

Fig. 2.13: Contigs and scaffolds
(Source: Based on review of literature, 2018)

DATA PROCESSING, SEQUENCING AND ANNOTATION

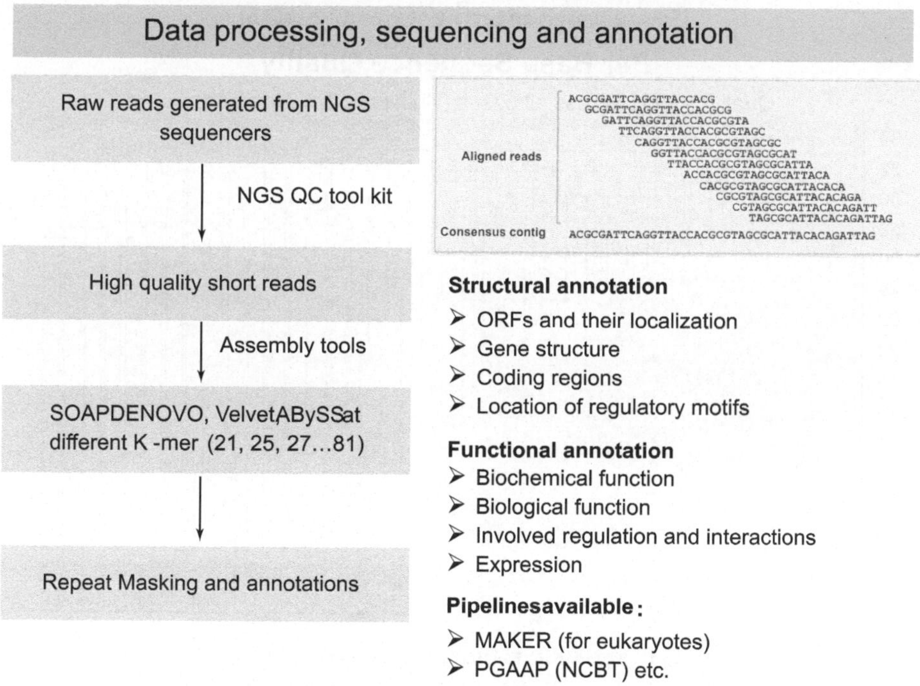

Fig. 2.14: Data processing, sequencing and annotation
(Source: based on review of literature, 2018)

Quality checks

R1 R2

FASTX
FASTQC
PRINSEQ (wip)
→
End bases in both R1, R2 have low base quality score. Possible reason:

- Adapter (seq data available)
- Illumina base calling error
- Real read problem??

Trouble-shooting:

- FASTX → Adaptor + Trimming + Quality-filter
- FASTQC (After every step)

Adaptor:

- Sequence available and can be removed.

Trimming:

- Different read length for R1 and R2
- Within R1 or R2 retain same length.

Quality-filter:

- 50%, 75% and 100% 3 parameter (p) values to try
- Q-score needs to be inspected (parameter q) (20, 25)

Fig. 2.15: Quality checks
(Source: based on review of literature, 2018)

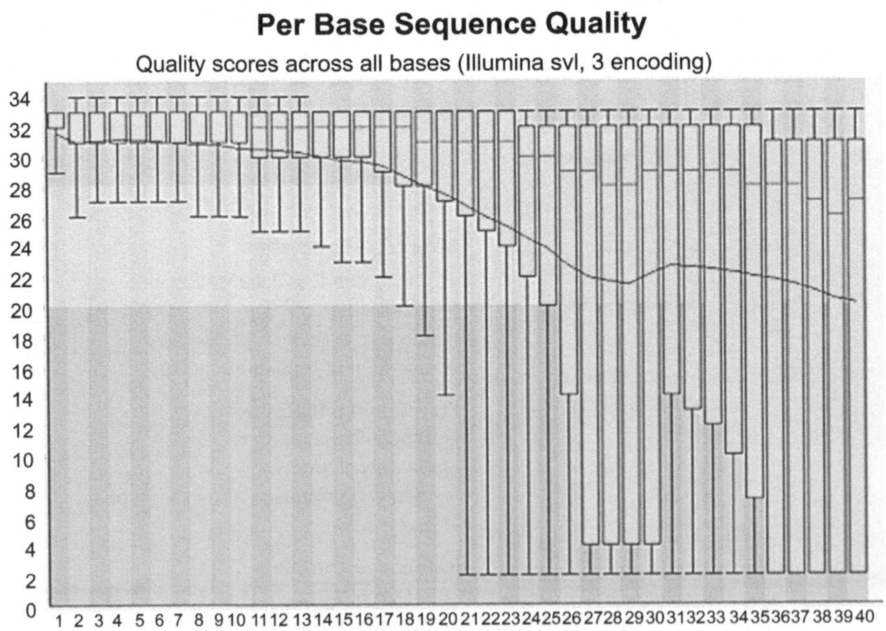

Fig. 2.16: Per base sequence quality
(Source: Based on review of literature, 2018)

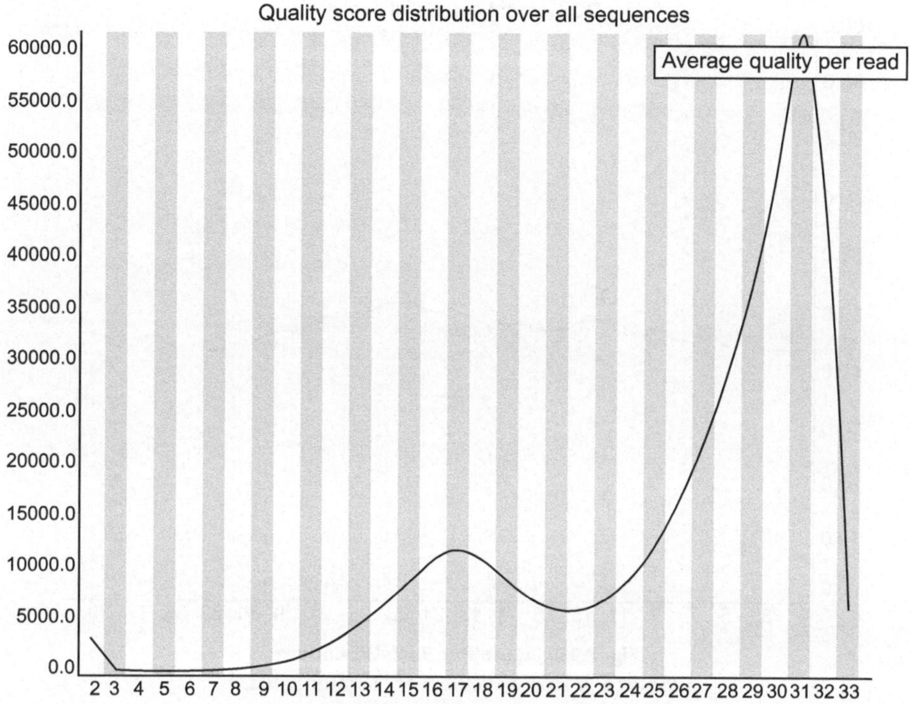

Fig. 2.17: Per Sequence Quality Scores
(Source: Based on review of literature, 2018)

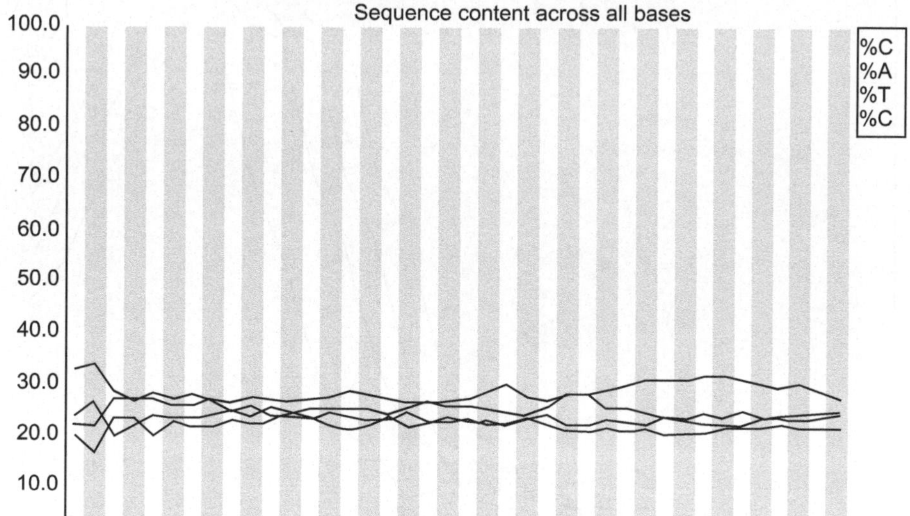

Fig. 2.18: Per Base Sequence Content
(Source: Based on review of Literature, 2018)

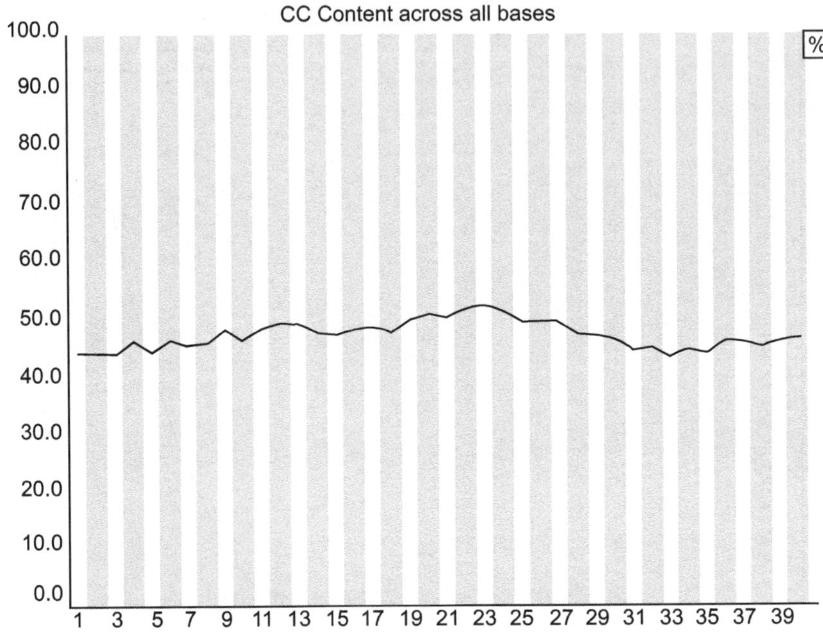

Fig. 2.19: Figure Per Base GC Content
(Source: Based on review of literature, 2018)

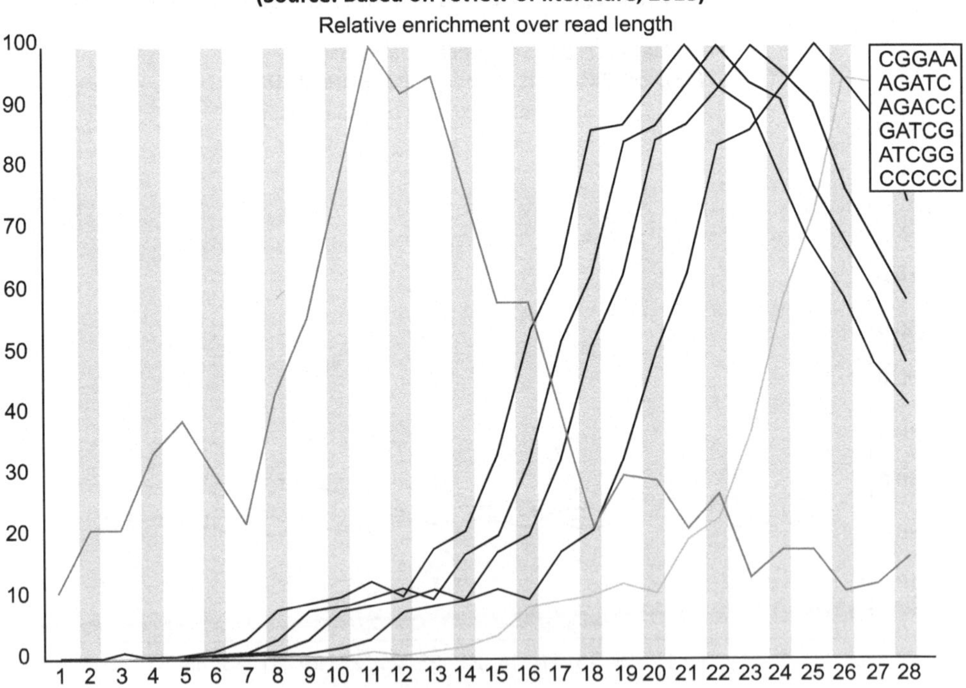

Fig. 2.20: Overrepresented Kmers
(Source: Based on review of literature, 2018)

Applications of Next Generation Sequencing

- Profiling of Variation
- Genetic variation
- Transcript variation
- Epigenetic variation

Metagenomic variation

- Discovery
- Novel genomes
- Novel genes
- Novel transcripts
- Small / long non-coding RNA

RNA Sequencing (RNASeq)

- Coding and non-coding transcript profiling
- Dynamic and Context dependent

Epigenomics

- Genome-wide protein-DNA interactions, DNA modifications
- Heritable and reversible regulation of gene expression

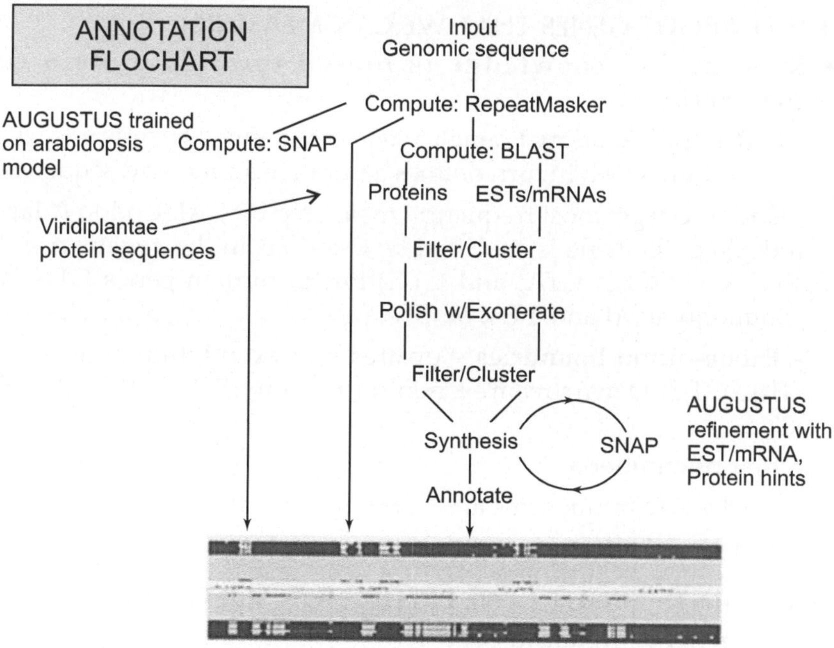

Fig. 2.21: Annotation flow chart
(Source: Based on review of literature, 2018)

DIFFERENT TYPES OF GENES

- **A. RNA genes**
  – tRNA, rRNA, snRNA, snoRNA, microRNA
- **B. Protein coding genes**
- **1. Prokaryotic**
- No introns, simpler regulatory features

2. Eukaryotic

- Exon-intron structure
- Complex regulatory features

APPROACHES TO GENE PREDICTION

- **Direct**

– Exact or near-exact matches of EST, cDNA, or Proteins from the same, or closely related organism

- **Indirect**
  1. Look for something that looks like one gene (***homology***)
  2. Look for something that looks like all genes (***ab initio***)
  3. Hybrid, combining homology and ab initio (and perhaps even direct) methods

WHAT IS IT ABOUT GENES THAT WE CAN MEASURE?

- **Most of our knowledge is biased towards protein-coding characteristics:**

  – **ORF (Open Reading Frame):** a sequence defined by in-frame AUG and stop codon, which in turn defines a putative amino acid sequence.

  – **Codon Usage**: most frequently measured by CAI (Codon Adaptation Index) eg., Leucine is specified by 6 codons in the genetic code (TTA, TTG, CTT, CTC, CTA, and CTG) but in human genes CTG is most commonly used and TTA, or CTA rarely.

  – **Exone-intron boundries** – upstream of exon-intron boundry: 5′-AG GTAAGT-3′. Down stream exon-intron boundry: 5′-PyPyPyPyPyPyNCAG -3′

- **Other phenomena**

  – Nucleotide frequencies and correlations: value and structure

  – **Functional sites:**splice sites, promoters, UTRs, polyadenylation sites

GENERAL POINTS ABOUT GENE PREDICTION SOFTWARE

- It is, in general, organism-specific
- It works best on genes that are *reasonably* similar to something seen previously

- It finds protein coding regions far better than non-coding regions
- In the absence of external (direct) information, alternative forms will not be identified
- It is imperfect! (It's biology, after all...)

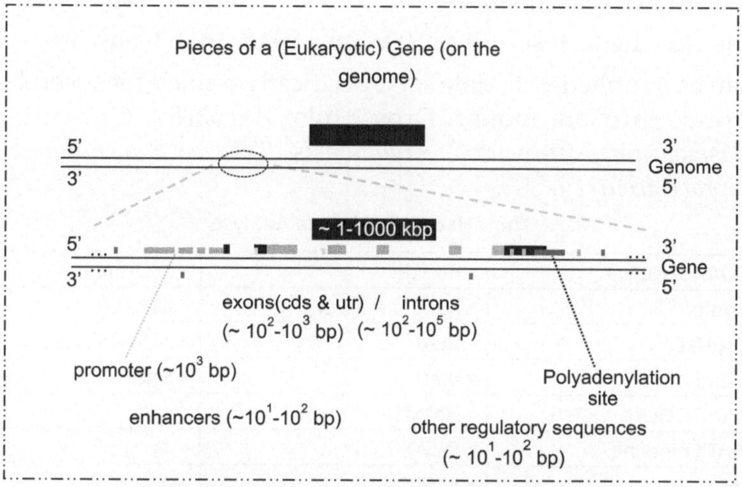

Fig. 2.22: Pieces of a eukaryotic gene on the genome (Source: based on review of literature, 2018)

Expression Stages and Structural Organization of Typical Eukaryotic Protein-coding Gene

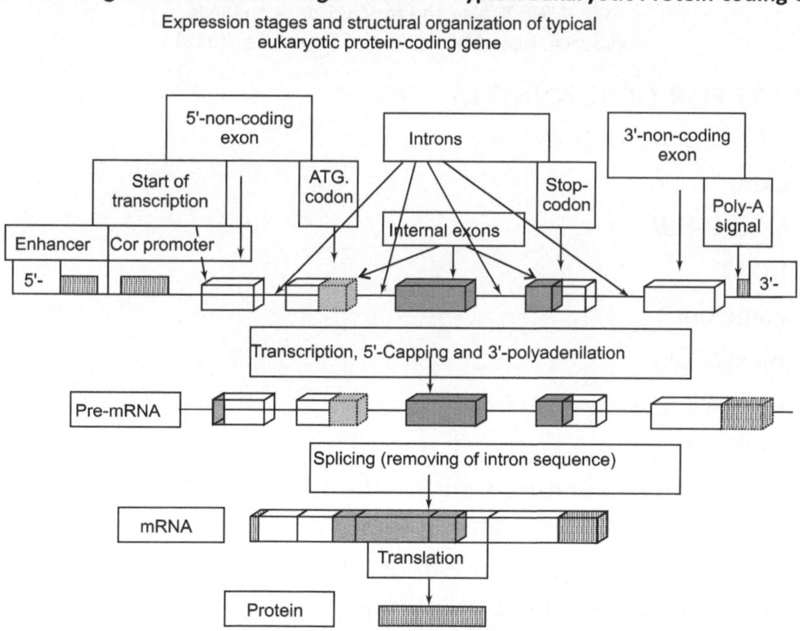

Fig. 2.23: Expression stages and structural organization of typical eukaryotic protein-coding gene (Source: Based on review of literature, 2018)

GENE FINDING FGENESH

- FGENESH: HMM-Based Gene Predictor For Wide Variety of Eukaryotic Genomes.
- FGENESH is HMM-based program for predicting multiple genes in genomic DNA sequences.
- It is also the fastest – 50 to 100 times faster than Genscan.
- Can be supplied with data sets specifically trained for several taxonomic groups (human, mouse, Drosophila, *Anopheles, C.elegans, SS.pombe, Plasmodium, Neurospora, Arabidopsis, Tobacco and monocot plants) to improve accuracy.*

Tools Used in NGS Data Analysis

• SOAPDENOVO	• Bowtie	• SEQ-map
• Trinity	• Reepat masker	• MAKER
• TopHat	• BLAT	• AUGUSTUS
• Cuttlinks	• Blast	• SNAP
• SAMTOOLS	• HMMER	
• GATK pipeline	• FASTX Tools	
• REAPER	• FASTQC	
• PICARDATOOLS	• VELVET	
• JELLYFISH	• R-SEQ	

Fig. 2.24: Tools used for NGS data analysis
(Source: Based on review of literature, 2018)

SOFTWARE FOR GENE ANNOTATION

- UCSC Genome Browser
- GeneMark
- GLIMMER
- BLAT
- Geneious
- Blast2GO
- BASys
- BioMart
- TRAPID is an online tool for the fast and efficient processing of assembled RNA-Seq transcriptome data.
- TRAPID offers high-throughput ORF detection, frameshift correction and includes a functional, comparative and phylogenetic toolbox, making use of 175 reference proteomes.
- http://bioinformatics.psb.ugent.be/webtools/trapid

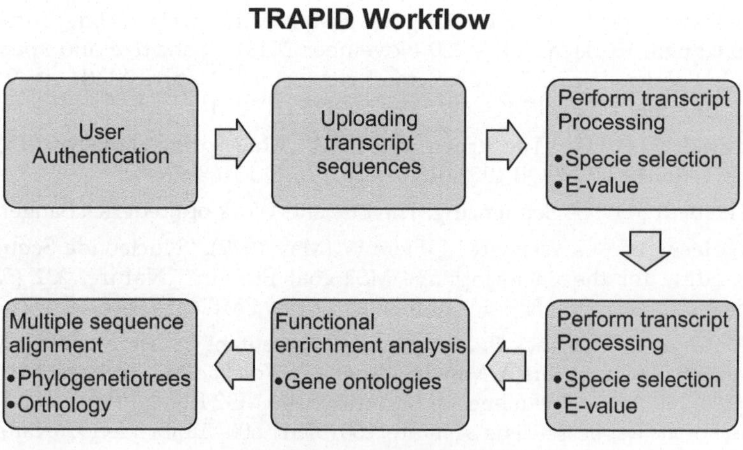

Fig. 2.25: TRAPID workflow
(Source: Based on review of literature, 2018)

CONCLUSION REMARKS

- Annotation accuracy is only as good as the available supporting data at the time of annotation- update information is necessary
- Gene predictions will change over time as new data becomes available (ESTs, related genomes) that are much similar than previous ones.
- Functional assignments will change over time as new data becomes available (characterization of hypothetical proteins)

REFERENCES

Olsvik O, Wahlberg J, Petterson B, Uhlén M, Popovic T, Wachsmuth IK, Fields PI (January 1993). "Use of Automated Sequencing of Polymerase Chain Reaction-generated Amplicons to Identify Three Types of Cholera Toxin Subunit B in Vibrio cholerae O1 strains". J. Clin. Microbiol. 31 (1): 22–25. PMC 262614. PMID 7678018.

Pettersson E, Lundeberg J, Ahmadian A (February 2009). "Generations of Sequencing Technologies". Genomics. 93 (2): 105 11. doi:10.1016/j.ygeno.2008.10.003. PMID 18992322.

Curtis, Caitlin; Hereward, James (29 August 2017). "From the Crime Scene to the Courtroom: the Journey of a DNA Sample". The Conversation.

Moréra, Solange; Larivière, Laurent; Kurzeck, Jürgen; Aschke-Sonnenborn, Ursula; Freemont, Paul S; Janin, Joël; Rüger, Wolfgang (August 2001). "High Resolution Crystal Structures of T4 phage β-glucosyltransferase: Induced Fit and Effect of Substrate and Metal Binding". Journal of Molecular Biology. 311 (3): 569–77. doi:10.1006/jmbi.2001.4905. PMID 11493010.

Ehrlich, Melanie; Gama-Sosa, Miguel A.; Huang, Lan-Hsiang; Midgett, Rose Marie; Kuo, Kenneth C.; McCune, Roy A.; Gehrke, Charles (1982). "Amount and Distribution of 5-methylcytosine in Human DNA from Different Types of Tissues or Cells". Nucleic Acids Research. 10 (8): 2709–21. doi:10.1093/nar/10.8.2709. PMC 320645 . PMID 7079182.

Ehrlich, M; Wang, R. (19 June 1981). "5-Methylcytosine in Eukaryotic DNA". Science. 212(4501): 1350–57. Bibcode:1981Sci...212.1350E. doi:10.1126/science.6262918. PMID 6262918.

Song, Chun-Xiao; Clark, Tyson A; Lu, Xing-Yu; Kislyuk, Andrey; Dai, Qing; Turner, Stephen W; He, Chuan; Korlach, Jonas (20 November 2011). "Sensitive and specific Single-Molecule Sequencing of 5-hydroxymethylcytosine". Nature Methods. 9 (1): 75–77. doi:10.1038/nmeth.1779. PMC 3646335 . PMID 22101853.

Watson JD, Crick FH (1953). "The Structure of DNA". Cold Spring Harb. Symp. Quant. Biol. 18: 123–31. doi:10.1101/SQB.1953.018.01.020. PMID 13168976.

Marks, L, The path to DNA Sequencing: The Life and Work of Frederick Sanger.

Min Jou W, Haegeman G, Ysebaert M, Fiers W (May 1972). "Nucleotide Sequence of the Gene Coding for the Bacteriophage MS2 coat Protein". Nature. 237 (5350): 82–8. Bibcode:1972Natur.237...82J. doi:10.1038/237082a0. PMID 4555447.

Fiers W, Contreras R, Duerinck F, Haegeman G, Iserentant D, Merregaert J, Min Jou W, Molemans F, Raeymaekers A, Van den Berghe A, Volckaert G, Ysebaert M (April 1976). "Complete Nucleotide Sequence of Bacteriophage MS2 RNA: Primary and Secondary Structure of the Replicase Gene". Nature. 260 (5551): 500–7. Bibcode:1976Natur.260..500F. doi:10.1038/260500a0. PMID 1264203.

Ozsolak, Fatih; Milos, Patrice M. (2011-02-01). "RNA Sequencing: Advances, Challenges and Opportunities". Nature Reviews Genetics. 12 (2): 87–98. doi:10.1038/nrg2934. ISSN 1471-0056. PMC 3031867 . PMID 21191423.

"Ray Wu Faculty Profile". Cornell University. Archived from the Original on 2009-03-04.

Padmanabhan, R; Ray Wu; Ernest Jay (June 1974). "Chemical Synthesis of a Primer and Its Use in the Sequence Analysis of the Lysozyme Gene of Bacteriophage T4". Proceedings of the National Academy of Sciences. 71 (6): 2510–14. Bibcode:1974PNAS...71.2510P. doi:10.1073/pnas.71.6.2510. PMC 388489 .

Onaga LA (June 2014). "Ray Wu as Fifth Business: Demonstrating Collective Memory in the History of DNA Sequencing". Studies in the History and Philosophy of Science. Part C. 46: 1–14. doi:10.1016/j.shpsc.2013.12.006. PMID 24565976.

16.Wu R (1972). "Nucleotide Sequence Analysis of DNA". Nature New Biology. 236 (68): 198–200. doi:10.1038/newbio236198a0. PMID 4553110.

Padmanabhan R, Wu R (1972). "Nucleotide Sequence Analysis of DNA. IX. Use of Oligonucleotides of Defined Sequence as Primers in DNA Sequence Analysis". Biochem. Biophys. Res. Commun. 48 (5): 1295–302. doi:10.1016/0006-291X(72)90852-2. PMID 4560009.

Wu R, Tu CD, Padmanabhan R (1973). "Nucleotide Sequence Analysis of DNA. XII. The Chemical Synthesis and Sequence Analysis of a Dodecadeoxynucleotide which Binds to the Endolysin gene of Bacteriophage Lambda". Biochem. Biophys. Res. Commun. 55 (4): 1092–99. doi:10.1016/S0006-291X(73)80007-5. PMID 4358929.

Jay E, Bambara R, Padmanabhan R, Wu R (March 1974). "DNA Sequence Analysis: A General, Simple and Rapid Method for Sequencing Large Oligodeoxyribonucleotide Fragments by Mapping". Nucleic Acids Research. 1 (3): 331–53. doi:10.1093/nar/1.3.331. PMC 344020 . PMID 10793670.

Sanger F, Nicklen S, Coulson AR (December 1977). "DNA Sequencing with Chain-terminating Inhibitors". Proc. Natl. Acad. Sci. USA. 74 (12): 5463–77. Bibcode:1977PNAS...74.5463S. doi:10.1073/pnas.74.12.5463. PMC 431765 . PMID 271968.

Maxam AM, Gilbert W (February 1977). "A New Method for Sequencing DNA". Proc. Natl. Acad. Sci. USA. 74 (2): 560–64. Bibcode:1977PNAS...74..560M. doi:10.1073/pnas.74.2.560. PMC 392330 . PMID 265521.

Gilbert, W. DNA Sequencing and Gene Structure. Nobel Lecture, 8 December 1980.

Gilbert W, Maxam A (December 1973). "The Nucleotide Sequence of the lac Operator". Proc. Natl. Acad. Sci. U.S.A. 70 (12): 3581–84. Bibcode:1973PNAS...70.3581G. doi:10.1073/pnas.70.12.3581. PMC 427284 . PMID 4587255.

Sanger F, Air GM, Barrell BG, Brown NL, Coulson AR, Fiddes CA, Hutchison CA, Slocombe PM, Smith M (February 1977). "Nucleotide sequence of bacteriophage phi X174 DNA". Nature. 265 (5596): 687–95. Bibcode:1977Natur.265..687S. doi:10.1038/265687a0. PMID 870828.

"The Next Frontier: Human Viruses", What is Biotechnology.org, Retrieved 3 May 2017.

Beck S, Pohl FM (1984). "DNA Sequencing with Direct Blotting Electrophoresis". EMBO J. 3 (12): 2905–09. PMC 557787 . PMID 6396083.

United States Patent 4,631,122 (1986)

Feldmann H, et al. (1994). "Complete DNA Sequence of Yeast Chromo-some II". EMBO J. 13 (24): 5795–809. PMC 395553. PMID 7813418.

Smith LM, Sanders JZ, Kaiser RJ, Hughes P, Dodd C, Connell CR, Heiner C, Kent SB, Hood LE (12 June 1986). "Fluorescence Detection in Automated DNA Sequence Analysis". Nature. 321 (6071): 674–79. Bibcode:1986Natur.321..674S. doi:10.1038/321674a0. PMID 3713851.

Prober JM, Trainor GL, Dam RJ, Hobbs FW, Robertson CW, Zagursky RJ, Cocuzza AJ, Jensen MA, Baumeister K (16 Oct 1987). "A System for Rapid DNA Sequencing with Fluorescent chain-Terminating Dideoxynucleotides". Science. 238 (4825): 336–41. Bibcode:1987Sci...238..336P. doi:10.1126/science.2443975. PMID 2443975.

Adams MD, Kelley JM, Gocayne JD, Dubnick M, Polymeropoulos MH, Xiao H, Merril CR, Wu A, Olde B, Moreno RF (June 1991). "Complementary DNA Sequencing: Expressed Sequence Tags and Human Genome Project". Science. 252 (5013): 1651–56. Bibcode:1991Sci...252.1651A. doi:10.1126/science.2047873. PMID 2047873.

Fleischmann RD, Adams MD, White O, Clayton RA, Kirkness EF, Kerlavage AR, Bult CJ, Tomb JF, Dougherty BA, Merrick JM (July 1995). "Whole-genome Random Sequencing and Assembly of Haemophilus Influenzae Rd". Science. 269 (5223): 496–512. Bibcode:1995Sci...269..496F. doi:10.1126/science.7542800. PMID 7542800.

Lander ES, Linton LM, Birren B, Nusbaum C, Zody MC, et al. (February 2001). "Initial Sequencing and Analysis of the Human Genome". Nature. 409 (6822): 860–921. Bibcode:2001Natur.409..860L. doi:10.1038/35057062. PMID 11237011.

Venter JC, Adams MD, et al. (February 2001). "The Sequence of the Human genome". Science. 291 (5507): 1304–51. Bibcode:2001Sci...291.1304V. doi:10.1126/science.1058040. PMID 11181995.

"Espacenet - Bibliographic Data". worldwide.espacenet.com.

Ronaghi M, Karamohamed S, Pettersson B, Uhlén M, Nyrén P (1996). "Real-time DNA Sequencing Using Detection of Pyrophosphate Release". Analytical Biochemistry. 242 (1): 84–89. doi:10.1006/abio.1996.0432. PMID 8923969.

Kawashima, Eric H.; Laurent Farinelli; Pascal Mayer (2005-05-12). "Patent: Method of Nucleic acid Amplification". Retrieved 2012-12-22.

Ewing B, Green P (March 1998). "Base-calling of Automated Sequencer Traces Using Phred. II. Error Probabilities". Genome Res. 8 (3): 186–94. doi:10.1101/gr.8.3.186. PMID 9521922.

"Quality Scores for Next-Generation Sequencing" (PDF). Illumina. 31 October 2011. Sci...309.1728S. doi:10.1126/science.1117389. PMID 16081699.

"Applied Biosystems - File Not Found (404 Error)". 16 May 2008.

Goodwin, Sara; McPherson, John D.; McCombie, W. Richard (17 May 2016). "Coming of Age: Ten Years of Next-generation Sequencing Technologies". Nature Reviews Genetics. 17(6): 333–51. doi:10.1038/nrg.2016.49. PMID 27184599.

Staden R (11 Jun 1979). "A Strategy of DNA Sequencing Employing Computer Programs". Nucleic Acids Research. 6 (7): 2601–10. doi:10.1093/nar/6.7.2601. PMC 327874. PMID 461197.

P. Mayer,L. Farinelli, G. Matton, C. Adessi, G. Turcatti, J. J. Mermod, E. Kawashima.DNA Colony Massively Parallel Sequencing ams98 presentation U.S. Patent 5,641,658.

Braslavsky I, Hebert B, Kartalov E, Quake SR (April 2003). "Sequence Information can be Obtained from Single DNA Molecules". Proc. Natl. Acad. Sci. USA. 100 (7): 3960–64. Bibcode:2003PNAS..100.3960B. doi:10.1073/pnas.0230489100. PMC 153030 . PMID 12651960.

de Magalhães JP, Finch CE, Janssens G (2010). "Next-generation Sequencing in aging Research: Emerging Applications, Problems, Pitfalls and Possible Solutions". Ageing Research Reviews. 9 (3): 315–23. doi:10.1016/j.arr.2009.10.006. PMC 2878865 . PMID 19900591.

Grada A (August 2013). "Next-generation Sequencing: Methodology and Application". J Invest Dermatol. 133 (8): 1–4. doi:10.1038/jid.2013.248. PMID 23856935.

Hall N (May 2007). "Advanced Sequencing Technologies and their Wider Impact in Microbiology". J. Exp. Biol. 210 (Pt 9): 1518–25. doi:10.1242/jeb.001370. PMID 17449817.

Church GM (January 2006). "Genomes for All". Sci. Am. 294 (1): 46–54. Bibcode: 2006SciAm.294a..46C. doi:10.1038/scientificamerican0106-46. PMID 16468433.

c Schuster SC (January 2008). "Next-generation Sequencing Transforms Today's Biology". Nat. Methods. 5 (1): 16–18. doi:10.1038/nmeth1156. PMID 18165802.

Kalb, Gilbert; Moxley, Robert (1992). Massively Parallel, Optical, and Neural Computing in the United States. IOS Press. ISBN .

ten Bosch JR, Grody WW (2008). "Keeping Up with the Next Generation". The Journal of Molecular Diagnostics. 10 (6): 484–92. doi:10.2353/jmoldx.2008.080027. PMC 2570630 . PMID 18832462.

Tucker T, Marra M, Friedman JM (2009). "Massively Parallel Sequencing: The Next Big Thing in Genetic Medicine". The American Journal of Human Genetics. 85 (2): 142–54. doi:10.1016/j.ajhg.2009.06.022. PMC 2725244. PMID 19679224.

Quail MA, Smith M, Coupland P, Otto TD, Harris SR, Connor TR, Bertoni A, Swerdlow HP, Gu Y (1 January 2012). "A Tale of Three Next Generation Sequencing Platforms: Comparison of Ion Torrent, Pacific Biosciences and Illumina MiSeq Sequencers". BMC Genomics. 13(1): 341. doi:10.1186/1471-2164-13-341. PMC 3431227 . PMID 22827831.

Liu L, Li Y, Li S, Hu N, He Y, Pong R, Lin D, Lu L, Law M (1 January 2012). "Comparison of Next-Generation Sequencing Systems". Journal of Biomedicine and Biotechnology. 2012: 1–11. doi:10.1155/2012/251364. PMC 3398667 . PMID 22829749.

"New Software, Polymerase for Sequel System Boost Throughput and Affordability - PacBio". 7 March 2018.

"After a Year of Testing, Two Early PacBio Customers Expect More Routine Use of RS Sequencer in 2012". Genome Web. 10 January 2012.

Inc., Pacific Biosciences,. "Pacific Biosciences Introduces New Chemistry With Longer Read Lengths to Detect Novel Features in DNA Sequence and Advance Genome Studies of Large Organisms".

Chin CS, Alexander DH, Marks P, Klammer AA, Drake J, Heiner C, Clum A, Copeland A, Huddleston J, Eichler EE, Turner SW, Korlach J (2013). "Nonhybrid, Finished Microbial

Genome Assemblies from long-read SMRT Sequencing Data". Nat. Methods. 10 (6): 563–69. doi:10.1038/nmeth.2474. PMID 23644548.

"De novo Bacterial Genome Assembly: A Solved Problem?". 5 July 2013.

Rasko DA, Webster DR, Sahl JW, Bashir A, Boisen N, Scheutz F, Paxinos EE, Sebra R, Chin CS, Iliopoulos D, Klammer A, Peluso P, Lee L, Kislyuk AO, Bullard J, Kasarskis A, Wang S, Eid J, Rank D, Redman JC, Steyert SR, Frimodt-Møller J, Struve C, Petersen AM, Krogfelt KA, Nataro JP, Schadt EE, Waldor MK (25 August 2011). "Origins of the Strain Causing an Outbreak of Hemolytic–Uremic Syndrome in Germany". N Engl J Med. 365(8): 709–17. doi:10.1056/NEJMoa1106920. PMC 3168948 . PMID 21793740.

Tran B, Brown AM, Bedard PL, Winquist E, Goss GD, Hotte SJ, Welch SA, Hirte HW, Zhang T, Stein LD, Ferretti V, Watt S, Jiao W, Ng K, Ghai S, Shaw P, Petrocelli T, Hudson TJ, Neel BG, Onetto N, Siu LL, McPherson JD, Kamel-Reid S, Dancey JE (1 January 2012). "Feasibility of Real Time Next Generation Sequencing of Cancer Genes Linked to Drug Response: Results from a Clinical Trial". Int. J. Cancer. 132 (7): 1547–55. doi:10.1002/ijc.27817. PMID 22948899.

Murray IA, Clark TA, Morgan RD, Boitano M, Anton BP, Luong K, Fomenkov A, Turner SW, Korlach J, Roberts RJ (2 October 2012). "The Methylomes of Six Bacteria". Nucleic Acids Research. 40 (22): 11450–62. doi:10.1093/nar/gks891. PMC 3526280. PMID 23034806.

Genetics and Bioengineering : *Concepts and Issues* **Pages 28-54**
***Edited by:* Dr. Ashok K. Rathoure and Dr. Pawan Kumar 'Bharti'**
ISBN: 978-93-86841-92-6
***Edition:* 2019**
***Published by:* Discovery Publishing House Pvt. Ltd., New Delhi (India)**

3 Adverse Effect of Transgenics Through Pollination or Gene Flow

[1]Basavaraj Makanur, [2]Dhirendra Kumar Singh and [3]Esakkimuthu

ABSTRACT

The rapid progress of transgenic biotechnology has significantly promoted the development and production of genetically modified (GM) crops. The current area under GM crops in world is 160 million hectares. The extensive global cultivation of GM crops has generated great benefits, which may provide opportunities for solving the problems inherent in world food security, but, it has also aroused considerable biosafety concerns worldwide. Among these, the potential environmental consequences created by possible transgene escape from a GM crop to its non-GM crop counterparts (crop-to-crop) and wild or weedy relatives (crop-to-wild) via gene flow are the most debated biosafety issues internationally. Gene flow indicates the movement of genes or genetic materials from one plant population into another The creation of the first transgenic organisms during the early 1970s initiated the debate about their risks that continues today. The major concerns of those who oppose GM foods center on the: potential danger to the environment and possible health risks to humans. There are a range of predicted possible environmental consequences (e.g., creation of new weeds, change of fitness-related characters, and loss of genetic diversity in crop landraces and wild relatives) caused by crop-to-crop and crop-to-wild transgene flow. Through pollen-mediated gene flow, a transgene can move from a GM crop into populations of a wild relative, and persist or disseminate in the wild population through further hybridization and introgression between the GM crop and wild relative and make the wild population more invasive and competitive. Without the consent of society at large, GE crops will fail in market place. While questions remain to be answered about the risk of each proposed trait on a case by case basis, there is little evidence that GM crops poses an inherent risk to food, feed, or the environment. The proper combination of transgene confinement and mitigation strategies will provide an effective management tool for minimising any environmental

[1,2] G. B. Pant University of Agriculture and Technology, Pantnagar, Uttarakhand, India
[3] Kerala Agricultural University, RARS, Pilicode, Kerala, India

consequences created by transgene escape to wild relatives via pollen-mediated gene flow.

Index terms: Adverse effect, biosafety, environment, gene flow and transgenic biotechnology.

Introduction

The rapid development of biological science and technology has brought the world into a new era of biotechnology. One of the most important characteristics of the biotechnology era is the wide application of genetic engineering (also referred to as genetic modification) technologies for the improvement of plant, animal, and microorganism species for human benefits. As a consequence, modern biotechnology has greatly promoted the research and development of genetically modified (GM), or transgenic crops worldwide. To date, a large number of modified genes conferring diverse traits have been successfully transferred into crop varieties through modern biotechnology. These traits include high protein content and unique nutritional compounds, disease and insect resistance, virus resistance, herbicide resistance, as well as salt and drought tolerances. The great success of GM crops has had an enormous impact on world crop production and cultivation patterns of agricultural species such as cotton, soya bean, oilseed rape, and maize (James, 2006).

On the one hand, the commercial production of GM crops with various agronomically beneficial traits has opened a new dimension for meeting the great challenge of world food security by enhancing the efficiency of crop production. But on the other hand, the extensive environmental release and cultivation of GM crop varieties have aroused tremendous biosafety concerns and debates worldwide (Ellstand, 2001, 2003; Pretty, 2001). Biosafety issues have already become a crucial factor in constraining the further development of transgenic biotechnology and the wider application of GM products in agriculture. Nowadays, it is not possible to circumvent biosafety issues when discussing the development and application of GM crops in the world. Therefore, it is a rational attitude to face the challenge of those biosafety issues aroused by the cultivation of GM crops and try to close the "knowledge gap" by providing solid data from sound scientific research.

Understanding what is the meaning of biosafety and its related issues will help make a correct decision when facing and dealing with the technology and its products. According to Food and Agriculture Organisation, the term "Biosafety" refers to "the avoidance of risk to human health and safety, and to the conservation of the environment, as a result of the use for research and commerce of infectious or genetically modified organisms". Therefore, this terminology is related to the safety aspects of GM products from transgenic biotechnology that may pose an impact on human health and environment during the entire procedures of research, exploration, production, and utilisation. There are a quite number of biosafety-related concerns in general, but the most important ones can be summarised as follows:

1. Food, feed, and health safety caused by GM products (Marshall, 2007);
2. Environmental safety (Sanvido *et al.*, 2007);
3. Labelling of GM products and the detection of possible transgene (or derived protein) presence in agricultural products (Phipps *et al.*, 2003; Vogel, 2006);
4. Socio-economical and ethic concerns aroused by the application of GM products and technology (Aerni, 2007; Einsele, 2007);
5. Regulatory procedures and acts for GM related issues (Schilter and Constable, 2002; Novoselova *et al.*, 2007);
6. General public perception or acceptance of GM products and transgenic biotechnology (Knight *et al.*, 2007); and
7. Risk assessment systems in relation to the environmental release and cultivation of GM products (Hooftman, *et al.* 2007; Johnson *et al.*, 2007).
8. The concerns of environmental or ecological biosafety aroused by the introduction of GM organisms are the most challenging issue, because it is difficult to determine the long-term environmental impacts caused by GMOs released to the environment in which unpredictable and complex situations are always expected. However, the most discussed environmental biosafety issues can be summarised as follows:
8. Direct and indirect effects of toxic transgenes (e.g. the *Bacillus thuringiensis* [Bt] insect resistance gene) on non-target organisms, sustainable utilisation of biotechnology and its products in our generation and generations to come. The most relevant questions regarding transgene escape and it environmental consequences include those as listed here:
9. Will transgene escape from a GM crop considerably influence the sustainable and safe use of crop biodiversity and impact agro-ecological systems?
10. How does transgene escape to non-GM crop varieties and to weedy/wild relatives happen in reality?
11. How could escaped transgenes actually affect the genetic diversity of crop landraces and wild populations?
12. What are the potential biosafety consequences caused by gene flow from an environmental perspective?
13. How can we assess the potential environmental risks caused by transgene outflow using a biosafety framework?
14. Can we mitigate environmental risks, if any, through the use of management measures?

These questions should and can be addressed, not only for the benefit of scientists and researchers, but importantly also for the public and consumers of biotechnology products within the international community. The objective of this review is to introduce: the concept and mechanisms of gene flow; the categories of possible consequences caused by pollen-mediated transgene outflow; the biosafety assessment framework for such consequences; and the theoretical means to mitigate and manage any potential environmental consequences, based on knowledge generated from past and current biosafety research.

Global Scenario of GM Crops

The rapid progress of transgenic biotechnology has significantly promoted the development and production of genetically modified (GM) crops. The current area under GM crops in world is 160 million hectares (**James, 2011**).

Table 3.1: Global Area of Biotech Crops in 2011: (by Country (Million Hectares)**

Rank	Country	Area (million hectares)	Biotech Crops
1.	USA*	69.0	Maize, soyabean, cotton, canola, sugarbeet, alfalfa, papaya, squash
2.	Brazil*	30.3	Soybean, maize, cotton
3.	Argentina*	23.7	Soybean, maize, cotton
4.	India*	10.6	Cotton
5.	Canada*	10.4	Canola, maize, soybean, sugarbeet
6.	China*	3.9	Cotton, papaya, poplar, tomato, sweet pepper
7.	Paraguay*	2.8	Soybean
8.	Pakistan*	2.6	Cotton
9.	South Africa*	2.3	Maize, soybean, cotton
10.	Uruguay*	1.3	Soybean, maize
	Total	160.0	

*17 biotech mega-countries growing 50,000 hectares, or more, of biotech crops
**Rounded off to the nearest hundred thousand
Source: Clive James, 2011.

Concept of Gene Flow

Gene flow is a natural process that contributes to species evolution. However, in the particular case of GM crops, the flow of one or more transgenes could have adverse environmental, socio-economic, or ethical impacts. Transgene flow from a GM crop to its non-GM crop counterparts (particularly conventional varieties) or to a population of weedy/wild relatives has been considerably discussed as one of the central ecological or environmental risks associated with the application of transgenic biotechnology to crop production (Committee on Scientific Evaluation of the Introduction of Genetically Modified Microorganisms and Plants into the Environment, 1989). Such environmental risks include potential adverse effects on natural biodiversity and the survival of wild populations. Assessing the consequences caused by transgene flow is challenging, because it is difficult to predict the ecological effects of transgenes that are integrated into different genetic backgrounds or expressed in different ecological contexts. Indeed, plants that acquire transgenes will continue to evolve, subject to natural and artificial selection pressures in the agricultural setting and beyond. Importantly, once transgenes have moved into new populations, it is impossible to remove them from the environment if the transgenes can successfully persist and spread in the population (Johnston et al., 2008). Therefore, understanding issues such as what is gene flow, what causes gene flow, and what will be the fate of a transgene that has moved into a recipient population through gene flow, is very useful for understanding their potential consequences.

Concept of Gene Flow

In simple terminology, gene flow is the movement of genetic materials (genes or alleles) from one organism to another. In population genetics, gene flow (also known as gene migration) refers to the transfer of alleles or genes from one population to another (Hartl and Clark, 1989). Theoretically, there are two types of gene flow: vertical gene flow and horizontal gene flow (Box 1), although the latter is commonly referred to as horizontal gene transfer. Horizontal gene flow occurs only among unrelated species, such as between plants and microbes, as well as between microorganisms (Thomson, 2001). The discussion of horizontal gene flow is based more on theory than practice, since it has never been shown to occur with transgenes outside an experimentally-enforced setting, even though this process is significant in the evolution of organisms. Therefore, this review will focus only on vertical gene flow.

Definition of Gene Flow

Vertical gene flow is the movement or transfer of genes or alleles by normal reproductive processes, between separate populations of plant and animal species. The horizontal gene flow: Introduction of genes into organisms by processes that are independent of organism reproduction; infectious. Gene flow (vertical) is a term extensively used in evolutionary biology and population genetics, long before the issue of transgene escape from GM crops was raised. It is a general understanding that many organisms (mostly plants and animals) are divided into spatially separate populations that have restricted contact with each other. Spatial separation will possibly lead to reproductive isolation among populations. Many factors can fragment a species into a series of isolated populations. For example, geographical or ecological isolation can cause differentiation of a plant species into populations with different levels of genetic barriers. Conversely, gene flow can also maintain populations with a certain degree of genetic relatedness. Isolation and gene flow are two different forces in the evolutionary process, with the former promoting speciation or diversity, whilst the latter maintains a species with the same genetic identity (Rieseberg *et al.,* 2004). Human activity, such as domestication, serves as a strong isolation force that can produce, by selection and cultivation, a separate population derived from a wild plant species. Therefore, gene flow is a natural process that occurs incessantly and permanently between biologically-compatible organisms and to which all genes are subject. In the case of transgene escape, gene flow serves as a medium that moves a transgene from a GM crop to its non-GM counterparts and wild relatives.

Avenues of Gene Flow

Since gene flow is defined as, for example in plants, the movement of genes from one plant population to another, any medium that can move genes around will lead to gene flow. Typically, there are three avenues for gene flow to be mediated; either by pollen, seed, or vegetative propagule (Box 2, Table 3.2). Pollen-mediated gene flow occurs when pollen grains travel from a plant individual to another individual resulting in fertilisation.

Avenues of Gene Flow

Pollen-mediated gene flow is the movement of genes through pollination between individuals of different populations. Seed-mediated gene flow is the movement of genes through seed dispersal between different populations. Vegetative-propagule-mediated gene flow is the movement of genes through dispersal of vegetative organs between different populations.

Table 3.2: Types of Gene Flow via Different Avenues and their Characteristics

Type of gene flow	Occurrence	Influenced by affinity between donors and recipients	Factors that constrain gene flow
Pollen-mediated	common	Yes	Outcrossing rate of recipients, pollen loads of donors, pollen competition between donors and recipients, the pollinating media (e.g. wind, animals), and climate conditions
Seed-mediated	common	No	Seed dispersal media (e.g. wind, water, animals, and humans) and sometimes climate conditions
Vegetative-propagule mediated (usually for perennial)	Not common	No	Vegetative-organ dispersal media (wind, water, animals, and humans)

This process can happen between individuals within the same population or among separate populations. In the latter case, wind, animals, water current and other factors can serve as media. Seed-mediated gene flow occurs through the natural dispersal of seeds by animals, wind, water, or other means from one population to another. Animals with long-range migration habits can transfer seeds over very long distances. Humans can also move seeds intentionally through seed-exchanging and trading within or between geographical regions, which can promote significant amounts of gene flow. The frequencies and patterns of human-influenced seed movement require sociological (seed exchange and distribution) and economic (regional and international trading) analyses and cannot be predicted using only knowledge related to plant biology. In the case of vegetative-propagule-mediated gene flow, the movement of genes takes place through the natural dispersal of vegetative organs (e.g. tillers,roots, tubers and rhizomes) of plant species by animals, wind, water, or other means. As for seed-mediated gene flow, the movement of vegetative organs, particularly by animals and humans, is difficult to estimate when based only on plant biology.

Pollen-mediated gene flow will be primarily determined by intrinsic biological features, particularly the pollination biology of the plant species, such as breeding systems, out-crossing rates, amount of pollen (pollen load) produced by pollen donors, and pollen competition between donors and recipients. Physical or environmental conditions, such as distances between pollen donors and recipients, the strength and direction of wind, temperature, light intensity, and air humidity, will also influence pollen-mediated gene flow to a great extent. It is very important to generate such baseline biological and physical data through a science-based approach for the accurate prediction of pollen-mediated gene flow. In agricultural ecosystems, humans can play an important role in seed and vegetative-organ dispersal and migration, as would be the case of seeds or vegetative organs falling on the ground during harvesting and picking, transportation to the processing manufacturers, and trading at the local, regional and international level. The intensity and avenues of gene flow in different crop species can vary significantly, depending on annual or perennial characteristics, the capacity for seed dormancy, the longevity of seeds or vegetative propagules during storage (under natural or artificial conditions), differences in breeding (mating) systems, the importance of such crops in national and international markets, and those parts of the crop that are consumed by humans. Given the complexity of gene movement through seeds or vegetative organs, seed-mediated gene flow and vegetative-propagule-mediated gene flow will not be discussed further in this review, but it is necessary to point out that these are very important avenues for gene flow in terms of evolutionary processes or GM-related biosafety issues.

Transgene Escape through Pollination, Hybridisation and Introgression

Transgene escape indicates a process in which a transgene(s) moves from a GM crop to its non-GM crop counterparts or to its wild or weedy relatives through gene flow. The escape of transgenes can be categorised into two major types, based on the gene flow avenues through which the transgenes have moved and the recipients. The first category concerning the various available gene flow avenues was discussed in the previous section. For the second category, transgene flow can usually be determined as crop-to-crop gene flow, crop-to-weedy gene flow, and crop-to-wild gene flow (Box 3), according to the type of recipient.

Recipient Based Types of Transgene Flow

Crop-to-crop transgene flow is transgene movement from a GM crop to its non-GM cropcounterpart. Crop-to-weedy transgene flow is transgene movement from a GM crop to conspecific weeds. Crop-to-wild transgene flow is transgene movement from a GM crop to wild relative species.

However, what is important to emphasise is that no matter which type of plant is the recipient, non-pollen-mediated gene flow only results in the physical movement of GM seeds or vegetative organs/propagules from one location to another. There is no hybridisation or introgression involved. Only pollination will cause hybridisation or further introgression of a transgene into wild populations, which will lead to different ecological and evolutionary consequences. It is therefore important to bear in mind that pollen-mediated gene flow is the first, but important, step in the persistence and spread of a transgene in wild populations. For example, pollen-mediated gene flow can produce a hybrid between cultivated rice and common wild rice, and further backcrosses between the hybrids and wild individuals will stimulate the spread of crop genes (including a transgene) in a wild rice population through introgression (Figure 3.2).

Fig. 3.1. Panicles of cultivated rice (*Oryza sativa* L., right), common wild rice (*O. rufipogon* Griffin, left), and the hybrid or introgressed progeny (middle) resulting from pollen-mediated gene flow.

Usually, pollen-mediated gene flow is a two-directional event under natural conditions (Lu, 2003). In other words, a crop gene can transfer to weedy and wild species, but a weedy or wild gene can also move to crop species (Figure 3.2).

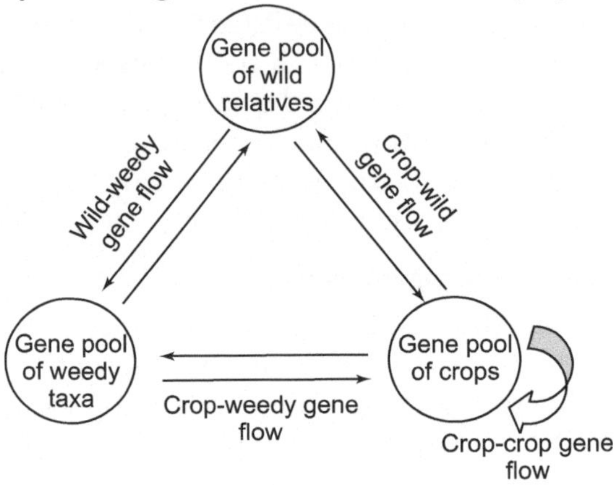

Fig. 3.2: Schematic illustration showing two-directional gene flow among cultivated plant species, weedy types, and wild relatives.

Such gene flow has been found to occur not only between different varieties of the same species (crop-to-crop), but also between crop species and their weedy/wild relatives (crop-to-weedy or crop-to-wild) (Figure 3.1). Occasionally, gene flow has also been found between a crop and less related wild species (Jenczewski, *et al.*, 2002; Heinemann, 2007) in the same taxonomic genus or different genera, as reported in the wheat grass tribe (Triticeae; Lu, 1993). The direction of gene flow among a crop species, a weedy type and a wild species can vary considerably, depending on the out-crossing rate of the pollen recipients.

In order for any transgene to escape (through pollination) and spread to wild populations, successful spontaneous hybridisation must happen between a sexually compatible crop plant and recipient species (for example, wild or weedy plants). In general, sexually compatible plants are usually members of the same species or closely related species. If hybrids between transgenic crops and weeds or wild plants produce viable seeds that develop into fertile plants, the offspring may cross with the weedy relative resulting in the introgression of the transgene into the weedy or wild population. The transfer or introgression of transgenes into subsequent generations will depend on the fertility of the hybrid progenies and the selection pressure on the recipient plants hosting the resident transgenes. Crop plants could also receive pollen from wild or weedy relatives resulting in possible hybrids for generation and dispersal. In principle, there will be no genetic recombination between GM seeds/propagules and those of non-GM crops or wild relative species if no further hybridisation and introgression occur following the physical movement of the transgenes. In this case, the environmental consequences caused by such gene flow may not be so serious, because the transgene(s) will not be integrated into the genomes of the recipient populations. However, if transgene flow mediated by pollination happens, it usually results in hybridisation between the pollen donors (in this case, a GM crop) and pollen recipients (non-GM crop counterparts or weedy/wild relatives) and further introgression.

Potential Consequences of Pollen-mediated Transgene Flow

From the above, it is easily understood that gene flow is a natural process, and a part of evolution that happens all the time. Therefore, gene flow per se is a widespread and natural event that should not generate any potential unwanted ecological risk. This is simply because such a process has been undertaken for many thousands of years during the evolution of vascular plants (higher plants). Even for gene flow between the major domesticated crop species and their wild relatives, such a process has continued for at least a few thousand years, from the onset of the domestication of wild ancestral species into cultivated forms by humans. To date, there has been no report of any major negative environmental consequences or disasters caused by such gene flow.

However, if a gene confers a sufficiently strong fitness advantage, like the case of transgenes with high expression levels and a unique function (such as the insect-resistant Bt transgene), it might spread quickly through crop-weedy or crop-wild hybrid progenies in the weedy and wild populations via hybridisation and introgression. Even with very low frequencies of gene flow from GM crops, a transgene can rapidly accumulate and disseminate in weedy and wild populations under favourable selection (e.g., Ellstrand, 2003; Snow *et al.* 2003; Lu and Snow, 2005). It is important to consider that seed-mediated gene flow can also be very extensive in both crop cultivars and their weedy forms due to intentional transportation and exchange of seeds by humans between regions. Strategies for confining the spread of certain transgenes need to consider the dispersal and longevity of pollen grains in air and seeds in transportation and storage. The estimation of the potential consequences caused by transgene escape, particularly into populations of wild and weedy species, should take the selective advantage of the specific transgenic trait into consideration.

The consequences caused by transgene escape into different recipients can vary significantly in terms of categories and magnitudes. Transgene escape from GM crops to their non-GM counterparts will have completely different affects compared with the escape to weedy and wild relative species. Even in the latter case, different types of transgenic traits will have different effects to wild populations under different environmental conditions. In principle, only transgenes that provide a selective advantage in the evolutionary process and that can change the fitness of the recipient individuals or populations will persist or quickly spread in the wild or weedy recipient populations following transgenes flow. Therefore, the case-by-case principle should be applied rigidly for biosafety assessments of transgene escape and its environmental consequences, and be dependent upon the types of recipients (e.g., crops or wild species) that may incorporate the transgene through gene flow. The potential or predicted consequences caused by different types of transgene flow are described next. Potential consequences of pollen-mediated transgene flow:

1. Contamination of non-GM crops
2. Impact on non-target species
3. Genetic Pollution
4. Issues with pharmaceutical and industrial GM crops
5. Development of Super Weeds
6. Spread of Engineered Genes to Wild Relatives
7. Multiple Resistance
8. Creation of male sterility
9. Allergenicity

Crop-To-Crop Gene Flow

Gene flow from one crop field to other adjacent fields planted with non-GM crop varieties of the same species can easily happen. The frequencies of transgene movement mediated by pollination between GM and non-GM crops depend essentially on the breeding (mating) systems and pollen quantity of the crops. Relatively high gene flow frequencies will be expected in out-breeding crops at the same spatial dimension from a pollen source under the same climate condition compared with autogamous crop species where low gene flow frequencies will be expected. On a very practical level, an understanding of crop-to-crop gene flow through both pollen and seeds is useful if different growers or countries want to separate GM crops from their non-GM varieties for marketing or regulatory reasons. This will help to determine the extent of consequences caused by crop-to-crop gene flow in different crops species. For example, cultivated rice is characterised by high rates of self-pollination and very little cross-pollination between adjacent plants or fields (typically less than 1.0%). Experiments in Italy showed that pollen-mediated gene flow from a transgenic, herbicide-resistant rice variety to adjacent plants of a non-transgenic counterpart was 0.05%-0.53%. Likewise in China, the average frequency of transgene flow from insect-resistant GM rice varieties and their non-GM counterparts was 0.02%-0.80% when the plants were grown at close spacing. Earlier, similar studies also indicated that gene flow frequencies between hybrid rice and traditional landraces grown next to each other were significantly different, with a much higher frequency of gene flow to the hybrid rice (Rong *et al.*, 2004). This asymmetric pattern of gene flow in rice suggests that the frequency is determined by the out-crossing rates of pollen recipients. A further study has shown that gene flow frequency dramatically reduced with the increase of spatial isolation distances from the GM rice pollen donors by only a few metres (Rong *et al.*, 2007). These findings are consistent with the small isolation distances that are recommended for maintaining the purity of cultivated rice grown in seed nurseries. In the USA, for instance, rice plants that are grown for certified seed to be sold to farmers must be isolated from other rice varieties by only 6 metres or less. Consequences caused by crop-to-crop gene flow in a cross-pollinating species like maize would be much more serious. This is reflected by the world debates caused by the "contamination" of traditional maize varieties in Oaxaca, Mexico. There are quite a number of predictions related to the consequences of crop-to-crop transgene flow, with only a few included below.

Contamination of Non-GM Crops

When transgenes move from GM crops to their non-GM crop counterparts, either through seed-, vegetative organ- or pollen-mediated gene flow, a major concern is the "adventitious mixing" (so-called "contamination") of GM and non-GM crop varieties. If the transgene or derived product becomes present in seeds or vegetative organs of non-GM crop to be consumed by human or used as animal feed, such a "contamination" may arouse food and feed safety concerns if the transgene is designed to alter the composition of food crops. There are already a few examples where the products of non-food GM crops have been found mixed with food and feed crops. One of the well known examples is the Starlink™ GM corn (transformation event CBH-351; OECD unique identifier ACS-ZMØØ4-3) that was only approved for use in animal feed. In 2000 the Bt (Cry9C) toxin from Starlink™ corn was detected in taco shells, sparking a whole-scale product recall. After three years of intense efforts to recall the seeds, the transgene was still present in detectable concentrations in the USA food supply (Heinemann, 2007). A recent evaluation strongly suggested that the amounts of Starlink™ corn still in circulation are underestimated and that there is no convincing data to suggest that present levels of "contamination" are reducing further (Marvier and Van Acker, 2005).

Another example is the herbicide resistant long grain GM rice (transformation event LLRICE601; OECD unique identifier BCS-OSØØ3-7) from the USA that was found in a number of European countries, as well as in Asian and African countries before it was approved for commercialisation. Recently, it was also found in China where GM rice is yet to be approved for environmental release and commercialisation in the market by the Chinese authorities.

These incidences of "contamination" of non-GM crops by GM crops illustrate the problems of crop-to-crop gene flow, as well as the challenges to maintaining segregation between GM crops and their non-GM counterparts. "Contamination" of non-GM crops, particularly organic agricultural products, usually creates social-economic and ethical biosafety concerns. Extensive and long-distance crop-to-crop gene flow will alter the deployment of GM and non-GM crop cultivation. The "co-mingling" of GM seeds or vegetative organs in non-GM crop varieties will cause disputes in regional or international trading, and may well cause legal disputes (Committee on the Biological Confinement of Genetically Engineered Organisms, 2004). A significant amount of gene flow to non-GM crops has the potential to increase opportunities for subsequent gene movement to weedy or wild rice populations. In these cases, the level of "mixture" or "contamination" from GM crop by gene flow is crucial. Different countries have set up a threshold to allow defined low levels of the adventitious presence of GM products in non-GM products, providing that the GM products are legally permitted to be commercialised in the exporting countries.

Change of Genetic Diversity of Traditional Crops

There is great concern that the extensive cultivation of GM crops will pose potential threats to the genetic diversity of traditional crops (Engels *et al.*, 2006). The loss of genetic diversity of crops in general will reduce the capacity to breed more productive and stress-resistant crop varieties. The concerns of genetic erosion are two fold. First, the extensive adoption of GM crops may lead to rapid losses of traditional crop varieties because of the continuous replacement of the traditional varieties by more commercially advantageous GM varieties. For example, after only a decade of adopting GM cotton, the current cultivation area of insect-resistant GM cotton (Bt) comprises more than 70 % of the total cotton cultivation area in China, and more than 40 % of the total cotton cultivation area in India. A similar situation is found with GM soya bean and GM oilseed rape in northern America. However, the counter argument is that losses to genetic diversity in traditional crop varieties have already taken place prior to the introduction of GM crops into modern agriculture, with its landscape fragmentation, adoption of improved crop varieties, and degradation of the agricultural environment. Second, the spread of transgenes from a GM crop variety to non-GM traditional varieties through gene flow may change the integrity of the traditional varieties if the transgenes have a selective advantage. During the process of cultivation and seed production, hybrids containing any beneficial transgenes may gradually accumulate unintentionally during selection to ultimately replace the original genotypes of the traditional varieties.

Change in Farming Practices

Some GM traits require specific management practices to remain effective. For example, the recommended management of a GM Bt crop is to have a high dose/refuge strategy, meaning to have a high dose of Bt toxin in the GM crops and to have a defined proportion of non-GM plants, capable of hosting the targeted pest species, sufficiently close to the Bt crops to allow mating of pests between the two locations. Extensive gene flow creates potential heterogeneity of traits in an environment and will likely change the concentration of Bt toxin in populations of GM crops, promoting the evolution of resistance to Bt among insects and lowering its strength and the effectiveness of high-dose/refuge strategies (Bates *et al.*, 2005). This can be accelerated by the practice of saving seeds that may lead to heterogeneous mixtures of Bt and non-Bt plants in subsequent generations. Insect-resistant plants are grown on approximately 12 million hectares globally, and adoption is growing (Bates *et al.*, 2005; Marvier and Van Acker, 2005). Moreover, the range of plants with Bt variants available or being developed is expanding, and includes cotton, maize, tomato, aubergine (otherwise known as eggplant or brinjal), soya bean, oilseed rape, potato, apple, peanut (groundnut) and broccoli (Bates *et al.*, 2005). This undoubtedly extends the variety of insects that will one day be exposed to Bt toxins, with the possible consequence that any management failures could extend to multiple crops and countries in a short period of time (Heinemann, 2007).

Another consequence brought about by gene flow is the creation of a landscape mosaic. Residual plants expressing Bt toxin-derived insect resistance, whether they be volunteer or feral crops or wild relatives, could undermine even region-wide efforts to coordinate Bt cropping practices. Stacked varieties might not significantly improve the management of Bt resistance if they are introduced after the same toxins have been individually introduced through commercialised varieties or if the toxin genes separate during transgene flow. The extensive cultivation of herbicide-resistant GM crops will also accelerate changes in farming practices by requiring the use of selective herbicides, thereby replacing traditional weeding practices that utilise broad spectrum herbicides or manual weeding, for example.

Issues with Pharmaceutical and Industrial GM Crops

One of the main concerns with crop species modified to produce pharmaceuticals is that they could harm humans or other species when accidentally consumed following unintentional "co-mingling" with conventional crops in the food chain. Some GM crops have been modified to serve as "bioreactors" for the production of pharmaceutical products and industrial chemicals, such as the GM rice that produces medicine. These GM crops are expected to be unsuitable as food for human consumption because they have no historical record of safe use (Heinemann, 2007). Gene flow from such GM crops into the general human food chain would certainly create adverse effects and greater concerns. The hazards will relate directly to the original transgenic crop. For example, a gene for the production of a vaccine protein may be transferred to a non-GM crop through extensive gene flow, with the same spectrum of concerns surrounding either the original or the hybrid crop entering the human food supply (Heinemann, 2007). Alternatively, novel hazards might arise from transgene flow, because the expression of a protein in one food crop may be significantly different from its expression in another. This was illustrated when a protein from a bean with a history of safe use as human food was demonstrated as being a potential allergen after it was transferred and produced in peas (Prescott et al., 2005). Care must also be taken to ensure that future GM crops specifically modified to have altered nutritional levels, such as the so-called "Golden Rice" (**Ye *et al.*, 2000**), will be safe for consumption by the general populace should they enter the human food chain in an unfettered manner.

Crop-to-Wild Gene Flow (Including Crop-to-Weedy Gene Flow)

Ecological studies have shown that some GM crops are viable in natural ecosystems and can interbreed with their wild relatives. The most publicized environmental consequence is that invasive weeds may be created if GM crops modified to tolerate herbicides or to resist diseases and pests transfer their transgenes to wild or weedy relatives via gene flow. Plants can also be modified with traits that allow them to grow faster (for example, by expressing a specific growth hormone), reproduce more (for example, by enhancing seed production), and live in new types of habitats (for example, by enhancing drought and cold tolerance). In principle, the potential environmental consequences caused by crop-to-wild or crop-to-weedy transgene flow can be effectively determined by the amount of transgenes that have outflowed to the wild and weedy populations, and by the characteristics of the GM traits that have or do not have evolutionary advantages under natural selection. When populations incorporate a GM trait likely to confer a selective advantage and are then exposed to a relevant selective pressure (e.g., pest attacks or drought/salinity stresses), the populations will most likely exhibit an enhanced performance (Ellstrand, 2003; Lu and Snow, 2005) leading to unwanted environmental consequences. It is necessary to point out that crop-to-wild or crop-to-weedy gene flow can recur over time. This is because plants of wild and weedy species generally persist in their habitats, or their seeds remain in the local soil seed-bank. The frequency of transgene flow can increase through recurrent gene flow over different years/seasons from GM crops cultivated in surrounding area. This is different from the case of transgene flow to cultivated species that are harvested at the end of the season. If the crops are consumed or used by industry/manufacturing, the transgenes do not accumulate in the crop populations. However, if the crops are to be used as seeds, the contaminated seeds may be propagated and disseminated to different regions.

Because of these unique features, the direct and immediate consequence of crop-to-wild gene flow will be changes in the genetic integrity of wild or weedy species by recurrently pumping transgenes into wild populations. In addition, if the transgene conveys a selectively advantageous trait(s), the movement of such a transgene into wild relatives may change the fitness of wild or weedy relatives, resulting in demographic alterations (either increase or decrease) of the wild and weedy populations, or rapid accumulation and spread of the transgenes in the populations by speeding up introgression of the transgene into wild or weedy populations. These changes will potentially lead to diverse environmental consequences. There are different possibilities for the fate of a wild population which incorporates a transgene. On the one hand, if the transgene can enhance the fitness of wild relatives through the expression of a favourable trait such as pest resistance, drought tolerance, or enhanced growth ability, the outflowed transgene will persist and quickly spread in the population through introgression. The individuals that express the transgene will out-compete those individuals without the transgene under natural selection. This process will promote a rapid increase of transgenic individuals and enhance their invasiveness, causing different degrees of weed problems by enabling the wild populations to expand into new territories. With the advent of herbicide resistant crops, oilseed rape being the most well known, there is strong public concern about the production of "super-weeds" that are resistant to multiple herbicides.

On the other hand, if the transgene reduces the fitness of receiving wild relatives, the frequencies of individuals that contain the disadvantageous transgene will decrease gradually. This process will be accelerated by recurrent gene flow and introgression from the nearby GM crop, possibly leading to the extinction of local populations by the so-called swarm effect. In many parts of the world, such swarm effects have already happened in the absence of GM crops through crop-to-wild gene flow, where populations of wild relatives are surrounded by crop fields in agricultural ecosystems and inhabit bordering areas between agricultural lands and natural habitats. If the transgene is selectively neutral and does not alter the fitness of the wild relatives, such as those genes encoding nutritional compounds and quality traits that are only favourable to human taste or health conditions, the outflow of such a transgene may not have considerable influences on the population dynamics of the wild relatives. In this case, the likelihood of environmental impacts of such gene flow should be low. Environmental consequences caused by crop-to-wild or crop-to-weedy gene flow are profound and need to be determined in the long-term. There are still many biological mechanisms underlying the process of gene flow and fitness change to be understood. Listed here are only some of the hypothesised/predicted consequences of crop-to-wild gene flow that are commonly discussed and debated worldwide, although most have never been found or proven. Science-based studies should be conducted to test whether in reality such consequences will happen under a case-by-case situation, and to measure the magnitude of such consequences should they occur.

Creation of New Weeds

Weeds can cause significant yield loss to a crop if the weed populations extensively infest agricultural fields, competing for resources with the crop (Hoagland and Paul, 1978). In addition, weeds can also lower the commercial quality or nutritional value of a crop by introducing undesirable grains, toxins, or allergens, whether they are sourced naturally or from GM plants. Any transgene-expressing weeds or wild populations are expected to create the same serious management problems as those currently experienced with their non-transgene-containing counterparts.

Crop-to-wild transgene flow may accentuate the characteristics of weediness, leading to greater persistence and invasiveness of already existing weeds. On the other hand, a GM crop may acquire genes for weediness leading to persistence and invasiveness of a crop species. Therefore, the concerns of gene flow with respect to weediness are mostly related to the following two aspects:

1. A wild or weedy species, for example a wild and weedy rice or oilseed rape that invades and persists in crop fields has the ability to become a more effective and aggressive weed; and
2. A GM crop volunteer or hybrid between the GM crop and wild relatives has the ability to become a more effective and aggressive weed, after incorporating transgenes that convey traits against biotic and abiotic stresses.

These concerns relate to the hypothesis that a transgene from GM crops will bring a fitness advantage to the populations of crop volunteer, weeds, and wild species (Ellstrand, 2001; Lu and Snow, 2005). Some noxious weeds, such as charlock (*Sinapis arvensis*) in the UK, have seeds that can persist in soil for up to 35 years. This observation is important due to the detection of a hybrid of charlock and herbicide-tolerant oilseed rape in a large UK study. While the seeds of the hybrid did not germinate, the pollen of the plant was not tested for the presence of the transgene. Thus, transgene flow could potentially make this important weed herbicide-tolerant. Traits that may influence invasiveness include fertility, vegetative vigour, tolerance of a wide range of environmental conditions, and the quality and dispersal range of viable material. Gene flow between crops and their weedy populations is relatively high, because the weedy populations are conspecific with the crops, usually derived from volunteers of the same crop species, or from offspring of hybrids between crops and their wild relatives (Lu, 2003). Recurrent or sequential transgene outflow from a GM crop may cause transgene stacking in the same type of wild relatives or volunteers. Cross pollination between varieties of oilseed rape (*Brassica napus*) in Canada has resulted in spontaneous triple-herbicide-resistant variants. Volunteers of oilseed rape are considered as among the 20 most common weeds in fields in Alberta, Canada, occurring as a residual weed in wheat and barley fields. Stacked herbicide tolerance in weeds or volunteers can significantly increase difficulties for weed control.

Effects of Other Fitness-related Transgenes

In many cases, transgenes do not encode traits with an evolutionary selective advantage. These types of transgenes are not expected to persist and spread in volunteer/weedy or wild populations of plant species. Therefore, the outflow of such transgenes is unlikely to result in environmental problems because frequencies of the transgenes would remain very low in populations. Likewise, transgenes that confer a fitness cost (in the form of reduced survival or fecundity) will be less likely to be passed on to host progeny. Many transgenic traits related to nutritional quality, manufacture processing quality, and grain composition are likely to have neutral or even negative effects on the fitness of weedy and wild relatives of the crop. These include for example, the psy, crtI, and Gt1 genes that increase the content of vitamin A (in the form of âß-carotene) in golden rice and the antisense Wx gene that improves the taste quality of rice grains (Chen *et al.*, 2006). These transgenes may pose limited environmental consequences should they escape to weedy or wild relative species through gene flow.

In contrast to the above cases, the fitness of wild and weedy populations might be enhanced by transgenes that confer a greater resistance to biotic stresses (such as insects and diseases), or a greater tolerance of abiotic stresses (such as drought and salinity), or an enhanced production of seeds or vegetative propagules. Depending on local environmental conditions, the flow of these types of "fitness-enhancing" transgenes to nearby recipients could release weedy or wild populations from ecological pressures that restrict their local abundance or limit their habitat requirements. If the transgene recipient population is already a weed or has the potential to become more invasive by acquiring specific transgenic traits, it might become more invasive in natural habitats. For example, if wild or weedy rice acquires transgenes that confer salt tolerance and faster growth rates, it will become more invasive in brackish and saline habitats. Another question concerning the consequences of gene flow from a transgenic crop relates to the magnitude of the transgene-derived fitness benefit and whether this will affect the population dynamics. This will largely depend on the extent to which insect and disease pressures regulate the wild relative populations. Therefore, fundamental ecological studies of wild populations are needed to help address this question. In wild sunflower, for example, the expression of a single Bt transgene resulted in less damage from insect larvae and a large boost in fecundity in field-grown experimental plants in Nebraska, USA (Snow *et al.*, 2003). Therefore, if certain transgenes can enhance the fitness of wild or weedy species, it is important to evaluate

1. The potential for creating more invasive weeds,
2. Any possible harm to non-target species, such as beneficial insects, and
3. Any possible effects of gene flow on the long-term durability of insect-resistant and glyphosate-resistant crops (e.g., Committee on Environmental Impacts Associated with Commercialization of Transgenic Plants, 2002).

Spread of Transgenic Herbicide Resistance

Transgenic herbicide resistance is the type of trait that could easily be acquired by wild and weedy species through gene flow. Weed control in crop fields is increasingly dependent on herbicides in both developed and developing countries, because of the shortage in agricultural labour and changes in farming practices, for example, the shift from transplanting plantlets to direct-seeding in rice. This transition has resulted in worse problems with weeds, due to weed seedlings out-competing, and suppressing the growth of, rice seedlings, as well as causing a severe occurrence of weedy rice in northeastern China (Cao *et al.*, 2006). Rice fields that become heavily infested with weedy rice can become unusable because the weed is an effective mimic of the crop and its longevity in the seed-bank makes it very difficult to eradicate. Thus, rice growers who can afford the cost of herbicides are eager to adopt herbicide-resistant rice varieties, even though the benefits of this strategy could be short-lived. The cultivation of herbicide-resistant rice varieties will certainly complicate the situation of weed control after a short period of time, because resistance to different types of herbicides is inherited as a dominant Mendelian trait that can easily spread to weedy rice by cross-pollination. If the same herbicide is used repeatedly, selection favouring the GM herbicide-resistant weedy rice will be very strong. Modelling studies by Madsen *et al.* (2002) estimated that herbicide resistance may become common in weedy rice populations within only 3-8 years of continuous rice cropping. A similar situation is expected with the cultivation of GM oilseed rape. Different herbicide resistant transgenes were found to be stacked in the same volunteers following recurrent gene flow, and the same transgenes are also expected to be taken up by any weedy types occurring in the neighbourhood.

Therefore, it seems extremely likely that new genes for herbicide resistance will spread to weedy types and volunteers, especially in regions where weed management is already difficult. In general, it seems likely that most fitness-enhancing traits will not be able to spread to weedy populations as quickly as those genes for herbicide resistance in populations that are frequently exposed to the herbicide in question. Even for self-pollinating wild or weedy species that can incorporate transgenes at very low rates, once transgene flow has occurred, those self-pollinating plants with a greater fitness will quickly increase the number of transgenic progeny in subsequent generations. In Costa Rica, for example, the rapid development of glyphosate-resistant weedy rice derived via gene flow from a herbicide resistant rice variety bred from a mutant has already become a major economic problem for rice farmers who rely on glyphosate for no-till rice production and who are not able to implement weedy rice control (Bernal E. Valverde, Tropical Agriculture Research and Development, Alajuela, Costa Rica, personal communication). Consequently, a number of rice scientists have recommended that herbicide-resistant rice should not be widely used without strict stewardship guidelines and effective biological confinement techniques to mitigate transgene flow (e.g., Madsen *et al.*, 2002).

Loss of Genetic Diversity in Wild Germplasm

Wild relatives of crop species are widely viewed as valuable resources of genetic diversity for future breeding (e.g., Ellstrand, 2003). Even if these wild relatives are somewhat weedy, germplasm experts believe that these reservoirs of diversity should be protected from population extinction and genetic "swamping," which results from a heavy influx of crop genes. To some people, the mere presence of transgenes in the wild germplasm of crop relatives represents a form of "contamination" or "genetic pollution".

There are two scenarios for the unwanted effects of transgenes on genetic diversity. First, it is theoretically possible that strong selection for fitness-enhancing transgenes could generate selective sweeps, in which portions of the crop genome that are linked to these transgenes displace corresponding portions of wild genomes (Ellstrand, 2003). This process is expected to be more common in self-pollinating species than in out-breeders, which have a greater potential for the mixing and dilution of crop alleles during sexual reproduction. Also, selective sweeps could be favoured by clonal reproduction, which might allow more vigorous transgenic crop-wild hybrids to out-compete the non-GM plants at the local level. The potential for rapid selective sweeps in most self-pollinating plants seems remote because 1) few transgenes seem likely to confer fitness benefits that are strong enough to lead to selective sweeps in wild populations, and 2) the extent of pollen-mediated gene flow is typically very low. However, massive transgene flow to wild relatives through recurrent pollination may pose threats to wild germplasm, particularly for out-breeders. Second, in some situations, a large influx of fitness-reducing transgenes could contribute to population declines or even local extinction of small, isolated populations of wild plants that occur near the crop. In populations of 100 individuals or more, frequencies of fitness-reducing transgenes would diminish due to the purifying force of natural selection. Therefore, current information suggests that gene flow from self-pollinating GM crops may not threaten the genetic diversity of wild and weedy relatives to a greater extent than current gene flow from conventional varieties (Ellstrand, 2003).

Gene flow may affect genetic diversity if it compromises the survival of populations of plants that are valued for not having a particular transgene. Biodiversity may be threatened by the escape and proliferation of a competitive accession expressing the transgene. Perhaps less well recognised is the loss of diversity through genetic erosion. While this is a natural process, GM agriculture can be conducted on scales that significantly distort the normal impacts of genetic erosion through gene flow. Not only are large areas covered in GM crops, but they are replenished frequently by human cultivation, leading to repetitive introductions of the exotic genes into an environment.

CASE STUDIES

Impact on Non-target Species

1. Effects of exposure to event 176 *Bacillus thuringiensis* corn pollen on monarchand black swallowtail caterpillars under field conditions by Zangerl *et al.* (2001)

The widespread planting of corn genetically modified to produce *Bacillus thuringiensis* endotoxin has led to speculation that pollen from these fields might adversely affect nearby nontarget lepidopterans.A previous study of *Bt* corn engineered with Monsanto event 810 failed to detect an effect of pollen exposure on the black swallowtail, *Papilio polyxenes*, in either the field or the laboratory. Here, we report results of a field study investigating the impact of exposure to pollen from a *Bt* corn hybrid containing Novartis event 176 on two species of Lepidoptera, black swallowtails and monarch butterflies, *Danaus plexippus*. Nearly half of the 600 monarch larvae died within the first 24 h; this and subsequent mortality was not associated with proximity to *Bt* corn and may have been due in part to predation. Survivorship of black swallowtails was much higher than that of the monarchs and was also independent of proximity to the transgenic corn. However, despite five rainfall events that removed much of the pollen from the leaves of their host plants during the experiment, we observed a significant reduction in growth rates of black swallowtail larvae that was likely caused by pollen exposure. These results suggest that *Bt* corn incorporating event 176 can have adverse sublethal effects on black swallowtails in the field and underscore the importance of event selection in reducing environmental impacts of transgenic plants.

2. Environmental risk assessment of transgene products using honey bee (*Apis mellifera*) larvae by Henrik *et al.* (2003)

An environmental concern regarding the cultivation of transgenic crop plants is their effect on non-target organisms. Honey bees are obvious non-target arthropods to be included in a risk assessment procedure but due to their complex social behaviour, testing transgene products on individual bees is not possible in bee colonies. We employed a laboratory larval rearing technique to test the impacts of such transgene products on honey bees. A serine proteinase inhibitor (Kunitz Soybean Trypsin Inhibitor, SBTI), that is a source of insect resistance in transgenic plants, was used as a model insecticidal protein on honey bee larvae reared individually in the laboratory. The addition of 1.0% SBTI (w:w of total protein) to the larval diet created significant additional larval mortality, slowed juvenile development and significantly decreased adult body mass. Our results suggest that the larval rearing technique can be used to monitor direct side-effects of transgene products on individual honey bee larvae.

Development of Super Weeds

1. Spread of Engineered Genes to Wild Relatives by Philip (1992): Wild species have been the source of many genes used in crop improvement, so there is information about the degree of sexual compatibility between crop species and their wild relatives. Potato (*Solanum tuberosum*) will cross-pollinate with wild diploid solanaceous species found at its place of origin in South America, but there is no evidence of cross-hybridization under field conditions with its relatives *S. nigrum* and *S. dulcamara*, which are common weeds of potato crops in Europe. In contrast, sugar beet will cross under field conditions with wild sea beets, and oilseed rape (*Brassica napus*) with *B. adpressa*. When there is poor sexual compatibility between a crop and its wild relatives, breeders may resort to ovary and embryo culture to obtain hybrids. By this means it is possible to obtain hybrids between *B. napus* and the common weed species *Sinapis arvensis* (charlock), but gene transfer in nature is unlikely. There is good evidence of coevolution of crop plants and certain wild species that have become important weeds of crops. Although coevolution can occur from genetic viability existing within the weed population, for example in *Echinocloa crusgalli* (bamyard grass), which is sexually incompatible with *Oryza sativa* (rice), in other instances there is evidence of genetic exchange between crop and weed. Hybridization between *O. sativa* and *O. perennis* under field conditions is reported to have produced *O. perennis* populations with reduced seed shattering, weak seed dormancy, and more synchronous germination, characteristics that would make them less likely to survive in wild habitats.

Although there is information in the literature on sexual compatibility between crop plants and related weed species, much of this is from controlled-hand pollination. More data are required to determine the extent of gene flow under field conditions, along with assessments of the competitiveness and fertility of those hybrids. Studies to estimate pollination distance have been important in the past to determine the isolation distance necessary for the multiplication of genetically pure seed stocks of plant varieties. Distances of 200 to 400 m are commonly used; however, it is reported that cultivated radish can cross pollinate with wild radish (both *Raphanus sativus* L.) over a distance of 1000 m. Transgenic plants generally contain convenient markers to estimate the distance of pollen movement and pollination, and data from a potato field trial using kanamycin resistance as a marker show 24% cross-pollination between adjacent potato plants (leaves touching), 0.017% at 10 m, and no evidence of cross-pollination at 20 m. Gene dispersal data from typical field test plots with transgenic plants are limited at present, and measurements of pollination distance could usefully be built into the field assessment programs currently being approved.

2. Transgenic crops : new weed problems for Canada? By Warwick *et al.* (1999): Over 25 000 transgenic field trials were conducted globally from 1986-1997, and many transgenic crops, including soybean *(Glycine max),* maize *(Zea mays),*tobacco *{Nicotiana tabaccum),* cotton *(Gossypium hirsutum),* canola *(Brassica napus, B. râpa),* tomato *(Lycopersicon esculentum)* and potato *(Solarium tuberosum)* have been commercially released. There has been a high adoption rate, with at least 28 million ha reported for 1998, with herbicide- and insect-resistant plants occupying 71 and 28% of the releases, respectively. The Current status of commercial production of transgenic crops in Canada is summarized. Transgenic crops have the potential to change weed communities/populations in three principal ways, via: 1. escape and proliferation of the transgenic plants as 'weedy' volunteers with subsequent displacement of the crop, weed and/or natural vegetation; 2. hybridization with and transgene infiltration into related weedy and/ or wild species, resulting in invigorated weeds and/or alteration of natural gene frequencies in these species; and 3. genetic changes in populations of unrelated species, as a result of changes to the environment, in particular herbicide resistant (HR) transgenic crops and the development of HR weeds. Potential risk can be estimated *a priori* using knowledge of the systematic of crop/wild/weed complexes. Risk must be assessed on a case-by-case basis for each crop, each country/ecological region, and for each trait. Potential weed risks will be greater if crop volunteers are predisposed to becoming weedy, are well adapted to the Canadian climate and if sexually compatible wild species are present.

Transgenic crops have the potential to change weed communities/ populations in three principal ways, via the: 1. escape and proliferation of the transgenic plants as 'weedy' volunteers in either agricultural/disturbed habitats or in natural habitats with subsequent displacement of crop, weed, or natural vegetation; 2.hybridization with and transgene infiltration (i.e., introgression) into related weed and non-weed species, resulting in invigorated weeds (often referred to as "super-weeds") and/or alteration of natural gene frequencies in these species; and 3. genetic changes in populations of unrelated species. For example, crops engineered to be herbicide or pest resistant may encourage greater use of particular herbicides and increase selection pressure for resistant biotypes in unrelated weeds or pests. These risks are illustrated in Figure 3.2.

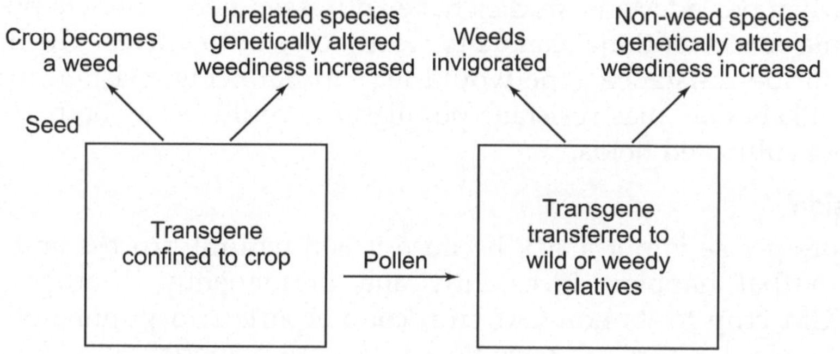

Fig. 3.2: Potential changes to weed populations due to crop transgenes

Consequences of Gene Transfer to Wild Species

1. Either the modified crops themselves, or wild species that receive the engineered genes by cross-pollination, may become plant pests.
2. If the resistant wild species happens to be a weed of that crop, this could make weed control difficult, especially if no suitable alternative control measures are available.

Herbicide Resistance

1. Herbicide Resistance: Toward an Understanding of Resistance Development and the Impact of Herbicide-Resistant Crops by William *et al.* (2012)

Gene flow via pollen in canola is significant. Out crossing rates as high as 47% have been reported. Canola pollen dispersal ranges from a few meters to 1.5 km. Pollen movement depends on wind direction and speed, surrounding vegetation, and topography. Bees are known to pollinate canola. Most bees forage close to their hive, but there are reports of bee movement up to 4 km. Because loose pollen grains can be picked up in a hive, a 4-km flying distance could result in pollen being moved 8 km. In Canada, gene movement between two genetically engineered canola lines was found at 800 m, which was the boundary of the study. In a Canadian field, volunteer canola plants were identified that contained transgenes for both glyphosate- and glufosinate-resistant canola. Although canola does not generally survive in undisturbed habitats, it can establish in areas adjacent to agricultural sites, roadsides, and field edges. The occurrence of glyphosate- and glufosinate-resistant canola plants along railways and roadways in Canada was measured in 2005. In Saskatchewan, 34% of 300 canola plants tested were glyphosate-resistant; in British Columbia, 43% of 81 plants tested were resistant. One hybrid between *B. rapa* and *B. napus* was identified as glyphosate-resistant. Volunteer canola plants can be a significant weed problem in subsequent crops. In 35 sampled fields, harvest seed loss ranged from 3 to 10%, with an average of about 6% or an equivalent of 107 kg/ha. In general, canola seedbanks decline quickly, but some seed may persist for several years. Canola seeds are reported to survive longer when buried.Many studies have addressed gene flow via pollen from transgenic or conventional canola to weedy or wild relatives. The movement of a herbicide-resistance gene would lead to herbicide-resistant individuals and the likelihood that resistant populations could occur both within and outside of cultivated fields.

Conclusion

Gene flow per se is not a risk because it is a natural process and a part of evolution that happens incessantly and permanently. Transgene escape from a GM crop to its non-GM crop counterparts and populations of wild or weedy relatives through gene flow may pose potential biosafety problems for food and health, environment, and socio-economics and ethics. Potential environmental consequences from transgene escape essentially depends on whether or not the transgenes will express normally in wild relatives, and whether or not the transgenes will change the fitness of introgressed plants, which will determine the dynamics of populations that have maintained the transgene under a selection pressure. Based on biological knowledge, the possibility of transgene escape can be assessed effectively, as well as the potential environmental consequences created by any transgene outflow (Lu, 2008). It is possible to significantly reduce transgene outflow by the use of a proper combination of confinement strategies and methodologies, applying both physical and biological means as use of any one method in isolation is likely to be ineffective. It is also possible to reduce the impacts of a transgene in the environment even further by the use of transgenic mitigation methods if confinement ultimately fails. Strategies or methodologies for transgene flow containment and mitigation are new and very little testing has been done to verify their long-term effectiveness. However, the availability of these strategies offers an opportunity for the future management of transgene escape to wild relatives and thereby further minimising any related environmental consequences.

REFERENCES

Aerni, P. (2007): Agricultural Biotechnology and Its Contribution to the Global Knowledge Economy. In: Green Gene Technology. Research in an Area of Social Conflict, Fiechter A & Sautter C (eds). *Series: Advances in Biochemical Engineering/ Biotechnology,* 107: 69-96.

Bates, S.L., Zhao, J.Z., Roush, R.T. and Shelton, A.M. (2005): Insect Resistance Management in GM crops: Past, Present and Future, *Nature Biotechnology,* 23: 57-62.

Cao, Q.J., Lu, B-R, Xia, H, Rong, J., Sala, F, Spada A and Grassi, F. 2006. Genetic Diversity and Origin of Weedy Rice (*Oryza sativa* f. *spontanea*) Populations Found in Northeastern China Revealed by Simple Sequence Repeat (SSR) Markers, *Annals of Botany,* 98: 1241-1252.

Chen, G., Wang, Z., Liu, Q.Q., Xiong, F., Gu, Y.J. and Gu, G.J. (2006): Development and Substance Accumulation of Caryopsis in Transgenic Rice with Antisense Wx Gene, *Rice Science,* 13: 106-112.

Einsele, A. (2007): The Gap Between Science and Perception: The Case of Plant Biotechnology in Europe, In: Green Gene Technology, Research in an Area of Social Conflict, Fiechter A & Sautter C (eds). *Series: Advances in Biochemical Engineering/ Biotechnology,* 107: 1-11.

Ellstrand, N. C. (2001): When Transgenes Wander, Should We Worry? *Plant Physiology,* 125:1543-1545.

Ellstrand, N. C. (2003): Current Knowledge of Gene Flow in Plants: Implications for Transgene Flow, Philosophical Transactions of the Royal Society, *Biological Sciences,* 358 (1434): 1163-1170.

Engels, J.M.M., Ebert, A.W., Thormann, I. and De Vicente, M.C. (2006): Centres of Crop Diversity and/or Origin, Genetically Modified Crops and Implications for Plant Genetic Resources Conservation, *Genetic Resources and Crop Evolution,* 53: 1675-1688.

Hartl, D.L. and Clark, A.G. (1989): Principle of Population Genetics (2nd Edition), *Sinauer Associates Inc.,* Sunderland MA, USA.

Heinemann, J.A. (2007): A Typology of the Effects of (Trans) Gene Flow on the Conservation and Sustainable Use of Genetic Resources, *Commission on Genetic Resources for Food and Agriculture, Background Study Paper,* Number 35 Rev. 1, Food and Agriculture Organization of the United Nations, Rome, Italy.

Henrik, F. B., Camilla, J. B., Henrik, H. and Gábor, L.L. (2003): Environmental Risk Assessment of Transgene Products using Honey bee (*Apis mellifera*) Larvae, *Apidologie,* 34: 139–145.

Hoagland, R.E. and Paul, R.V. (1978): A Comparative SEM Study of Red Rice and Several Commercial Rice (*Oryza sativa*) varieties, *Weed Science,* 26(6): 619-625.

Hooftman, D.A.P., Jong, M.J.D., Oostermeijer, J.G.B. and Nijs. H.J. (2007): Modelling the Long-term Consequences of Crop-wild Relative Hybridization: A Case Study Using Four Generations of Hybrids, *Journal of Applied Ecology,* 44(5): 1035-1045.

James, C. (2006): Global Status of Commercialized Biotech/GM Crops:ISAAA Brief No. 35. *International Service for the Acquisition of Agri-Biotech Applications (ISAAA),* Ithaca, NY, USA.

James, C. (2011): Global Status of Commercialized Biotech/GM Crops- 2011, ISAAA Brief No. (43), Ithaca, New York.

Jenczewski, E., Ronfort, J. and Chèvre, A.M. (2002): Crop-to-Wild Gene Flow, Introgression and Possible Fitness Effects of Transgenes, *Environment Biosafety Research,* 2: 9-24.

Johnson, K.L., Raybould, A.F., Hudson, M.D. and Poppy, G.M. (2007): How does Scientific Risk Assessment of GM Crops Fit within the Wider Risk Analysis?., *Trends in Plant Science,* 12: 1-5.

Knight, J.G., Mather, D.W., Holdsworth, D.K. and Ermen, D.F. (2007): Acceptance of GM food - An Experiment in six Countries, *Nature Biotechnology,* 25: 507-508.

Lu, B. R. (2008): Transgene Escape from GM Crops and Potential Biosafety Consequences: An Environmental Perspective, *Collection of Biosafety Reviews,* 4: 66-141.

Lu, B.R. (1993): Biosystematic Investigations of Asiatic Wheatgrass - Elymus L. (Triticeae: Poaceae), PhD thesis, Department of Plant Breeding Research, Swedish University of Agricultural Sciences, Svalöv, Sweden, pp. 563.

Lu, B.R. (2003): Transgene Containment by Molecular Means-is it Possible and Cost Effective?., *Environmental Biosafety Research,* 4: 3-8.

Lu, B.R. and Snow, A.A. (2005): Gene Flow from Genetically Modified Rice and Its Environmental Consequences, *BioScience,* 55: 669-678.

Madsen, K.H., Valverde, B.E. and Jensen, J.E. (2002): Risk Assessment of Herbicide Resistant Crops: A Latin American Perspective using Rice (*Oryza sativa*) as a Model, *Weed Technology,* 16: 215-223.

Marshall, A. (2007): GM Soybeans and Health Safety - A Controversy re-examined, *Nature Biotechnology*, 25: 981-987.

Marvier, M. and Van Acker, R.C. (2005): Can Crop Transgenes be Kept on a Leash?., *Frontiers in Ecology and the Environment*, 3: 99-106.

Novoselova, T.A., Meuwissen, M.P.M. and Huirne, R.B.M. (2007): Adoption of GM Technology in Livestock Production Chains: An Integrating Framework, *Trends in Food Science and Technology*, 18: 175-188.

Philip, J. D. (1992): Spread of Engineered Genes to Wild Relatives, *Plant Physiol.*, 100: 13-15.

Phipps, R. H., Deaville, E.R. and Maddison, B.C. (2003): Detection of Transgenic and Endogenous Plant DNA in Rumen Fluid, Duodenal Digesta, Milk, Blood and Feces of Lactating Dairy Cows, *Journal of Dairy Science*, 86: 4070-4078.

Pretty, J. (2001): The Rapid Emergence of Genetic Modification in World Agriculture: Contested Risks and Benefits, *Environmental Conservation*, 28: 248-262.

Rieseberg, L.H., Church, S.A. and Morjan, C.L. (2004): Integration of Populations and Differentiation of Species, *New Phytologist*, 161: 59-69.

Rong, .J, Lu, B.R., Song, Z.P., Su, J., Snow, A.A., Zhang, X.S., Sun, S.G., Chen, R. and Wang, F. (2007): Dramatic Reduction of Crop-to-crop Gene Flow within a Short Distance from Transgenic Rice Fields, *New Phytologist*, 173: 346-353.

Rong, J., Xia, H., Zhu, Y.Y., Wang, Y.Y. and Lu, B.R. (2004): Asymmetric Gene Flow between Traditional and Hybrid Rice Varieties (Oryza sativa) Estimated by Nuclear SSRs and Its Implication in Germplasm Conservation, *New Phytologist*, 163: 439-445.

Sanvido, O., Romeis, J. and Bigler, F. (2007): Ecological Impacts of Genetically Modified Crops: Ten Years of Field Research and Commercial Cultivation, In: Green Gene Technology. Research in an Area of Social Conflict, Fiechter A & Sautter C (eds)., *Series: Advances in Biochemical Engineering/ Biotechnology*, 107: 235-278.

Schilter, B. and Constable, A. (2002): Regulatory Control of Genetically Modified (GM) Foods: Likely Developments, *Toxicology Letters*, 127: 341-349.

Snow, A.A., Pilson, D., Rieseberg, L.H., Paulsen, M.J., Pleskac, N., Reagon, M.R., Wolf, D.E. and Selbo, S.M. (2003): A Bt Transgene Reduces Herbivory and Enhances Fecundity in Wild Sunflowers, *Ecology Applications*, 13:279-286.

Thomson, J.A. 2001. Horizontal Transfer of DNA from GM Crops to Bacteria and to Mammalian Cells, *Journal of Food Science*, 66: 188-193.

Vogel. G. (2006): Genetically Modified Crops - Tracing the Transatlantic Spread of GM Rice, *Science*, 313: 1714-1714.

Warwick, S. I., Hugh, J. B. and Ernest, S. (1999): Transgenic Crops : New Weed Problems for Canada?., *Phytoprotection*, 80 : 71-84.

William, K. V., Robert, L. N., Theodore, M. W., John, K. S., Carol, S., Nilda, R.B., William, G.J. and Marilyn, R. (2012): Herbicide Resistance: Toward an Understanding of Resistance Development and the Impact of Herbicide-Resistant Crops, *Weed Science*, Special Issue: 2–30.

Ye, X., Al-Babili, S., Klöti, A., Zhang, J., Lucca, P., Beyer, P. and Potrykus, I. (2000): Engineering the Provitamin A (Beta-carotene) Biosynthetic Pathway into (carotenoid-free) Rice Endosperm, *Science*, 287: 303-305.

Zangerl A. R., D. McKenna, C. L. Wraight, M. Carroll, P. Ficarello, R. Warner, and M. R. Berenbaum. (2001): Effects of Exposure to Event 176 *Bacillus thuringiensis* Corn Pollen on Monarch and Black Swallowtail Caterpillars Under Field Conditions, *PNAS*, 98 (21): 11908–11912.

Genetics and Bioengineering : *Concepts and Issues* **Pages 55-71**
Edited by: **Dr. Ashok K. Rathoure and Dr. Pawan Kumar 'Bharti'**
ISBN: 978-93-86841-92-6
Edition: **2019**
Published by: **Discovery Publishing House Pvt. Ltd., New Delhi (India)**

4

Modern Molecular Techniques for New Innovation

[1]Prasann Kumar, [2]Shweta Pathak

ABSTRACT

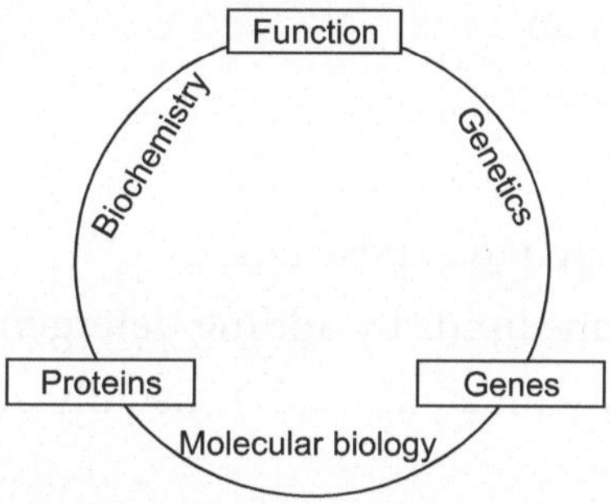

Schematic relationship between biochemistry, genetics and molecular biology

Researchers in molecular biology use specific techniques native to molecular biology but increasingly combine these with techniques and ideas from genetics and biochemistry. There is not a defined line between these disciplines. The figure to the right is a schematic that depicts one possible view of the relationships between the fields.

Keywords: Agriculture, Biotic, Crop, Molecular, Techniques.

INTRODUCTION

Before any type of DNA Based study DNA must be extracted. A need of the source of biological samples.

- Samples from Prokaryotes
- Samples from Eukaryotes

Why DNA Extraction

- The extraction of DNA from a cell is often a first step for scientists who need to obtain and study a gene.

[1] Department of Agronomy, School of Agriculture, Lovely Professional University, Jalandhar, Punjab, 144411, India

[2] Department of Plant Physiology, I.Ag. Sci., BHU., Varanasi, 221005, U.P., India

- The total cell DNA is used as a pattern to make copies (called clones) of a particular gene. These copies can then be separated away from the total cell DNA, and used to study the function of that individual gene.
- There is basic need of DNA in all the biological fields.
- With the help of genomic DNA extraction we can establish desirable, sustainable changes for "HUMNITY".

Methods of DNA Samples Preparation for Genetic Analysis

Old trend of DNA analysis

- Phenol-chloroform DNA extraction.
- Salting out DNA extraction etc.

Recent trend in DNA analysis

- FTA Card technology

Steps to DNA Extraction

1. Break the cells open to expose DNA.
2. Remove membrane lipids by adding detergent.
3. Precipitate DNA with an alcohol — usually ethanol or isopropanol.

Why Add Detergent?

- A cell's membranes have two layers of lipid (fat) molecules with proteins going through them (Figure 4.1).

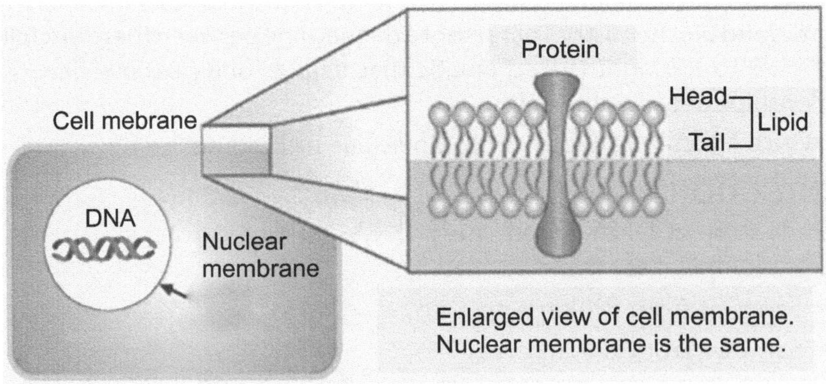

Fig. 4.1: Enlarge view of cell membrane and nuclear membrane (Source: Based on a review of Literature, 2018)

- When detergent comes close to the cell, it captures the lipids and proteins (Figure 4.2).

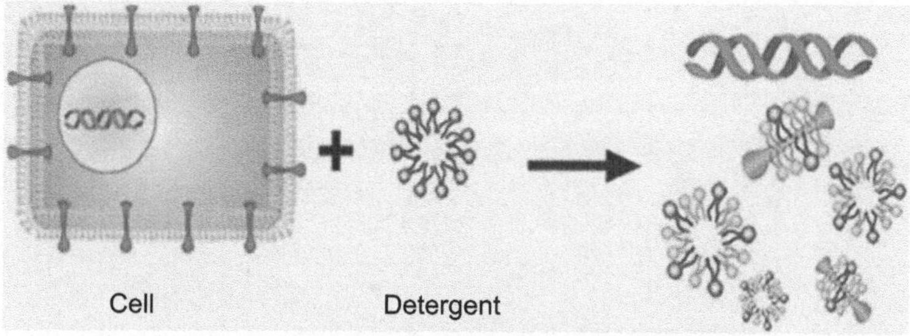

Fig. 4.2: Cell and Detergents interaction
(Source: Based on a review of Literature, 2018)

Why Add Enzyme?

- After the detergent step, the last question is: what you have now in your organism soup?
- The cell and nuclear membranes have been broken apart, as well as all of the organelle membranes.
- So what is left?
  * Proteins
  * Carbohydrates (sugars)
  * DNA

The DNA in the nucleus of the cell is molded, folded, and protected by proteins. The enzymes cuts the proteins away from the DNA (Figure 3).

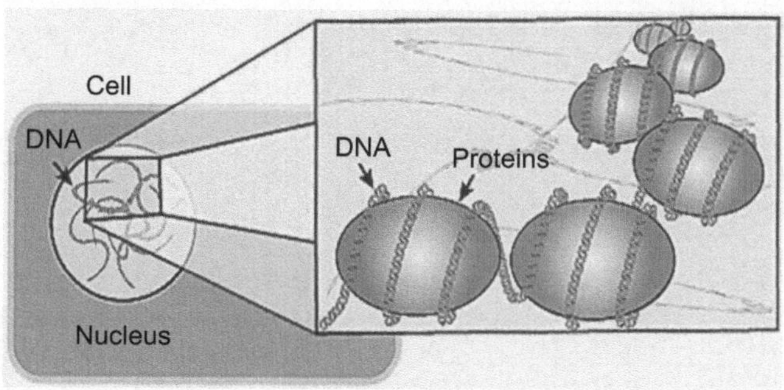

Fig. 4.3: Cell and DNA integration
(Source: Based on a review of Literature, 2018)

Quality and Quantitation of DNA

- Determination of DNA concentration by Spectrophotometer or nano-drop.
- If the ratio of OD values at 260 nm and 280 nm is

Within 1.6 to 2 = pure DNA, Less than 1.6 = contamination of protein or phenol, More than 2.0 = RNA contamination (Figure 4.4 & 4.5)

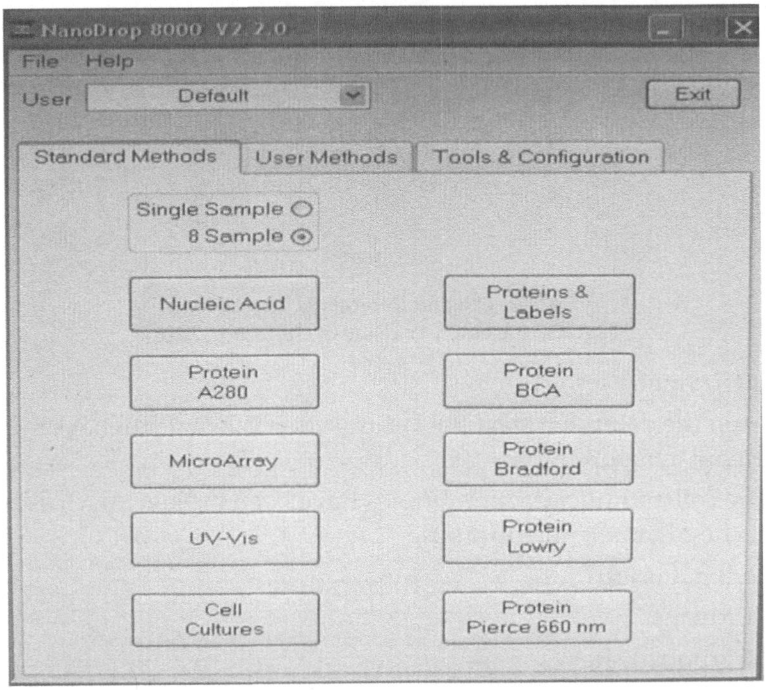

Fig. 4.4: Display of Nano Drop
(Source: Based on a review of Literature, 2018)

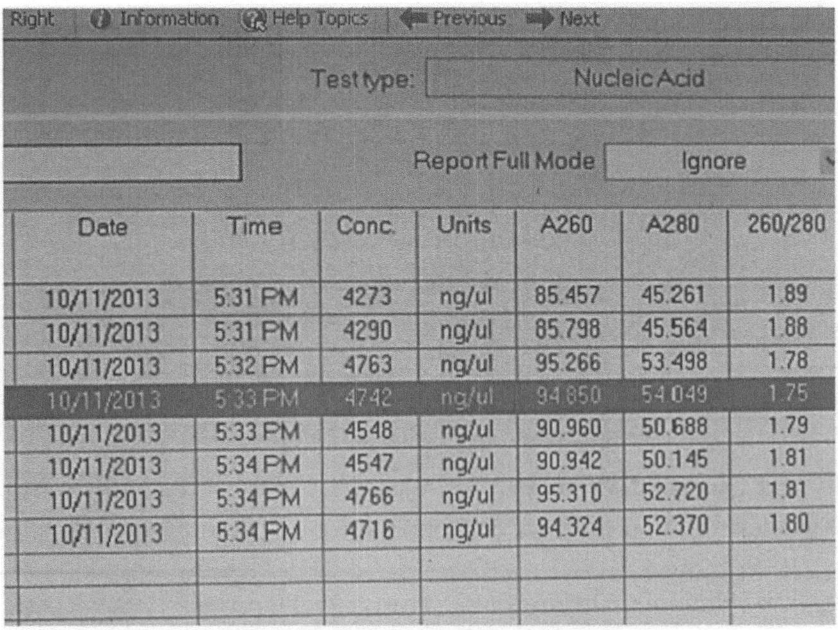

Date	Time	Conc.	Units	A260	A280	260/280
10/11/2013	5:31 PM	4273	ng/ul	85.457	45.261	1.89
10/11/2013	5:31 PM	4290	ng/ul	85.798	45.564	1.88
10/11/2013	5:32 PM	4763	ng/ul	95.266	53.498	1.78
10/11/2013	5:33 PM	4742	ng/ul	94.850	54.049	1.75
10/11/2013	5:33 PM	4548	ng/ul	90.960	50.688	1.79
10/11/2013	5:34 PM	4547	ng/ul	90.942	50.145	1.81
10/11/2013	5:34 PM	4766	ng/ul	95.310	52.720	1.81
10/11/2013	5:34 PM	4716	ng/ul	94.324	52.370	1.80

Fig. 4.5: Measured amount in nano-drop
(Source: Based on a review of Literature, 2018)

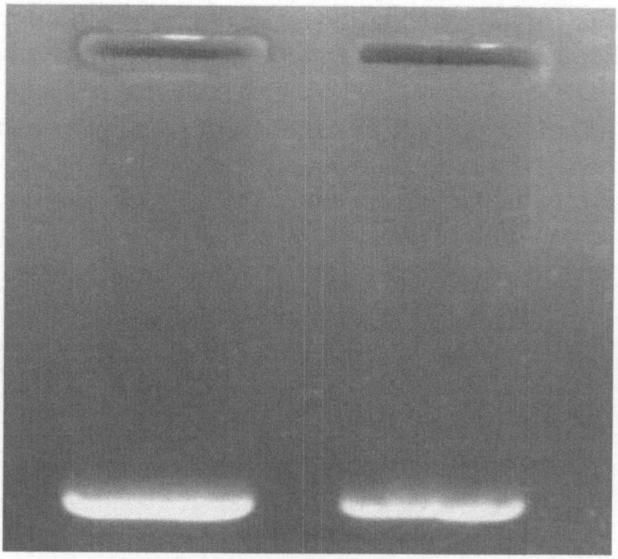

Fig. 4.6: Amount of genetic materials
(Source: Based on a review of literature, 2018)

Polymerase Chain Reaction

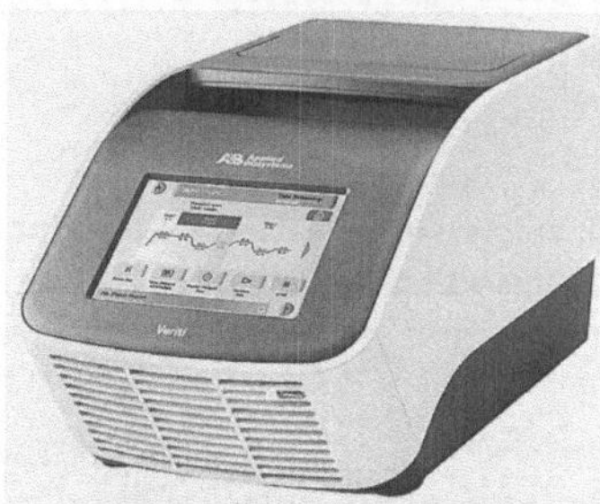

Fig. 4.7: PCR Machine
(Source: Based on a review of Literature, 2018)

Fig. 4.8: The Nobel Prize in Chemistry 1993
(Source: Based on Review of Literature, 2018)

Kary B. Mulis, for the contribution to the developments of methods within DNA-based chemistry for his invention of the polymerase chain reaction (PCR) method

Taq Polymerase is an enzyme extracted from *Thermus aquaticus,* a bacterium found in the hot springs of Yellowstone National Park. Who would have thought a bacterium hangingout in a hot spring in Yellowstone National Park would spark a revolutionary new laboratories techniques? (Figure 4.9 & 4.10).

Fig. 4.9: Yellowstone National Park Hot Spring
(Source: Based on Review of Literature, 2018)

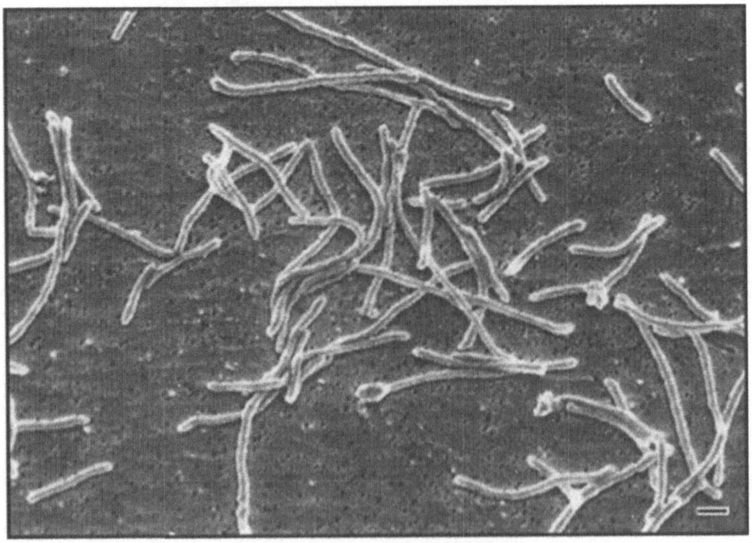

Fig. 4.10: Thermus aquaticus
(Source: Based on Review of Literature, 2018)

Master mix by mixing PCR component as following (Figure 4.11 & 4.12): (For 25 microliter reaction) buffer 10X = 2.5 micro liter, dNTPs (10 mM) = 0.5 micro liter, MgCl2 (50 mM) = 0.75-1 microliter primer forward (10 pico liter) = 0.8-1.5 primer reverse (10 pico liter) = 0.8-1.5 Taq polymerase (5U/microliter) = 0.15-0.25 microliter RNase-free water = variablekeep the PCR tube on ice (when working).

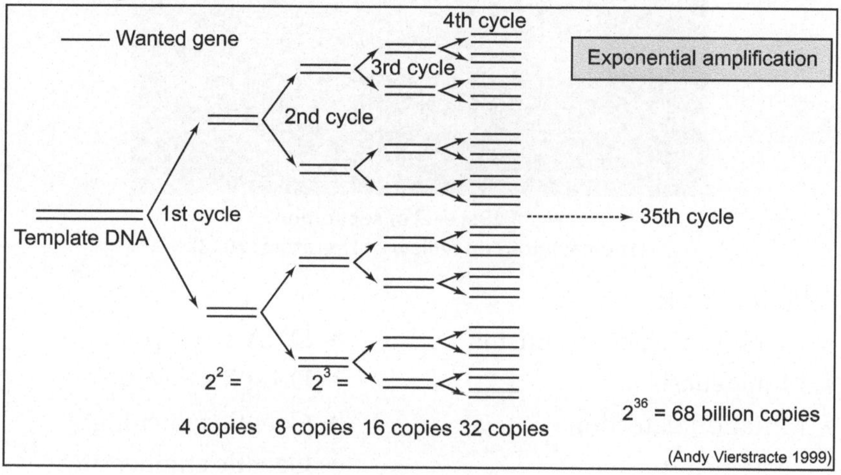

Fig. 4.11: Process of PCR
(Source: Based on review of Literature, 2018)

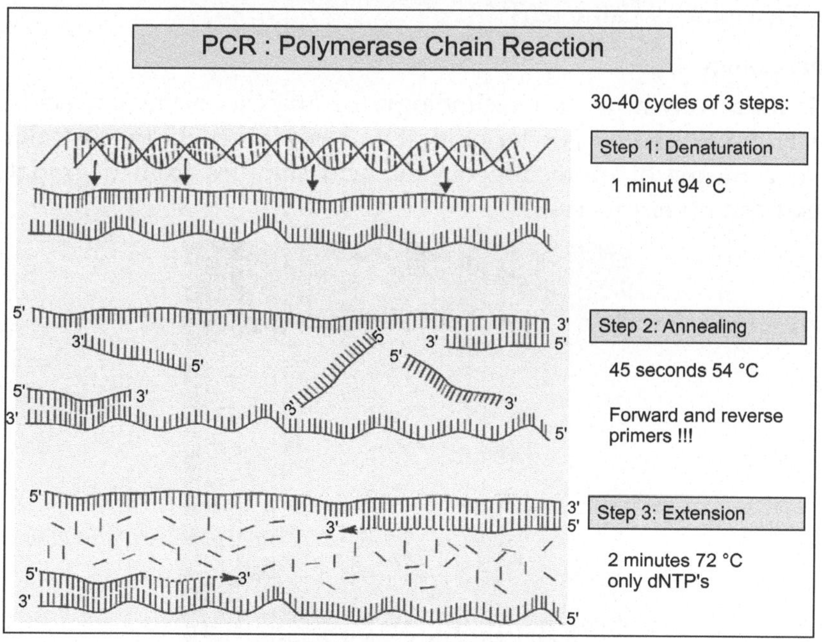

Fig. 4.12: PCR Chain Reaction
(Source: Based on a review of literature, 2018)

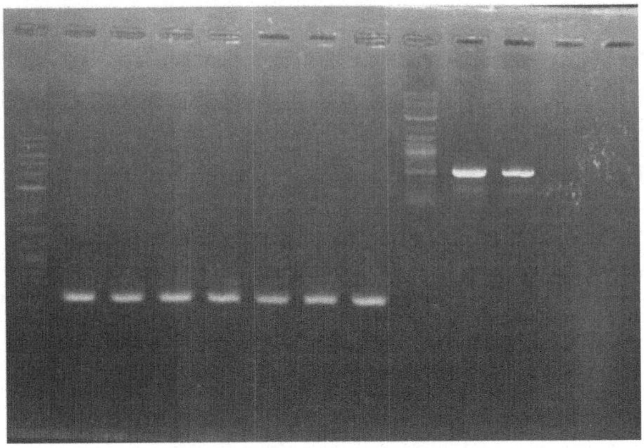

Fig. 4.13: Level of separation
(Source: Based on review of Literature, 2018)

Applications of PCR

- Classification of organisms
- Mutagenesis
- Mutation detection
- Sequencing
- Cancer research
- Detection of pathogens
- DNA fingerprinting
- Drug discovery
- Genetic matching
- Genetic engineering
- Pre-natal diagnosis

FTA Technology

FTA® is an acronym for fast technology for analysis of nucleic acids.It was originally developed by Fowler et al., Flinders University in Australia in the 1980s as a means of protecting nucleic acid samples from degradation by nucleases and other processes.

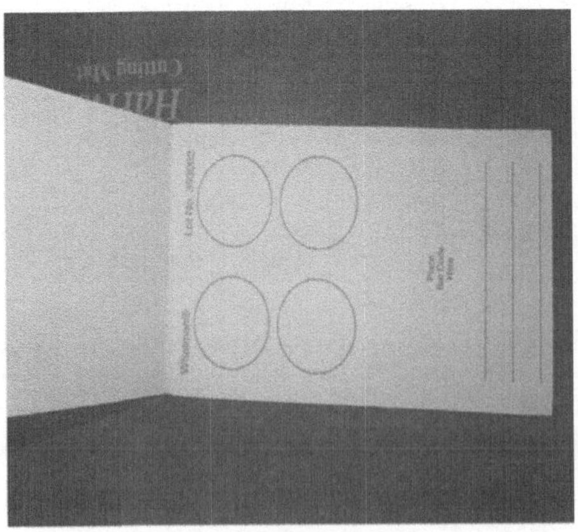

Fig. 4.14: FTA analysis of Nucleic acid
(Source: Based on Review of Literature, 2018)

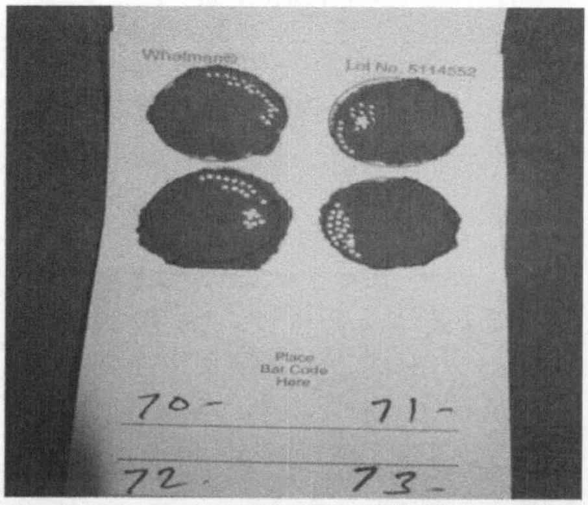

Fig. 4.15: FTA Analysis of nucleic acid
(Source: Based on a review of literature, 2018)

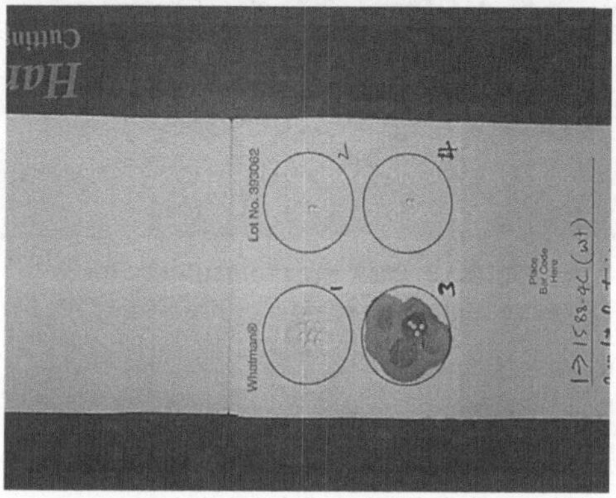

Fig. 4.16: Analysis of nucleic acid with the help of FTA
(Source: Based on review of Literature, 2018)

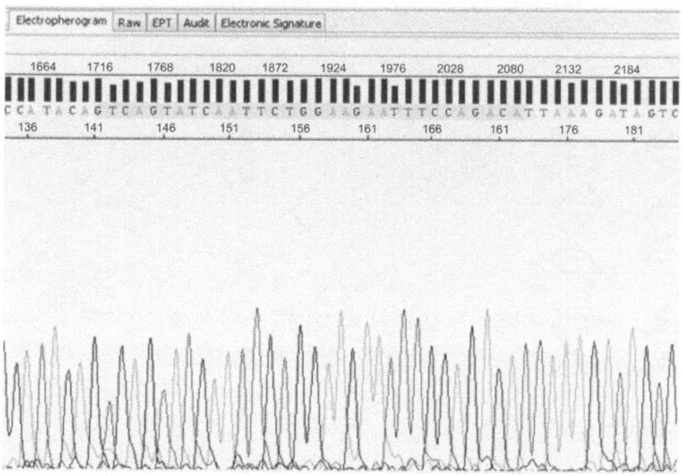

Fig. 4.17: Electropherogram of nucleic acid
(Source: Based on review of Literature, 2018)

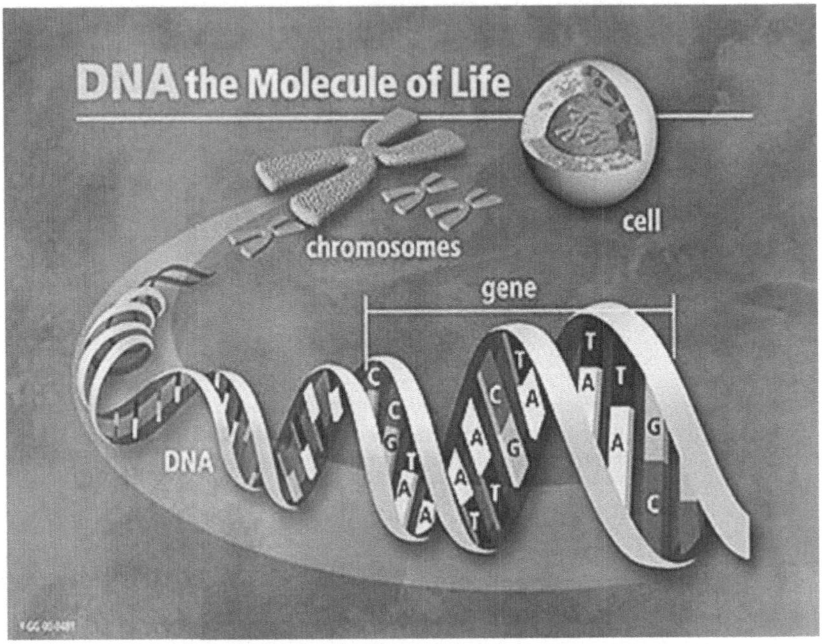

Fig. 4.18: DNA the molecules of life
(Source: Based on review of literature, 2018)

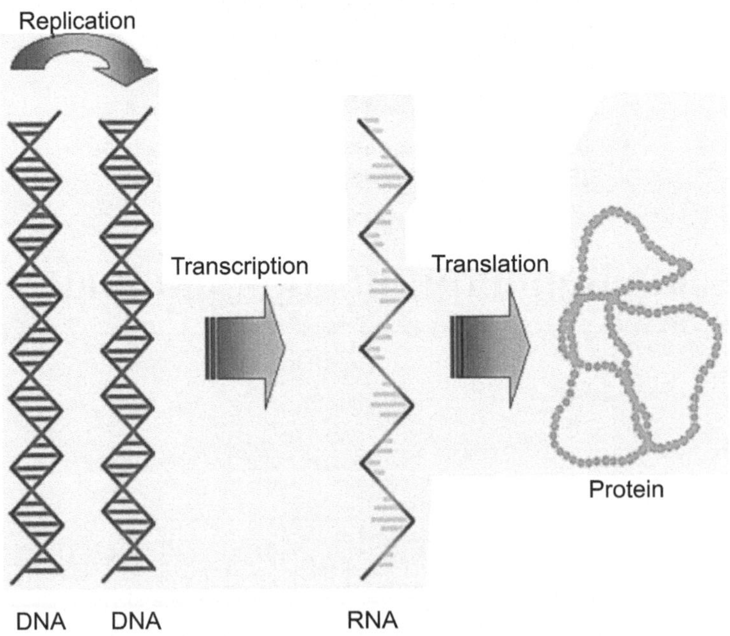

Fig. 4.19: Molecular mechanism of genetic materials
(Source: Based on review of literature, 2018)

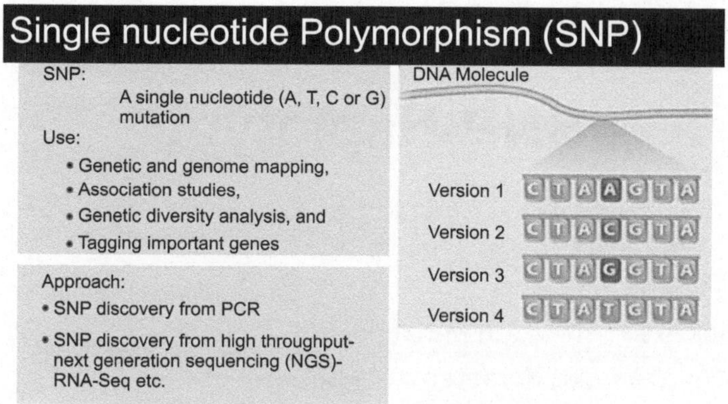

Fig. 4.20: Sequence of Nucleic acid
(Source:Based on review of Literature, 2018)

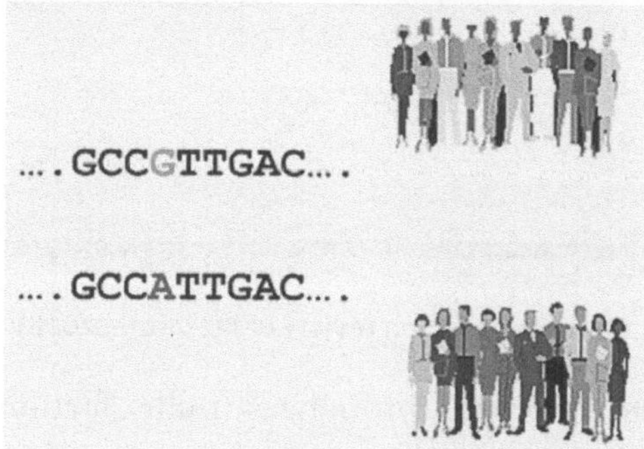

Fig. 4.21: Different type of markers
(Source: Based on review of literature, 2018)

BRCA1 gene SNPs:
- rs1799950, known as Q356R
- rs4986850, known as D693N
- rs2227945, known as S1140G
- rs16942, known as K1183R
- rs1799966, known as S1613G

BRCA2 gene SNPs:
- rs766173, known as N289H
- rs144848, known as N372H
- rs4987117, known as T1915M
- rs1799954, known as R2034C
- rs11571746, known as S2835P
- rs11571747, known as E2856A
- rs4987047, known as I2944F
- rs11571833, known as K3326stop

ATM gene SNPs:
- rs3218707, known as V182L
- rs4987945, known as L546V
- rs4986761, known as S707P
- rs3218695, known as D814E
- rs1800056, known as F858L
- rs1800057, known as P1054R
- rs3092856, known as H1380Y
- rs1800058, known as L1420F
- rs1801673, known as D1853V

CHEK2 gene SNPs:
- rs17879961, known as I157T

TP53 gene SNPs:

Fig. 4.22: SNP haplotype
(Source: Based on review of literature, 2018)

In humans, mitochondrialinfluences male fertility. Sperm races: H haplotype best, T haplotype worst.

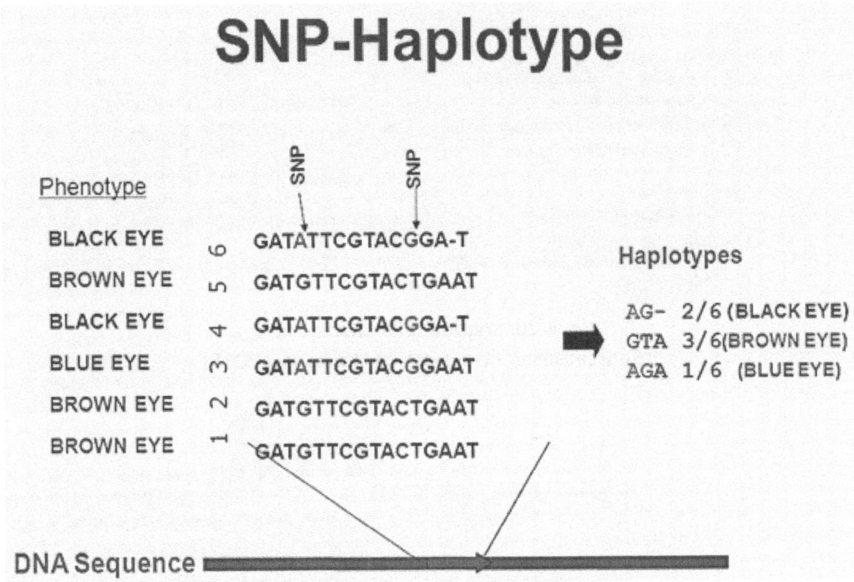

(Source: Based on review of literature, 2018)

In humans, mitochondrial influences male fertility. Sperm races: H haplotybe best, T haplotype worst.

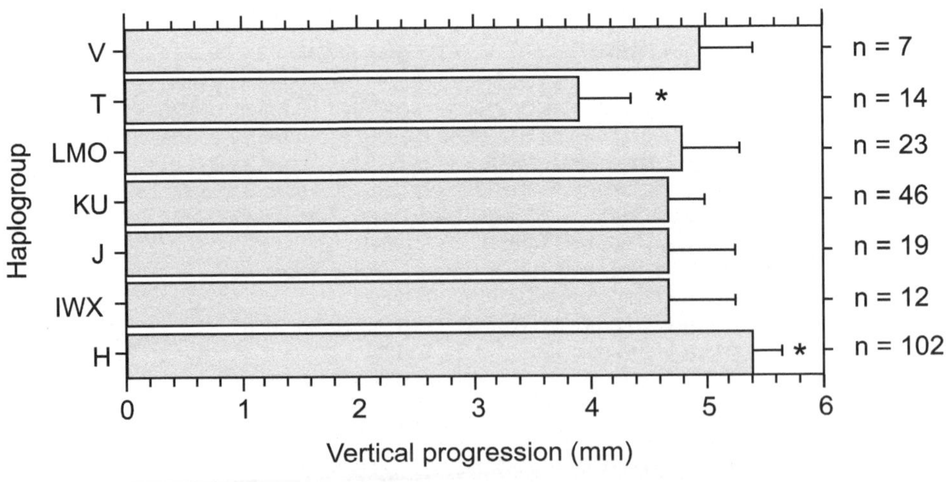

Fig. 4.23: Haplogroup and Vertical progression (mm)
(Source: Based on review of literature, 2018)

The Effects of Mutation: Sickle Cell Anemia

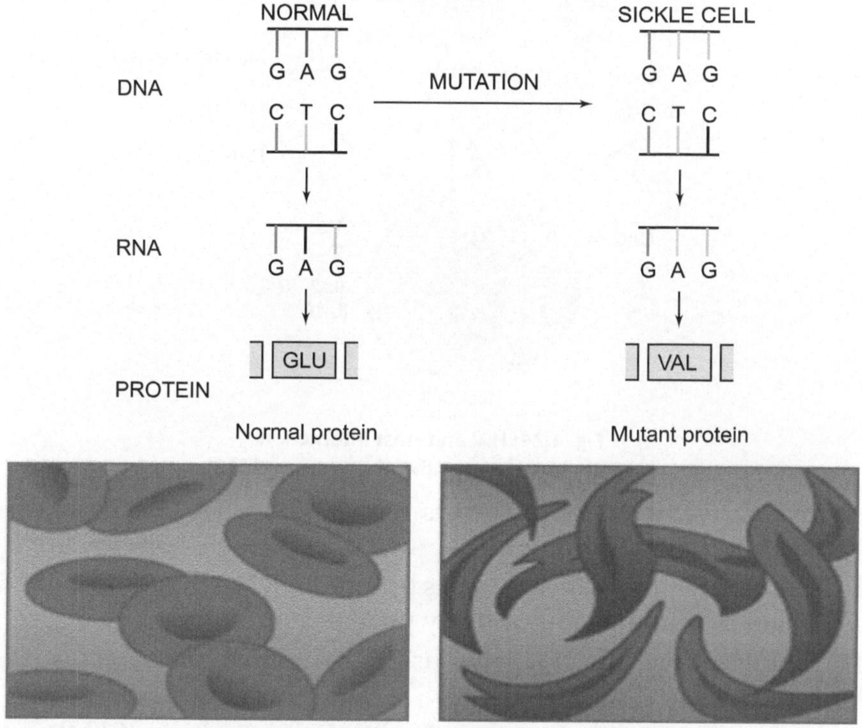

(Source: Based on review of literature, 2018)

Analysis of SNP and RFlp

Study of Stromal cell derived factor 1 gene in caste population of MP using PCR-RFLP method:

- The Human Immunodeficiency Virus (HIV) which cause Acquired Immune Deficiency Syndrome (AIDS) in Human was first time reported in the early 1980s.
- According to naco the prevalence of HIV in India, recorded around 0.26%. During 2015.
- SDF1 is present on chromosome no. 3 and acts as a chemokine ligand for CXCR4.
- SDF-1 forms a barrier for HIV-1 to enter the cell by specifically blocking the binding of CXCR4.

The SDF1-32A is a single nucleotide polymorphism present in conserved sequence of 32 UTR (untranslated region).The difference in AIDS progression depends on factors like host, virus and environmental factor.

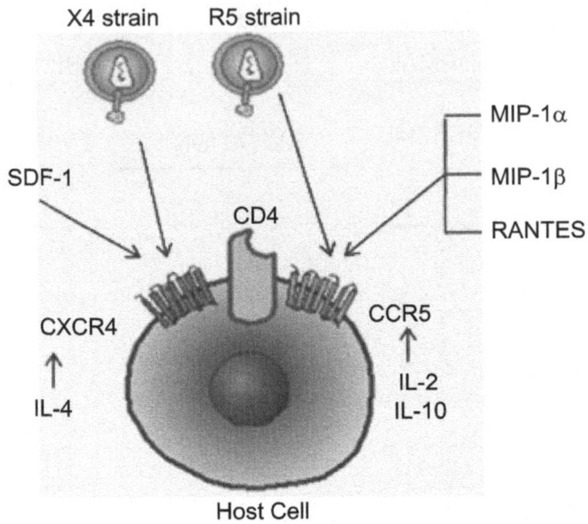

Fig. 4.24: HIV and Host interaction
(Source: based on review of literature, 2018)

Stromal-derived factor-1 (SDF-1) is ligand of CXCR4 which play crucial role during infection of T-tropic HIV-1 with the following objectives:

To isolate DNA from saliva samples using FTA DNA isolation method and extraction of DNA from blood using by phenol chloroform method.

To amplification of SDF1gene using respective primers using PCR technique.

To perform Restriction Fragment Length Polymorphism (RFLP) method for confirmation of the presence or absence of mutation in SDF1 gene.

To perform Restriction Fragment Length Polymorphism (RFLP) method for confirmation of the presence or absence of mutation in SDF1 gene.

MATERIALS AND METHODS

Collection of saliva and blood samples: A total 22 blood samples has been collected each from Caste population of Madhya Pradesh. Isolation of DNA from Blood samples using Phenol-chloroform DNA extraction(after-Sambrooket al., 1989).

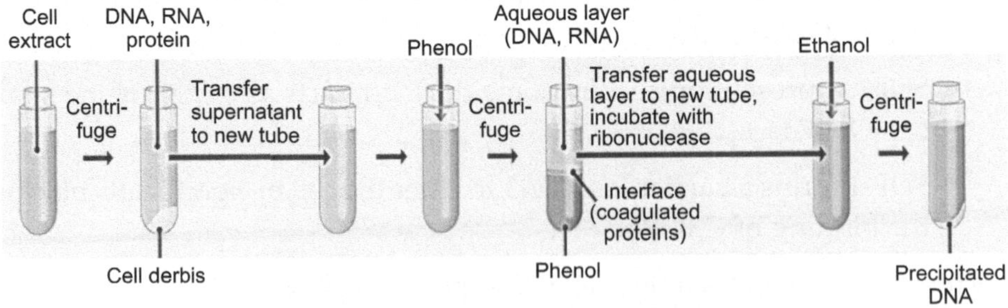

Fig. 4.25: Isolation of DNA from the blood of animals
(Source: Based on Review of Literature, 2018)

POLYMERASE CHAIN REACTION (PCR)

Samples are amplified using SDF1 primer by PCR technique as follows:

SDF1 FW 5 CAGTCAACCTGGGCAAAGCC 3

SDF1RV 5 AGCTTTGGTCCTGAGAGTCC 3

Table 4.1: Treatments, Temperature and Duration

S. No.	Treatments:	Temperature	Duration
1.	Predenaturation	95°C	5 min
2.	Denaturation	95°C	30 sec
3.	Annealing	60.0°C	30 sec
4	Primer extension	72°C	30 sec
5.	Final extension	72°C	7 min

(**Source:** Based on review of literature, 2018)

Table 4.2: Contents to be added in a PCR tube (for 20 µl)

Primer (forward) 0.4 µl	
Primer (reverse)	0.4 µl
DNTPs	0.3 µl
Mgcl2	0.3 µl
Buffer	2.0 µl
Taq polymerase 0.2 µl	
DNA Sample	1.0 µl

RESTRICTION ENZYME DIGESTION

Restriction enzymes are named based upon the organism it was discovered in for example HindIH is the third enzyme discovered in *Haemophilus influenza,* strain Rd.Restriction enzymes are bacterial enzymes that cleave double –stranded DNA at specific sites to produce discrete fragments.Certain restriction enzymes exhibit "star activity", which means that under varying conditions that specificity of the enzyme is relaxed.

The MspI enzyme recognizes the following restriction site to produce blunt end fragments in SDF1 gene.

DNA Restriction Enzyme: MspI

C I CGG

GGC I C

Source: E. coli carrying the plasmid encoding the Msp I gene from Moraxella speciesReaction mixture for RFLP

1. PCR product 3 microlitre
2. Cut smart buffer 1 microlitre (10x)
3. Restriction enzyme 0.2 microlitre

4. MQ water 5.8
5. Total volume = 10 microlitre

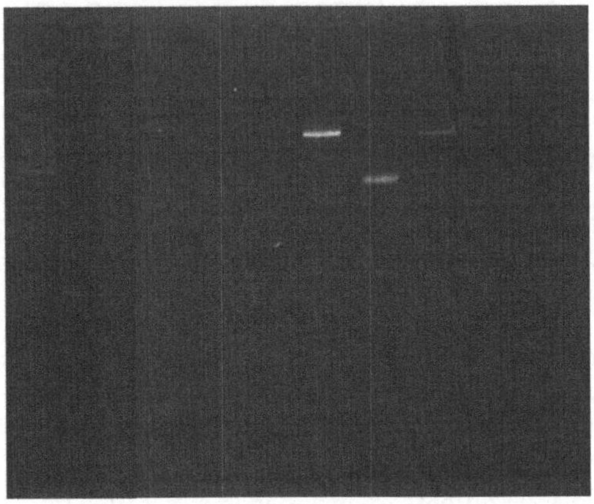

Fig. 4.26: Identification of antimicrobial genes direct through PCR (Source: Based on review of literature, 2018)

Table 4.3: Genotype distribution of SDF-1 genes

S. No.	Gene	Caste population	
		Major allele	Minor allele
3.	SDF1	0.978	0.022

CONCLUSIONS

In present study less frequency was recorded in minor allele of SDF1, which indicate less protection from host duringHIV1 virus infection

REFERENCES

Poste G (May 2001). "Molecular Diagnostics: A Powerful New Component of the Healthcare Value Chain". Expert Review of Molecular Diagnostics. 1 (1): 1–5. doi:10.1586/14737159.1.1.1. PMID 11901792

Burtis CA, Ashwood ER, Bruns DE (2012). Tietz Textbook of Clinical Chemistry and Molecular Diagnostics. Elsevier. ISBN 1-4557-5942-2.

Hamburg MA, Collins FS (July 2010). "The Path to Personalized Medicine". The New England Journal of Medicine. 363 (4): 301–4. doi:10.1056/NEJMp1006304. PMID 20551152.

Grody WW, Nakamura RM, Strom CM, Kiechle, Frederick L. (2010). Molecular Diagnostics: Techniques and Applications for the Clinical Laboratory. Boston MA: Academic Press Inc. ISBN 978-0-12-369428-7.

Kan YW, Lee KY, Furbetta M, Angius A, Cao A (January 1980). "Polymorphism of DNA Sequence in the Beta-globin Gene Region. Application to Prenatal Diagnosis of Beta 0 Thalassemia in Sardinia". The New England Journal of Medicine. 302 (4): 185–8. doi:10.1056/NEJM198001243020401. PMID 6927915.

Cohn DV, Elting JJ, Frick M, Elde R (June 1984). "Selective Localization of the Parathyroid Secretory Protein-I/Adrenal Medulla Chromogranin A Protein Family in a Wide Variety of Endocrine Cells of the Rat". Endocrinology. 114 (6): 1963–74. doi:10.1210/endo-114-6-1963. PMID 6233131.

Persselin JE, Stevens RH (August 1985). "Anti-Fab Antibodies in Humans. Predominance of Minor Immunoglobulin G Subclasses in Rheumatoid Arthritis". The Journal of Clinical Investigation. 76 (2): 723–30. doi:10.1172/JCI112027. PMC 423887/. PMID 3928684.

Kaplan G, Gaudernack G (October 1982). "In Vitro Differentiation of Human Monocytes. Differences in Monocyte Phenotypes Induced by Cultivation on Glass or on Collagen". The Journal of Experimental Medicine. 156 (4): 1101–14. doi:10.1084/jem.156.4.1101. PMC 2186821/. PMID 6961188.

Fausto N, Kaul KL (1999). "Presenting the Journal of Molecular Diagnostics". The Journal of Molecular Diagnostics. 1: 1. doi:10.1016/S1525-1578(10)60601-0. PMC 1906886/.

Atanasovska B, Bozhinovski G, Chakalova L, Kocheva S, Karanfilski O, Plaseska-Karanfiska D (December 2012). "Molecular Diagnostics of â-Thalassemia". Balkan Journal of Medical Genetics. 15 (Suppl): 61–5. doi:10.2478/v10034-012-0021-z (inactive 2017-01-15). PMC 3776673/ PMID 24052746.

Sharples A (2011-03-23). "Gene Patents in Europe Relatively Stable Despite Uncertainty in the U.S." Genetic Engineering and Biotechnology News. Retrieved 2013-06-13.

Bravin J, Kendall B (13 June 2013). "Justices Strike Down Gene Patents". The Wall Street Journal. Retrieved 15 June 2013.

Barnes R, Brady D (13 June 2013). "Supreme Court Rules Human Genes May not be Patented". The Washington Post. Retrieved 15 June 2013.

Gibbs JN (1 August 2008). "Regulatory Pathways for Molecular Diagnosis. Detailing the Various Options Available and what Each Requires". 24 (14). Genetic Engineering & Biotechnology News. Retrieved 4 September 2013.

Gibbs JN (1 April 2011). "Uncertainty Persists with RUO Products. FDA may be Considering More Restrictive Approach with Research Use Only Assays". 31 (7). Genetic Engineering & Biotechnology News. Retrieved 4 September 2013.

Tomiello K (21 February 2007). "Regulatory Compliance Drives LIMS". Design World. Retrieved 7 November 2012.

Mackinnon AC, Wang YL, Sahota A, Yeung CC, Weck KE (November 2012). "Certification in Molecular Pathology in the United States: An Update from the Association for Molecular Pathology Training and Education Committee". The Journal of Molecular Diagnostics. 14 (6): 541–9. doi:10.1016/j.jmoldx.2012.05.004. PMID 22925695.

Molecular Diagnostics: Current Technology and Applications (Horizon Bioscience). 7 July 2006. p. 97. ISBN 1-904933-19-X.

van Ommen GJ, Breuning MH, Raap AK (June 1995). "FISH in Genome Research and Molecular Diagnostics". Current Opinion in Genetics & Development. 5 (3): 304–8. doi:10.1016/0959-437X(95)80043-3. PMID 7549423.

Hammerling JA (2012). "A Review of Medical Errors in Laboratory Diagnostics and Where We are Today". Laboratory Medicine. 43 (2): 41–44. doi:10.1309/LM6ER9WJR1IHQAUY.

Khodakov D, Wang C, Zhang DY (October 2016). "Diagnostics Based on Nucleic Acid Sequence Variant Profiling: PCR, Hybridization and NGS Approaches". Advanced Drug Delivery Reviews. 105 (Pt A): 3–19. doi:10.1016/j.addr.2016.04.005. PMID 27089811.

Genetics and Bioengineering : *Concepts and Issues* **Pages 72-97**
Edited by: **Dr. Ashok K. Rathoure and Dr. Pawan Kumar 'Bharti'**
ISBN: 978-93-86841-92-6
Edition: **2019**
Published by: **Discovery Publishing House Pvt. Ltd., New Delhi (India)**

5 Effect of Replacement of Fish Meal by Broiler *by-products Meal in Rearing Stage of Genetically Improved Farmed Tilapia (GIFT) Diet*

[1]Madusanka WAN, [2]Athauda ARSB,
[3]Esakkimuthu M [4]Ranathunga LN

ABSTRACT

Aquaculture of GIFT is becoming popular now in Sri Lanka. However, for aquaculture practices the feed cost was the highest among variable cost incurred. The main protein supplement such as fish meal and soybean meal prices are highly effect on feed price. This could be solved if a cheap feed can be formulated using locally available broiler by-products as a protein replacer. The main objective of this study was to investigate the effect of replacing of imported fish meal (IFM) by Broiler by-product meal (BBM) in GIFT fry feed. GIFT fry were collected from Aquaculture Development Centre at Udawalawe and the experiment was also carried out at the same venue. Three isonitrogenous and isocaloric experimental diets were formulated by replacing fish meal by broiler by- products meal (BBM) by different proportions. Total of 6600 GIFT fry were stocked in 09 cemented tanks (8m x2.75m x1m) and experimental feeds were provided for 40 days at a rate of 10% in first ten days, 08% in 10 to 20 days and 05% in 20 to 40 days according to their body weight, respectively. Feeding was done daily at 8 am, 11 am and 2 pm. Growth parameters such as weight and length were measured in every 10 days while Body Weight Gain (BWG), Body Length Gain (BLG), Specific Growth Rate (SGR), Feed Conversion Ratio (FCR), Condition Factor (CF) and Survival Rate (SR) were calculated at the end of the experiment. Data were analysed using ANOVA for experimental designs of Complete Randomized Design (CRD) to observe any differences among treatments. Mean comparison was done using Least Significant Method (LSD). The means of BWG, BLG. SGR, FCR, CF and SR have not shown any significant difference (P>0.05) for all three treatments. Further, diet 1 (IFM 20%+ 0% BBM), Diet 2 (IFM 10%+ BBM 10%) and Diet 3 (IFM 5%+ BBM 15%) showed similar performance in GIFT fry stage. Hence, IFM can be replaced up to 15% by BBM in GIFT fry feed without any effect for their performances.

Keywords: GIFT, Body Weight Gain, Fish meal, Broiler By-product Meal, Fry Diet.

[1,2] Department of Animal Science, Faculty of Agriculture, University of Peradeniya, Sri Lanka
[3] Kerala Agricultural University, RARS, Pilicode
[4] Faculty of Agriculture, Aquinas College of Higher Studies, Colombo, Sri Lanka

INTRODUCTION

Sri Lanka has immense water resources, both fresh and brackish water bodies. Freshwater bodies comprise of over 260,000 ha of large irrigation reservoirs, medium irrigation reservoirs, minor irrigation reservoirs, seasonal village tanks, flood lakes, upland reservoirs/estate tanks and Mahaweli river basins. These resources play a vital role in increasing protein supply of the island and meeting the population's nutritional and livelihood needs. Each and every kind of freshwater habitats are inhabited by a wide spectrum of freshwater fauna. Around 151 species of freshwater fish are found in Sri Lanka today. There are 94 species of indigenous fish and 24 exotics. Of them 33 species are endemic which are identified as threatened and out of them 9 species are globally threatened (Edirisinghe, 2009).

Contribution of the indigenous species for fish production is low in Sri Lanka. Hence, Exotic fish species were introduced for inland fisheries mainly as a solution to the low availability of protein for the rural people. This is relatively a new development since the introduction of exotic cichlid species *Oreochromis mossambicus* into Sri Lankan freshwaters in 1950s. (Amarasinghe, 1992). Tilapia is a unique fish in the inland fish production of Sri Lanka with maximum contribution coming from reservoir fisheries catches (Ariyaratne, 2007). Tilapia is mainly a freshwater fish, inhabiting shallow streams, ponds, rivers and lakes, and less commonly found living in brackish water. *Oreochromis niloticus, O. aureus, O. mossambicus and,* GIFT (Genetically Improved Farmed Tilapia) are the major culture species of the tilapia species. The Genetically Improved Farmed Tilapia (GIFT) strain developed through selective breeding in a base population derived from eight strains of Nile tilapia, (*Oreochromis niloticus*).The culture of an improved tilapia strain characterized with fast growth rate and low Feed Conversion Ratio would have great economic benefit for the fanners, to the improved production potential of tilapia.

Fish feed plays an important role for the production of fish at a satisfactory level. Different feed mills and industries produce commercial fish feeds of different protein levels which are used in fish farms. But, the demand and supply do not match and farmers always face scarcity of feed (Hossen *et al.*, 2011). In addition, the development of fish culture is adversely affected by high cost of fish feed. In fish 2 farming, nutrition is critical because feed represents 40-50% of the production costs (Abowei and Ekubo, 2011). In fertilized ponds, proteins are often that limiting factor. Providing protein in feeds can be cost-effective by increasing the growth rate of fish stocked in a pond and allowing more fish to be stocked in the same water volume. But dietary protein is often expensive to incorporate into a diet.

The typical sources of proteins are fish meal and soybean oil meal. These are relatively expensive ingredients that are useful in other animal feeds. With the recent financial problems in Asia and the devaluation of local currencies, fishmeal costs have risen to new highs. Providing less expensive sources of protein has been a goal of numerous other nutrition studies in the past, which have examined many ingredients including plants, agricultural processing wastes, and even brewery wastes (Fitzsimmons *et al.*, 2011). For an economical and intensive fish culture, the knowledge on nutritional requirements is indispensable; especially in the economical view point it is necessary to rear fish by using a well balanced diet which is composed of cheap and abundant sources and enables to attain high growth rate (Teshima, 1978). To fish farmers, in order to minimize running cost, it is important to use cheaper alternative feed ingredients that are locally available to produce good quality, suitable and palatable fish feeds. Nonconventional feed-stuffs and by-products for aqua feeds would reduce the unit cost of fish production.

Fish meal is the major protein source in aquaculture feeds. There has been a considerable research effort towards utilization of less expensive renewable ingredients in fish diet formulations to alleviate problems related to shortage of quality fishmeal. In order to sustain aqua feed industry, a great part of nutritional research has been focused on the search for alternative proteins. Protein is usually the most expensive component in the diet of cultured fish; hence dietary protein levels directly affect production cost (Lazo *et al.*, 1998). Fishmeal is a quality protein source commonly added to fish diets (Turker *et al.*, 2005). It is a rich source of essential amino and fatty acids, energy and minerals, highly digestible and very palatable to most fish. The increasing cost of fishmeal together with decrease in its quality have necessitated the search for less expensive plant or animal protein sources as partial or total replacements for fishmeal in aqua feeds. One of the alternative ingredients to fish meal is poultry by-product meal (PBM). PBM is made of ground, rendered, or clean parts of the carcass of slaughtered poultry. PBM has been tested at varying success so far in tilapia (Sadiku and Jauncey, 1995; El-Sayed, 1998). Huge quantities of different types of poultry wastes are generated daily in the retail markets mainly from the dressing of poultry birds. Careless disposal of these wastes results in pollution of environment and loss of enormous quantities of nutrients contained in the wastes By-products of the Broiler processing industry are high in protein and contain favourable profiles of indispensable amino acids (IAA) for fish production.

The Objectives of the research to evaluate the effect of replacing imported fish meal by broiler by-product (BBM) meal in rearing stage of GIFT (Genetically Improved Farmed Tilapia) fish. To find out a suitable low cost ration for GIFT fry by replacing fish meal from broiler by-Product meal.

Aquaculture in Sri Lanka

The aquaculture industry in Sri Lanka started in the early 1980s with few large multinational companies and few medium scale entrepreneurs embarked on shrimp farming. Aquaculture is culturing of aquatic biota in freshwaters, brackish waters or in sea waters (aquatic resources), by human as an economic activity (Edirisinghe, 2009).

Sri Lanka is now in the process of embarking on a very ambitious aquaculture development plan. It is important as a cheap source of protein in the diet of rural community. And aquaculture is one of the most rapidly expanding activities which has become a major non-traditional foreign exchange earner in Sri Lanka. Aquaculture in Sri Lanka can be classified according to the nature of the operation. They are capture fisheries and culture fisheries (Jayantha and De Silva, 2010). Government of Sri Lanka has taken initial steps to develop reservoir fisheries and inland fish production early 1950s' by introducing *Oreochromis mossambicus* (De Silva, 1985).

Freshwater Fisheries in Sri Lanka

Sri Lanka, with a total land area of 65,610 km2, is truly a unique tropical island in the Indian Ocean. The country has a variety of lentic and lotic freshwater habitats distributed throughout the island. The lotic habitats comprise a large number of rivers and streams while lentic habitats of the island include man-made lakes, reservoirs as well as natural stagnant water bodies (Jayaratne and Surasinghe, 2010). Nowadays Sri Lanka has a limited, but stable, shrimp production and a growing aquaculture production of finfish. Traditional earthen pond farming of shrimp and finfish is slowly increasing, and farmers are now following a strict coastal zone management plan regulating the time for stocking and harvest in different farming regions. The land-based farming sector in Sri Lanka is also receiving increased attention.

Introduction of Exotic Fish into Freshwaters

The average annual fish yield from the reservoirs of Sri Lanka was low. So steps were taken to overcome this deficiency by introducing suitable exotic fish species by introducing *Oreochromis mossambicus*. Several species of Chinese carps and lndian carps were introduced to Sri Lanka at a later stage in 1970s and 1980s respectively.

Tilapia Species in Freshwater

Tilapia are mainly freshwater fish, inhabiting shallow streams, ponds, rivers and lakes, and less commonly found living in brackish waters. Tilapias are second only to the carps as a farmed food fish (Fitzsimmons, 2011). Tilapia is the common name of several kinds of fish belonging to the Family Cichlidae, including three major genera, such as Tilapia, Sarotherodon and Oreochromis. *Oreochromis niloticus, O. aureus, O.mossambicus* and GIFT (Genetically Improved Farmed Tilapia) are the major culture species of the tilapia species.

The Nile tilapia, (0. *niloticus*) is presently the dominant species in freshwater tilapia culture (Mair *et al.,* 2002). Genetically Improved Farmed Tilapia (GIFT) is established as a good strain for aquaculture and has been widely distributed throughout Asia (Mair *et al.,* 2002), Recently, the Genetically Improved Farmed Tilapia (GIFT) strain developed through selective breeding in a base population derived from eight strains of the Nile tilapia. The introduction of the GIFT (Genetically Improved Fanned Tilapia) strain was aimed at improving the genetic quality of farmed tilapia in order to give better growth, higher survival rates and delayed sexual maturation (Mamun *et al.,* 2005).

Taxonomy of Tilapia

Kingdom -Animalia

Phylum - Chordata

Class - Actinopterygii

Order - Perciformes

Family - Cichlidae

Sub family - Pseudocrenilabrinae

Genus – *Oreochromis*

Species - *Oreochromis niloticus*

Biological features: Tilapia are shaped much like sunfish or crappie but can be easily identified by an interrupted lateral line characteristic of the Cichlid family of fishes. They are laterally compressed and deep-bodied with long dorsal fins. The forward portion of the dorsal fin is heavily spined. Spines are also found in the pelvis and anal fins. There are usually wide vertical bars down the sides of fry, fingerlings, and sometimes adults (http://www.daff.qld.gov.au).

Habitats characteristics: Those fish can tolerate wide range of temperature such as 8-42 °C and prefers temperatures between 28-30 °C depending on acclimation temperature. However they can tolerate low dissolved oxygen (0.1 ppm) and can withstand salinity range of 11 to 29% (http:/el.erdc.usace.army.mil).

Reproduction: In all *Oreochromis* species the male excavates a nest in the pond bottom (generally in water shallower than 3 feet) and mates with several females. After a short mating ritual the female spawns in the nest (about two to four eggs per gram of brood female), the male fertilizes the eggs, and she then holds and incubates the eggs in her mouth (buccal cavity) until they hatch. Fry remain in the female's mouth through yolk sac absorption and often seek refuge in her mouth for several days after they begin to feed. (http://www.daff.qld.gov.au)

Production Cycle

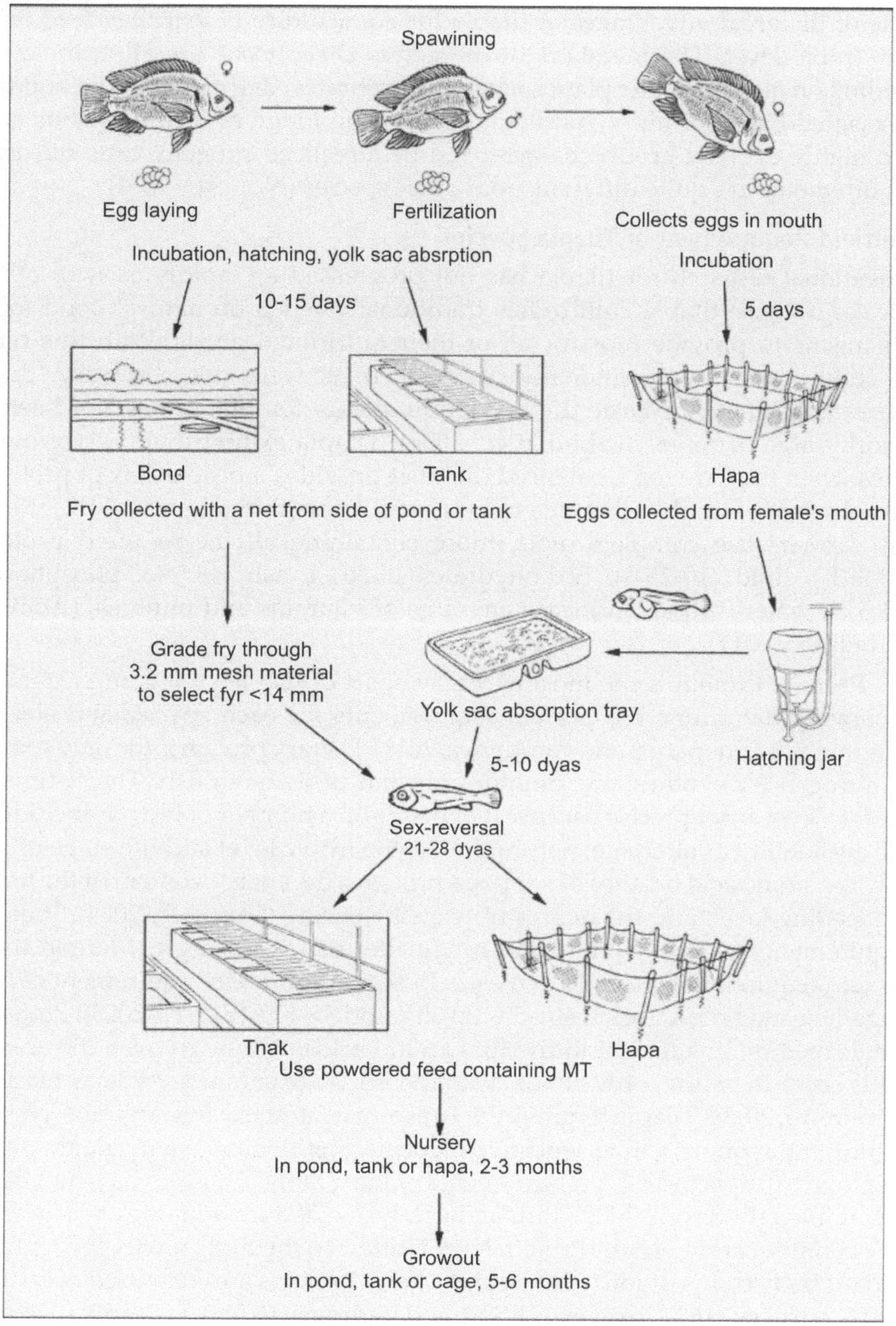

Fig. 5.1: Production cycle of Tilapia species.

Feeding Habits of Tilapia Species

One of the great advantages of tilapia for aquaculture is that they feed on a low tropic level. The members of the genus *Oreochromis* are all omnivores, feeding on algae, aquatic plants, small invertebrates, detritus material and the associated bacterial films. As tilapia has a wide range of feeding habits and is a highly evolved group characterized by advanced progeny care, nutrient requirements are quite different from other species (Noticias, 2002).

Nutrient Requirement of Tilapia Species

Nutritional research for tilapia has not progressed as rapidly as with other species because tilapia culture has traditionally relied on natural pond food organisms to provide most or all of their nutritional needs. With this type of culture system, nutritionally complete diets were not necessary, thus, the establishment of basic dietary requirements for tilapia has not been a priority area of research (Lim *et al.,* 1993). Tilapia exhibit their best growth rates when they are fed a balanced diet that provides a proper mix of protein, carbohydrates, lipids, vitamins, mineral and fiber (Fitzsimmons, 2012). Most fish farmers use complete diets, those containing all the required protein (18-50%), lipid (10-25%), carbohydrate (15-20%), ash (<8.5%), phosphorus (<1.5%), water (<10%), and trace amounts of vitamins and minerals (Abowei and Ekubo, 2011).

Protein: Protein is the most expensive part of fish feed, it is important to accurately determine the protein requirements for each species and size of cultured fish (Adeparusi and Famurewa, 2011). Dietary protein is the only source of nitrogen for synthesizing amino acids and proteins in fish. The optimum protein level is not precise because it depends on a number of factors, including the availability of alternate, natural foods, the tropic level and life stage of the fish, the amino acid balance of supplied proteins, the energy content of the food, the feeding level, and the degree of protein sparing (Somsueb, 2004). Protein requirements generally are higher for smaller fish. As fish grow larger, their protein requirements usually decrease. In sequent, protein requirement of fry, fingerling and brood stock is 40-45%, 30-35% and 35-40% (Eid *et al* 2003). Proteins are formed by linkages of individual amino acids. Although over 200 amino acids occur in nature, only about 20 amino acids are common (Adeparusi and Famurewa, 2011). Tilapia requires the 10 essential amino acids (arginine, lysine, histidine, threonine, valine, leucine, isoleucine, methionine, phenylalanine, and tryptophan). Specific EAA requirements of most fanned tilapias have not been determined (El-Sayed, 2002). But, of these, lysine and methionine are often the most limiting amino acids. Protein level is affect to the fish growth, feed intake and the body composition (Ahmad *et al.,* 2005). Proteins are composed of carbon (50%), nitrogen (16%), oxygen (21.5%), and hydrogen (6.5%). Fish are capable of using a high protein diet, but as much as 65% of the protein may be lost to the environment. Most nitrogen is excreted as ammonia (NH3) by the gills of fish, and only 10% is lost as solid wastes (Adeparusi and Famurewa, 2011).

Lipids: Dietary lipids are an important source of highly digestible energy and are the only source of essential fatty acids required by fish for normal growth, development and maintaining health. They are also carriers and assist in the absorption of fat-soluble nutrients such as sterols and vitamins A, D, E and K. In addition, dietary lipids serve as a source of phospholipids and participate in the synthesis of hormones, prostaglandin and other metabolically active compounds (Lim *et al.*, 2008). Tilapia does not tolerate as high a dietary lipid level as salmonids. Minimum lipid level of the diet should be 5%. High levels of dietary lipid may adversely affect the fish carcass / body composition and reduce feed intake (El Hammady, 2002).

The lipid requirement of different fish species varies. Most of the carnivorous fish species appear to digest and utilize dietary lipids more effectively as compared to omnivorous and herbivorous fishes (Ali, 2000). EFA requirements of fish may be variable with environmental factors such as water temperatures and salinities besides the genetic differences of fish (Teshima *et al.*, 1982).

Carbohydrates: Carbohydrates (starches and sugars) are the most economical and inexpensive sources of energy for fish diets (Davis, 2009). Although not essential, carbohydrates are included in aquaculture diets to reduce feed costs and for their binding activity during feed manufacturing (Adeparusi and Famurewa, 2011). The relative utilization of dietary carbohydrates by fish varies and appears to be related to their complexity (Solomon *et al.*, 2007). The effect of dietary carbohydrate on fish growth seems to depend on the source, dietary concentration and digestibility, the level of dietary intake, rearing conditions and fish species. Prepared feeds for carnivorous fish usually contain less than 20% soluble carbohydrate, while feeds for omnivorous species usually contain 25 to 45% (Gatlin, 2010). Warm water fishes are able to utilize much higher levels of carbohydrate compared to cold water fishes (Gaber, 2002). No dietary requirement for carbohydrate has been demonstrated in fish. However, if carbohydrates are not provided in the diet, other nutrients such as protein and lipids are atabolised for energy and to provide metabolic intermediates for the synthesis of other biologically important compounds.

Vitamins: Commercial production of tilapia requires the use of high quality, complete feed (Campeche *et al.*, 2009). Vitamins are organic substances that are essential for growth, health, reproduction and maintenance in animals, but required in small amounts (Shiau and Lin, 2006). Increasing vitamin supplementation of complete diets decreases stress caused by high stocking density and boosts immunological system of fish. On the other hand, inadequate dietary vitamin supplementation can result in disease outbreaks or reduced growth in a confined fish population.

The two groups of vitamins are water-soluble and fat-soluble. Water-soluble vitamins include such as the B vitamins, choline, inositol, folic acid, pantothenic acid, biotin and ascorbic acid (vitamin C). Of these, vitamin C probably is the most important because it is a powerful antioxidant and helps the immune system in fish. Water-soluble vitamins are abundantly found in various foods, including yeast, leafy plants, algae and cereals. The fat-soluble vitamins include A vitamins, retinols (responsible for vision); the D vitamins, (bone integrity); E vitamins (antioxidants); and K vitamins such as menadione (blood clotting, skin integrity). Deficiency of each vitamin has certain specific symptoms, but reduced growth is the most common symptom of any vitamin deficiency (Adeparusi and Famurewa, 2011). Fat-soluble vitamins are found in various fats and oils. The needs for the vitamins differ according to the species, age and raising period.

Minerals: Minerals are inorganic elements necessary in the diet for normal body functions. They can be divided into two groups such as macro-minerals and micro-minerals, based on the quantity required in the diet and the amount present in fish. Common macro-minerals are sodium, chloride, potassium and phosphorous. These minerals regulate osmotic balance and aid in bone formation and integrity. Micro-minerals (trace minerals) are required in small amounts as components in enzyme and hormone systems. Common trace minerals are copper, chromium, iodine, zinc and selenium (Adeparusi and Famurewa, 2011).

A dietary source of 23 minerals has been demonstrated as essential in one or more animal species. Ten minerals (Calcium, Phosphorous, Magnesium, Potassium, Copper, Iron, Zinc, Manganese, Selenium and Iodine) may be essential for fish. Minerals serve a variety of functions as both intra and extra-cellular components, structural components of hard and soft tissues, component of metalloproteinase and serve as cofactors and activators of variety of enzymes (Davis and Gatlin, 1996). Fish can absorb many minerals directly from the water through their gills and skin, allowing them to compensate to some extent for mineral deficiencies in their diet.

Low Cost Feeding for Tilapia Species

Seasonality in the availability of ingredients is one major problem in the feed industry. It may not always possible to store large quantities of ingredients, and so it becomes necessary to vary ingredient composition according to availability. In many developing countries where feedstuffs are scarce, one cannot expect sufficient priority to be given to their use in aquaculture. Even when a particular feedstuff is available for purchase, increased prices may make it necessary to use substitutes in order to obtain a least-cost ration (Pillay, 1993). In the economical view point it is necessary to rear fish by using a well-balanced diet which is composed of cheap and abundant sources and enables to attain high growth rate (Teshima *et al.,* 1978). Feed ingredients used in commercial tilapia diets in many developing countries in Asia are mostly imported. As feed incurs up to 60% of the production cost in aquaculture, knowledge of nutrition and the feeding management is important Alternative cheap feeds for tilapia have been tried e.g. fruit and vegetable wastes, crop by-products, leguminous fodders and aquatic plants (Noticias, 2002). Several feed ingredients have been investigated in an attempt to find substitutes for fish meal in the diets of tilapia. These include animal protein sources and plant protein sources. These feeds are not only considerably cheaper than fish meal but also enjoy high availability and accessibility in certain regions of the world (Ogunji *et al.,* 2008).

Preparation of Poultry–by Product Meal

Poultry offal without feathers produced in Poultry processing plants together with hatchery waste is converted into a meal called poultry by-product meal. Poultry offal contains head, feet, viscera and fat in processing plant. The protein content usually deferens from 45-60%. The nutritional value of poultry by-product meal varies with the composition of the input materials.

Benefits of Poultry –by Product Meal Incorporated in to Fish Diet

Addition of poultry by-product meal in to animal diets reduce feeding costs. Poultry by-product meal is cheaper than fishmeal in the market. Poultry by-product meal of high quality provides amino acids, phospholipids, and fatty acids for optimum development, growth and reproduction, especially of larvae and brood stock. Incorporation of poultry by-product meal into diets of aquatic animals helps to reduce pollution from the poultry waste.

Nutrient Value of Poultry –by Product Meal

The range of dry weight proximate composition of poultry by-product meal samples have 55-74% of protein, 10-19% of lipid and 11-23% of ash (Dong *et al.,* 1993). The Poultry by-products meal can be used as protein and energy sources for growing fish.

Feed Formulation

Fish food consists of natural food and artificial (supplementary) feeds. When fish have balanced diet to eat, they grow fast and stay healthy. Feed formulation is the process of matching the fish's nutrient requirements with the nutrients supplied by available ingredients, in the most economical mariner possible. For a successful fish feed formulation, a fish farmer must be acquainted with the nutrient requirement of the fish (amino acids, carbohydrates, fatty acids, vitamins and minerals) and nutrient composition of feedstuffs (National Agricultural Extension and Research Services, 2002).

Feed Formulation Methods

Feed formulation and preparation is the process of combining feed ingredients to form a mixture that will meet the specific goals of production (Adeparusi and Famurewa, 2011).

Pearson Square method: Pearson Square is an established method that is popular due to its simplicity. However, its simplicity is also its weakness. It functions well only in very simple diets. It is best used in diets containing only two ingredients. For more complex situations, other methods are preferable (Omidiora *et al.,* 2013).

Linear programmed: The speed and simplicity of computer formulation of diets makes it the most effective and popular method. Rather than use the more simplistic and slower algebraic methods or Pearson Square, the computer can handle many simultaneous equations in a fraction of a second. Because of this simplicity and speed, the computer allows nutritionist to consider more ingredients and more nutrients, and pay for greater attention to cost than would otherwise be the case (Omidiora *et al.,* 2013).

Algebraic Formulae: In the absence of computers, sometimes simple calculations are required to balance a simple ration involving only a few ingredients. In such cases, algebraic methods are often selected because they are more accommodating. However, for those not comfortable with algebra, they may be a bit confusing at first (Omidiora *et al.,* 2013).

Trial and Error method: This is the most popular method of formulating ration. As the name implies, the formulation is manipulated until the nutrient requirements of the animal are met. This method makes possible the formulation of a ration that meets all the nutrient requirements of the animal (Omidiora *et al.,* 2013).

Two-By-Two Matrix Method: This method solves two nutrients requirement using two different feed ingredients. A 2 by 2 matrix is formed a set and a series of equations are solved to come up with the solution to the problem (Omidiora *et al.,* 2013).

Imami Method: This is an educational way to describe and balance simple rations by a common calculator with a high accuracy for farmers who do not have access to the computer (Omidiora *et al.,* 2013).

Feed Preparation

The feeds formulated may be dry with a final moisture content of 6-10%, semi moist with 35-40% water or wet with 50-70% water content. Most of the feeds used in intensive production systems or in home aquaria are commercially produced as dry feeds. The dry feeds may consist of loose mixtures of dry ingredients, such as mash or meals, to more complex compressed pellets or granules. Pellets are often broken into smaller sizes known as crumbles

(Pandey, 2013). Pellets are most popular and their shape and size would depend on the age of the fish. Mash feeds are good for fry and pellets (0.8-Imm) for fingerlings, juveniles (2 mm-3 mm) and adults (4.5 mm) depending on pellet sizes (National Agricultural Extension and Research Services, 2002).

There is no single way for preparation of formulated fish feed. Use finely ground ingredients of similar particle size. Dissimilar sizes results in an unstable pellet. Individual ingredients should be ground using a hammer mill, or other type of grinder or even a mortar and pestle. A sieve can also be used to remove large particles or foreign materials like stones, pieces of metal etc. that can damage machinery. Then weigh or measure ingredients. Take particular care when weighing micro-nutrients (vitamin and mineral premixes) as these are used in very small quantities and are very expensive (Gonzalez and Allan, 2007).

However, most methods begin with the formation of dough like mixture of ingredients. The dough is then kneaded and water is added to produce desired consistency for whatever fish is going to be fed. Pelleting and rolling converts the dough into pellets or flakes, respectively. The amount of water, pressure, friction and heat greatly affects pellet and flake quality. For instance, excess water in the mixture results in a soft pellet. Too little moisture and pellet will crumble (Pandey, 2013). After pelleting, the pellets should be dried in the sun or oven and packed in water impermeable bags. This is to prevent attack by mould and other pests (National Agricultural Extension and Research Services, 2002).

Storage of Feed

Keep feeds and ingredients dry, cool and away from pests. Poor storage of feeds and ingredients will waste money and can kill fish. Any feed requires special care during storage to prevent deterioration in quality. Environmental factors, such as moisture, temperature, light and oxygen influence deterioration and losses in feedstuff's. High levels of moisture favour growth of fungus or insect infestation. Fungal growth can be retarded by the use of mould inhibition agents (e.g. Myocurb). High temperatures also affect the rate of loss of heat liable vitamins and other nutrients (Gonzalez and Allan, 2007).

Quality of Formulated Feed

The limited availability of ingredients, lack of information on fish nutrition and on how to make and deliver feeds often results in poor quality feed and reduced production and profitability (Gonzalez and Allan, 2007). Availability of high quality fish feed is one of the greatest problems that affects the expansion of the small scale fish industries in the country. Due to some kinds of technical flaws such as bad palatability and poor floating, fish feed pellets sink to the bottom immediately before eaten thus leading to waste of materials and low nutrition intake (http://www.fishfeecUnachine.com, 04 Nov.).

Characteristics of Ingredients

There are 3 factors to consider in the choice of ingredients.

- Quality - nutrient composition and presence of any anti-nutrients (substances that interfere directly with the absorption of nutrients or contaminants).
- Quantity - how much is available locally & is the supply regular.
- Price or cost.

The raw materials are collected or delivered in jute or polythene or plastic sacks/bags or containers. Special care should be taken to inspect the materials for wetness, mould growth, insects and parasites. The inspection procedure starts with visual examination of a sample for the colour and texture and smelling for obvious contamination or rancidity. When preparing feed, use finely ground ingredients of similar particle size. Dissimilar sizes results in an unstable pellet (Gonzalez and Allan, 2007).

Nutrition of Fish Feed

Knowing the composition of the available ingredients and the basic nutritional requirements of the fish being cultured, it is usually possible to formulate a diet that will promote optimum survival and growth. Fish need energy and essential nutrients for maintenance, movement, normal metabolic functions and growth. The major components of feeds are moisture, protein, lipid, carbohydrate, minerals and vitamins (Gonzalez and Allan, 2007).

Growth Parameters

Generally, growth and feed conversion increase with feeding frequency (Adeparusi and Famurewa, 2011).

Growth: Generally in fish culture, the major factors affecting fish growth are stocking rate, stocking density, the water temperature, the quantity (adequacy) and quality of feeds, and the feeding method and frequency (National Agricultural Extension and Research Services, 2002).Although environment of aquaculture is complex, management of the water quality parameters is essential especially if the fish are to be grown in pond culture systems because environmental factors affects the fish body condition, growth performance and yield (Nehemia *et al.,* 2012).

Condition Factor: Knowledge of some quantitative aspects such as length-weight relationship is important in studying fish biology. The condition factor which show the degree of well-being of the fish in their habitat is expressed by 'coefficient of condition' also known as length - weight factor. When condition factor value is higher it means that the fish has attained a better condition (Nehemia *et al.,* 2012).Fishes are said to exhibit isometric growth when length increases in equal proportions with body weight for constant specific gravity (Mortuza and Misned, 2013).

Feed Conversion Ratio: The feed conversion ratio (FCR) is a good tool to measure the acceptability and suitability of artificial feed for fish (Jabeen *et al.*, 2004).Feed Conversion Ratio (FCR) is an important calculation for the fish. FCR is calculated as the weight of the feed fed to the fish divided by the weight of fish growth (Adeparusi and Famurewa, 2011). Feed conversion ratio will vary among species, sizes and activity levels of fish, environmental parameters and the culture system used.

Feed Efficiency: FE is simply the reciprocal of FCRs (1/FCR). Fish are not completely efficient (FEs of 100%, FCRs of 1.0), when fed 5 kg of feed, fish cannot exhibit 5 kg of growth because they must use some of the energy in feed for metabolic heat, digestive processing, respiration, nerve impulses, salt balance, swimming, and other living activities (Adeparusi and Famurewa, 2011).

MATERIALS AND METHODS

Location

GIFT (Genetically improved farmed Tilapia) Tilapia fish samples were collected and fish feed preparation and feeding trials were carried out at the National Aquaculture Development Authority (NAQDA) Tilapia Breeding Centre at Udawalawe. Feed ingredients were collected from Weeraketiya and Kuliyapitiya area. Laboratory analyses for proximate composition of ingredients and formulated feed rations were carried out at the Department of Animal science, Faculty of Agriculture, University of Peradeniya.

Preparation of Broiler by-Product Meal

Broiler by-products (head, feet and viscera) were collected from Broiler processing plant in Weeraketiya (Madamulana) area in Hambantota district. They were cut in to small pieces .Those samples were boiled in water on a stove for 10 minutes. Processed sample were dried at 60 0C for 72 hours and then ground into a fine powder by using a grinder. This powder was stored air tied in polythene bags until use for feed preparation.

Fish Feed Preparation

Feed Formulation: Three "Isonitrogenous" and "Isocalaric" diets was formulated by using of computer software method for nutritional requirement of GIFT (Genetically improved farmed Tilapia) fish. Amount of feed ingredients in fish diets are shown in Table 5.1.

Table 5.1. Composition of the Experimental Diets.

Feed Ingredients	Diet 1 (Control)	Diet 2	Diet 3
Imported fish meal.	200 g	100 g	50 g
Broiler by products Meal.	0	100 g	150 g
Soya bean meal.	229 g	243.7 g	250.5 g
Corn flour.	100 g	100 g	100 g

Rice polish.	250g	250g	243.1g
Coconut poonac.	115.6g	100.4g	100g
Wheat flour.	80g	80g	80g
Vitamin and mineral Complex.	10g	10g	10g
soya oil.	15.4 ml	14.9 ml	15.4 ml

The first diet was formulated without Broiler by- products meal and considered as a control diet. Diet 2 and 3 were formulated to be comprised level of 50% and 75% Broiler by-products meal, respectively.

Feed Preparation

Feed ingredients were properly dried at 60°C in an oven to prevent deterioration. Individual ingredients were ground using a grinder. A sieve was used to remove large particles and foreign materials like stones, pieces of metal etc. Then weighed the required quantities of ingredients with using an electronic balance. Weighed of all ingredients were mixed evenly with water and fish oil by hand into it to obtain stiff dough. Then using a pelleting machine mixture of ingredient was converted to pellets. Then pellets were steamed for 5 minutes. Next, Pellets were dried overnight at room temperature. After drying Pellets were grounds in to fine particles. Feed was stored in polythene bags until use for Gift Tilapia (Genetically improved farmed Tilapia) fish.

Proximate Analysis of Diet

Fish feed and feed ingredients proximate analysis was carried out according to the standard method of AOAC (2005) for Dry matter, Crude fat, Crude fibre, Crude protein, and ash in the Nutrition laboratory, Department of Animal Science, faculty of Agriculture, University of Peradeniya. Dry matter was obtained after drying in an oven at 105°C for overnight until constant weight. Protein content was determined by using kjeldhal method. Ash content was determined by incineration in a muffle furnace at 520°C for four hours. Crude fat was find out by ether extract in the laboratory.

Preparation of Tanks

Feed trial was conducted at cement tanks in National Aquaculture Development Authority (NAQDA) at Udawalawe. Tanks were cleaned and dried properly. Bleaching powder ($CaOCl_2$) at a rate of 35 g/m^2 was added as disinfection agent and was applied manually into the tanks floor. Tanks were allowed for the disinfection for 2 days Before stocking the fish. Fry were transferred to stocked tank after one day from disinfection. cement fish tanks of volume 8m × 2.75m × 1 m were used for this experiment. All the tanks filled with water up to 0.7 m and label according to the experimental design before stocking fish.

Stocking of GIFT (Genetically Improved Farmed Tilapia) fry into Tanks

GIFT (Genetically improved farmed Tilapia) Tilapia fry were collected from the rearing pond NAQDA at Udawalawe. Initial weight and length was taken of 100 fry from random sampling of the stock. Length and weight measurements were taken using a ruler and an electronic balance. Then average weight and length were record. 59 400 fry were stocked in 9 experimental tanks. (300 per $m^{2)}$ Stocking of fry was done at morning period to reduce the stress.

Feeding of Fry

Three feed rations were given to fish in each tanks at a rate of 10% in first ten days, 08% in 10 to 20 days and 05% in 20 to 40 days of their body weight. Daily feeding was practiced at 8 am, 11 am and 2 pm in each day . Fish were randomly taken for measurement of body weight, standard length and total length. In every 10 day of period during experimental period.

Determination of Growth Parameter

Initial measurements as length and weight were recorded and subsequent growth of the fish was measured at 10 day intervals. Length and weight of fry were measured with a measuring ruler and an electronic balance. After recording weight and length, Fish were carefully released into the labelled tanks. Growth of fish was measured consequently four times at intervals of 10 days, while the experiment was continued up to 40 days. Body Weight Gain, Body Length Gain, Specific Growth Rate (SGR), Condition Factor, Feed Conversion Ratio and survival rate were calculated by using the following formulae.

Body Weight Gain (BWG)

It was calculated using initial and final body weight of fry.

$$\frac{\text{Body Weight Gain (\%)} = \text{Final body weight (g)} - \text{Initial body weight (g)} \times 100.}{\text{Initial body weight (g).}}$$

Body Length Gain (BLG)

It was calculated using final and initial total length of fry.

$$\frac{\text{Body Length Gain (\%)} = \text{Final total length (cm)} - \text{Initial total length (cm).} \times 100.}{\text{Initial total length (cm).}}$$

Specific Growth Rate (SGR)

$$\frac{\text{SGR} = \ln \text{final mean weight (g)} - \ln \text{initial mean weight (g)} \times 100}{\text{Experimental days.}}$$

Condition Factor (CF)

$$\frac{\text{Condition Factor} = \text{Weight of fish (g)} \times 100.}{(\text{Total length of fish (cm)})^{3.}}$$

Feed Conversion Ratio (FCR)

Feed conversion ratio (FCR) is the amount of feed intake to produce unit weight of fish.it was calculated from quantity of feed taken to weight increased.

$$\text{Feed Conversion Ratio} = \frac{\text{Feed fed (g).}}{\text{Gain in weight of fish (g).}}$$

Survival Rate (SR)

Survival rate was calculated from subtracting the total number of death fish during the culture period from the stocked fish and divided it from the number of fish stocked on the first day.

$$\frac{\text{Survival rate \%} = \text{No. of Remaining fish during the culture period} \times 100.}{\text{No. of fish stocked in the first day.}}$$

Measurement of Water Quality Parameter

Dissolved Oxygen (DO), Temperature, PH and Light penetration were measured with every 5 days interval throughout the experimental period. pH was measured using pH meter at the morning. Temperature was measured by thermometer at 70cm depth of water. Dissolved Oxygen was measured using a DO meter, three time a day at 8 am, 12 noon and 2 pm.

Experiment Design

All data analysed using ANOVA for experimental design arranged with Complete Randomized Design (CRD) for finding differences among treatment diets. Mean comparison were done using least significant Method (LSD) test.

RESULTS AND DISCUSSION

Proximate Composition of Feed Ingredients

Proximate composition of selected feed ingredients are shown in Table 5.2.

Table 5.2: Proximate Composition of Feed Ingredients

Feed Ingredients	Crude protein (%)	Crude fat (%)	Crude Fibre (%)	Ash (%)	Dry Matter (%)
Imported fish meal	62.31	3.47	1.02	14.49	90.74
Broiler by products Meal	54.18	26.23	1.23	7.48	91.47
Corn flour	11.14	4.16	2.41	3.45	90.47
Soya bean meal	44.81	6.74	7.34	6.22	90.35
Rice polish	13.54	14.73	8.23	7.42	84.61
Coconut poonac	21.12	7.5	13.48	7.34	89.47
Wheat flour	9.71	2.10	3.25	4.30	98.24

Imported fish meal and Broiler by-product meal (BBM) were showed high crud protein level. But imported fish meal is a relatively expensive ingredient than a Broiler by product meal. Therefore preparing a low cost and quality fish feed by using of replacement of fish meal by Broiler by-product meal.

Proximate Composition of Feed Diets

Proximate composition of three fish diets were showed in Table 5.3. according to the proximate analysis.

Table 5.3: Proximate Composition of Feed Diets

Feed ingredients	Diet 1	Diet 2	Diet 3
Dry matter %	95.26±0.260	94.86±0.140	93.95±0.164
Crude Protein %	31.78±0.150	31.66±0.017	31.65±0.069
Crude Fat %	11.20±0.177	11.08±0.018	11.19±0.011
Crude Fibre %	6.56±0.144	6.61±0.020	6.57±0.030
Ash %	7.54±0.182	8.18±0.014	8.29±0.014
Energy (kcl/kg)	3150±0.882	3149±0.881	3151±0.577

Values are expressed as means ± SE

Growth Measurements in Rearing Stage

Average Body Length (ABL):

Table 5.4: Average Body Length Measurement

	Days of measurements				
	Initial cm	1-10 cm	11-20 cm	21-30 cm	31-40 cm
Diet 1	1.141	1.496	2.129	2.433	2.997
Diet 2	1.141	1.492	2.140	2.411	2.986
Diet 3	1.141	1.455	2.118	2.406	2.952

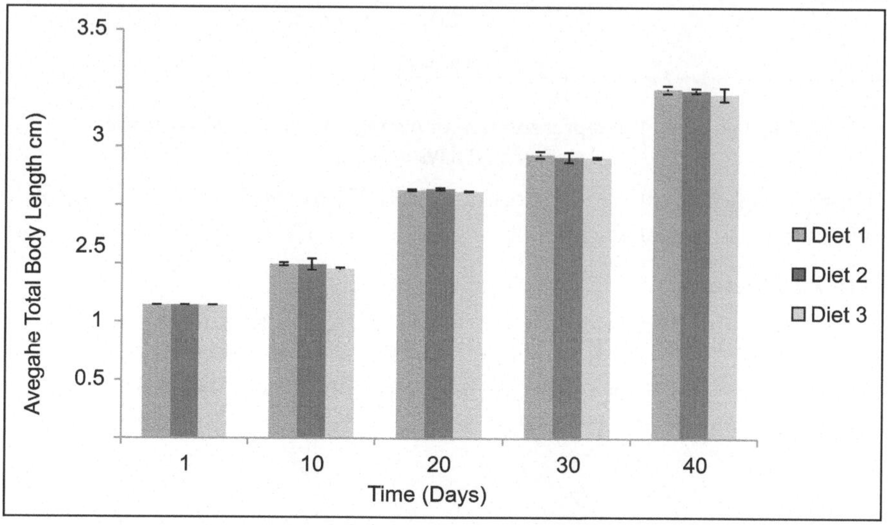

Fig. 5.2 Graphical representation of (ABL) of fry in 10 days interval

There was no significant difference (P>0.05) in total Average length of fry fed with three formulated diets.

Average Body Weight (ABW)

Table 5.5. Average Body Weight Measurements with Different Fish Diets

	Days of measurements				
	Initial g	1-10g	11-20g	21-30g	31-40g
Diet 1	0.014	0.058	0.175	0.314	0.659
Diet 2	0.014	0.051	0.178	0.304	0.650
Diet 3	0.014	0.050	0.172	0.301	0.621

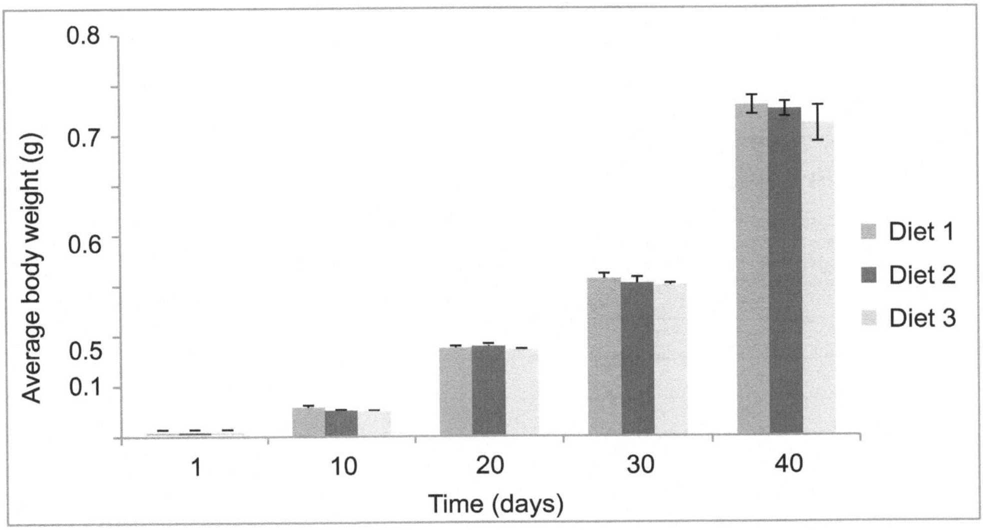

Fig. 5.2: Graphical representation of Average weight measurement of fry in 10 days interval

There was no significant difference (P>0.05) in total Average Weight of fry fed with three formulated diets.

Growth Parameter

Body Weight Gain, Body Length Gain, Specific Growth Rate, Feed Conversion Ratio, Condition factor and Survival Rate were considered. These parameters were calculated according to the initial weight, final weight, initial total length and final total length of GIFT fry.

Body Length Gain (BLG)

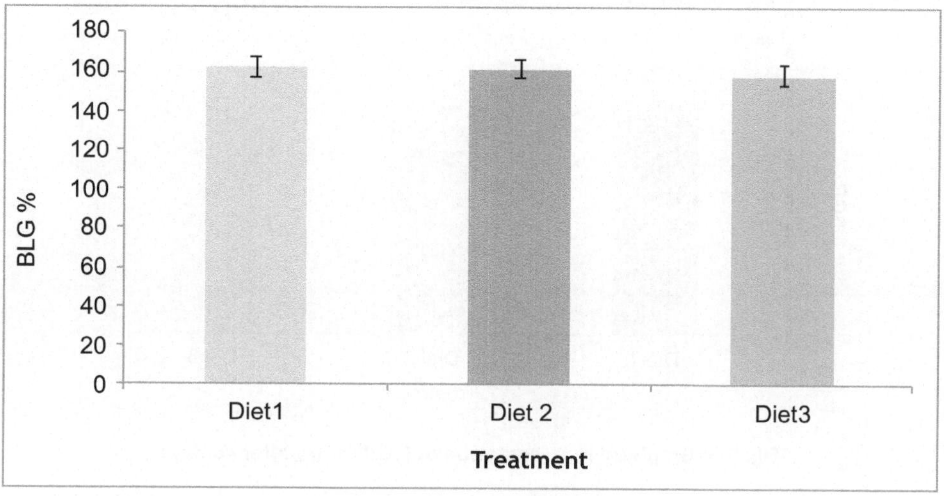

Fig. 5.3: Graphical representation of Body Length Gain of Tilapia fry after 40 days

There was no significant difference (P>0.05) in BLG of fry fed with three formulated diets.

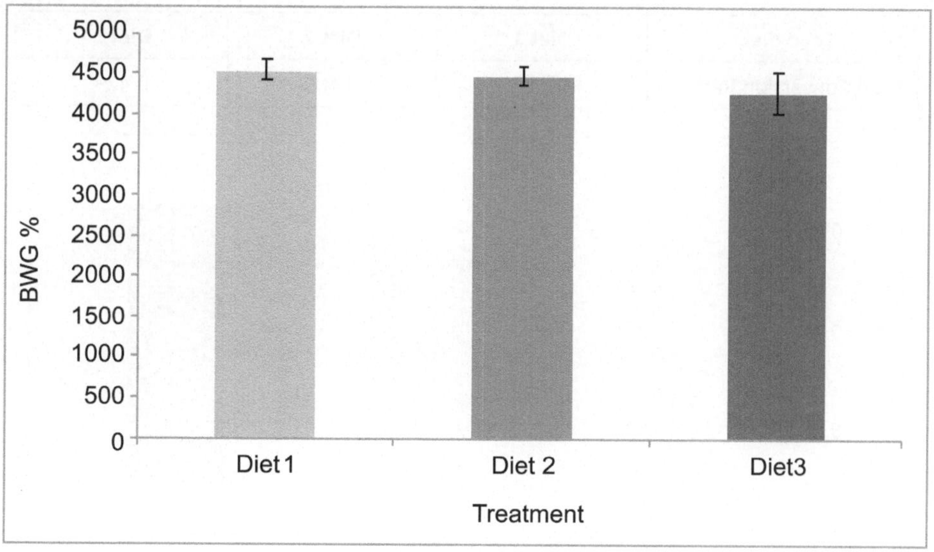

Fig. 5.4: Graphical representation of Body Weight Gain (BWG) of fry after 40 days

There was no significant difference (P>0.05) in BWG of fry fed with three formulated diets.

Specific Growth Rate (SGR)

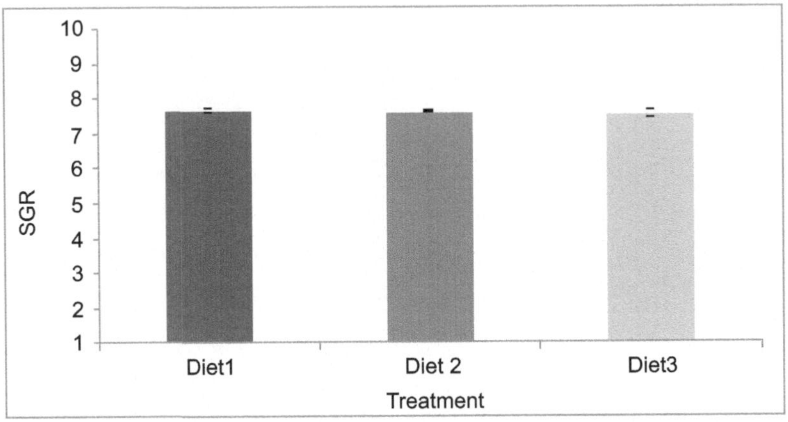

Fig. 5.5: Graphical representation of (SGR) of fry after 40 days

There was no significant difference (P>0.05) in SGR of fry fed with three formulated diets.

Feed Conversion Ratio (FCR)

Table 5.6: Feed Conversion Ratio (FCR) Measurements for Different Fish Diets

Feed diets	Diet 1	Diet 2	Diet 3
Feed Conversion Ratio	0.419	0.409	0.429

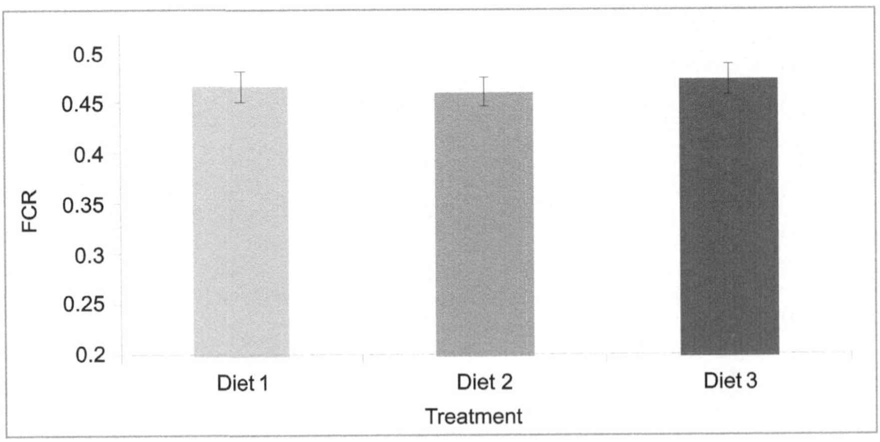

Fig. 5.6: Graphical representation of (FCR) of fry after 40 days

There was no significant difference (P>0.05) in FCR of fry fed with three formulated diets.

Condition Factor (CF)

Table 5.7: Condition Factor measurements for different fish diets

Feed diets	Diet 1	Diet 2	Diet 3
Condition Factor	2.447	2.443	2.412

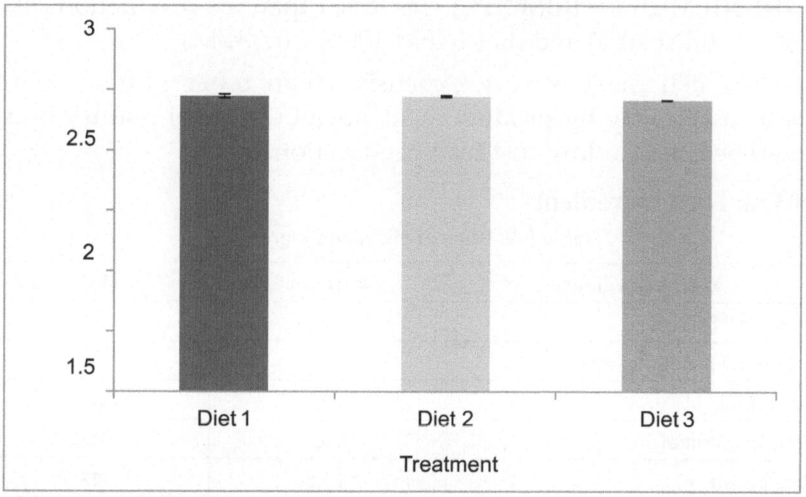

Fig. 5.7 Graphical representation of Condition Factor (CF) of fry after 40 days

There was no significant difference (P>0.05) in CF of fry fed with three formulated diets.

Survival Rate (SR)

Table 5.8: Survival Measurements with Different Fish Diets

Feed diets	Diet 1	Diet 2	Diet 3
Survival Rate(SR) %	80.98	78.65	77.44

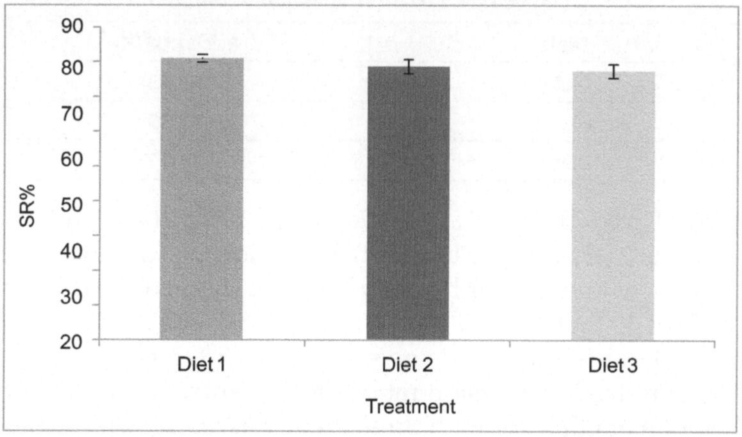

Fig. 5.8: Graphical representation of Survival Rate (SR) of fry after 40 days

There was no significant difference (P>0.05) in SR of fry fed with three formulated diets.

Cost of Feed

The estimated total cost of production for 1 kg of formulated diets. Production cost of diet 3(IFM 25% + BBM 75%) was lesser than the production cost of diet 2 (IFM 50% + BBM 50%) and diet 1(IFM 100% + 0%BBM).

Imported fish meal is very expensive than other protein source feed ingredients as Poultry by product meal, soya bean meal poultry by-product meal could be used for low cost feed preparation.

Price of Fish Feed Ingredient

Table 5.9: Price of Fish Feed Ingredient

Feed Ingredients	Amount	Price (Rs) in LKR
Imported fish meal	1 kg	158
Broiler by products Meal	1 kg	30
Corn flour	1 kg	80
Soya bean meal	1 kg	100
Rice polish	1 kg	25
Coconut poonac	1 kg	28
Wheat flour	1 kg	90
Vitamin and mineral Complex	1 kg	600
soya oil	1 L	600

Estimation of the Total Cost of Production of Formulated Feed (1 Kg)

The estimated total cost of production for 1 Kg of formulated feed as diet 1, diet 2 and diet 3.

Table 5.10: Cost of Production of Diets

Diets	Price (Rs)/Kg
Diet 1	94.43
Diet 2	82.37
Diet 3	76.77

Diet 3 (IFM 5%+ BBM 15%) was lower in price than Diet 1(IFM 20%+ 0%BBM) and Diet 2 (IFM 10%+ BBM 10%). Diet 2 and Diet 3 were prepared using imported fish meal and Broiler by-product meal showed similar performance compare to Diet 1, that was contain imported fish meal without broiler by-product meal. Because there were no significant difference (p>0.05) in weight gain, length gain, feed conversion ratio, specific growth rate, condition factor and survival rate of GIFT fry with three diets. Therefore, Diet 3 could be used as a low cost feed than other two formulated feed for rearing stage of GIFT fry.

CONCLUSION AND RECOMMENDATIONS

There was no significant difference (P>0.05) BWG, BLG, SGR, CF and SR of GIFT fry fed with three diets. Cost of diet 3 was less than the diet 1 and the diet 2. Therefore, it can be reduced feed cost for GIFT fry by replacing 15% of fish meal by BBM meal as a protein source for formulated feed given in the rearing stage. Do further research with replacing of fish meal by BBM in fish diet. Conduct this study with other species. Diet 3(IFM 25%+PBM 75%) can be developed as a low cost feed for mini hatchery farmers.

REFERENCES

Abowei, J.F.N, and Ekubo, A.T. (2011): Some Principles and Requirements in Fish Nutrition, *British J. of Pharmacology and Toxicology,* Vol. 2(4): 163-178.

Adeparusi, E.O. and Famurewa, J.A.C. (2011): Water Temperature and Surface Coating Effect on Floatability, Water Absorption and Thickness Swelling of Feed, *J. of Agricultural Science,* Vol. 3(4) 254 - 260.

Amarasingha U. S. A Synthesis on the Management of the Capture Fisheries of Sri Lanka Peranial Reservoirs.

Ariyarathne M. H. S. (2007): "Economically Feasible Feed for GIFT Tilapia Food Fish Culture in Sri Lanka.

Chiu, A. et al. (2013): Feed and Fishmeal Use in the Production of Carp and Tilapia in China, Aquaculture, (pp. 414-415).

Edirisinghe, U. (2009): *Freshwater Capture Fisheries and Aquaculture of Sri Lanka:* Aruna Printers, Kurunagala, Sri Lanka.

Eid, A.L., Saiid, M.M. and Salama, A.A. (2003): Effect of Protein Levels on Growth Performance and Economical Evaluation of Nile Tilapia *(oreochromisniloiicus), Egypt. J. Aquat. BfoL& Fish,* Vol.7(3): 309 - 318.

El Hammady, A.K.I. (2002): Carbohydrate to Lipid Ratio (CHO:L) in Practical Tilapia Diets: 1- Effect of Dietary Carbohydrate to Lipid Ratio on Growth Performance of Hybrid Tilapia *(oreochromisniloticus x o aureus), Egypt. J. Aguat. Boil & Fish,* Vol.6(3): 17 -38.

El-Sayed, A.F.M. (2002): Protein Nutrition of Farmed Tilapia: Searching for Unconventional Sources, Oceanography Department, Faculty of Science University of Alexandria, Alexandria, Egypt.

Ensminger, M. E., Olentine Jr, C. G. (1978): Feeds for Fish. In *Feeds & Nutrition*-(pp.1029–1037).

Fitzsimmons, K., Circa, A., Jimenez, E.B. and Pereda, P. (2011): Development of Low-cost Supplemental Feeds for Tilapia in Pond and Cage Culture, Eighth Work Plan, Philippines Research 1 (PHR1), Progress Report, 57 - 63

Gaber, M.M. (2002): Effects of Dietary Carbohyrate-to-lipid Ratios on Growth Performance and Body Composition of Nile tilapia, *Oreochromisniloticus* Fingerlings, *Eypt. J. Agut. Bio.& Fish$_y$*Vol. 6(2):25 - 40.

Gatlin, D.M. (2010): Principles of Fish Nutrition, SRAC Publication No. 5003.

Glencross, B. D., Booth, M., & Allan, G. L. (2007): A Feed is only as Good as Its Ingredients - A Review of Ingredient Evaluation Strategies for Aquaculture Feeds. *Aquaculture Nutrition.* http://doi.org/10.1111/j.1365-2095.2007.00450.x.(2017-08-20)

Gohl, B. (1981): Tropical Feeds. Feed Information Summaries and Nutritive Values. FAO Animal Production and Health Series 12 (pp. 528), FAO, Rome.

Higgs, D.A., Markert, J.R., Macquarrie, D.W., McBride, J.R., Dosanjh, B.S., Nichols, C. and Hoskins, G. (1979): Development of Practical Dry Diets for Coho Salmon, *Oncorhynchus kisutch,* using Poultry by-product Meal, Feather Meal, Soybean Meal and Rapeseed Meal as Major Protein Sources. Inc: J.E. Halver and K. Tiews (Editors), Fintish Nutrition and Fish Feed Technology, Vol. II, Heenemann, Berlin, (pp. 191-218).

Hossen M. D. N. (2011): Effect of Storage Time on Fish Feed Stored at Refrigeration Temperature and Room Temperature.

Hasan, M.R., Haq M.S., Das, P.M. and Mowlah, G. (1997): Evaluation of Poultry Feather Meal as a Dietary Protein Source for Indian Major Carp *Labeo rohita* fry. *Aquaculture,* 151 (pp. 47-54).

Ighwela, K.A., Ahmad, A.B. and Abol-Munafi, A.B. (2013): Water Stability and Nutrient Leaching of Different Levels of Maltose Formulated Fish Pellets, *J. Global Veterinarian* Vol. 10(6): 638 - 642.

Jabeen, S., Salim, M. and Akhtar, P., (2004): Feed Conversion Ratio of Major Carp Cirrhinusmrigala Fingerlings Fed on Cotton Seed Meal, Fish Meal and Barley, *Pakistan Vet. /.,* Vol. 24(l).

Jayaratne, R and Surasinghe, T. (2010): General Ecology and Habitat Selectivity of Fresh Water Fishes of the Rawan Oya, Kandy, Sri Lanka, *J. Sabaramuwa University,* Vol. 9: 11-43.

Kaviraj, A., Mondal, K., Mukhopadhyay, P.K. and Turchini, G.M. (2012): Impact of Fermented Mulberry Leaf and Fish Offal in Diet Formulation of Indian Major Carp *(Labeo rohita).* Proc. Zool. Soc.,DOI 10.1007/s12595-012-0052-1.

Keong Ng, W. and Chong, C.Y. (2007): An Overview of Lipid Nutrition with Emphasis on Alternative Lipid Sources in Tilapia Feeds, Fish Nutrition Laboratory, School of Biological Sciences, UniversitiSains Malaysia, Penang, Malaysia, 241-248.

Little, D.C. and Tuan, P.A. (1999): Common Carp Indigenous Ricefield based culture in Northern Vietnam. AARM Newsletter, 4(3):4-5.

Lim, C. (2008): Effects of Varied Dietary Lipid Sources Tested in Tilapia Study, *Global Aquaculture Advocate,* 68 - 70.

Lim, C, Aksoy, M.Y., Li, M.H., Welker, T.L. and Klesius, P.H. (2009): Influence of Dietary Levels of Lipid and Vitamin E on Growth and Resistance of Nile Tilapia to Streptococcus Iniae Challenge, *J. Aquaculture,* Vol. 298:76 - 82.

Lim, C, leamaster, B. and Brock, J.A. (1993): Riboflavin Requirement of Fingerling Red Hybrid Tilapia Grown in Seawater, *J. Of the world aquaculture society,* Vol. 24(4): 451 -458.

Mair, G.C. (2000): Programme Development Research Completion Report: Socioeconomic and Environmental Impacts of the Introduction of Genetically Improved Fish in Vietnam. Report to the DFID Fish Genetics Programme. 3p.

Mair G. C and Tuna P.A. Stock Coparison poly Culture and National Breeding Program.

Mondal, K., Kaviraj, A. and Mukhopadhyay, P. K. (2011): Partial Replacement of Fishmeal by Fermented Fish-offal Meal in the Formulation of Diet for Indian Minor Carp *Labeo bata. J. Apl. Aqa.,* 23: (pp. 41-50).

Mortuza, M.G. and Al-Misned, F.A. (2013): Length-Weight Relationships, Condition Factor and Sex-Ratio of Nile Tilapia, *Oreochromisniloticus*in WadiHanifah, Riyadh, Saudi Arabia, *World J. of Zoology,* Vol. 8(l): 106 -109.

Nehemia, A., Maganira, J.D. and Rumisha, C. (2012): Length-Weight Relationship and Condition Factor of Tilapia Species Grown in Marine and Fresh Water Ponds, *Agriculture and Biology J. of North America,* Vol. 3(3): 117 - 124.

Nengas, I., Alexis, M.N. and Davies, S.J. (1999): High Inclusion Levels of Poultry Meals and Related Byproducts in Diets for Gilthead Seabream, *Sparus aurata* L. Aquaculture, (*179*: pp. 13-23).

Ogunji, J .,Toor, R.U.A.S., Schulz, C. and Kloas, W. (2008): Growth Performance, Nutrient Utilization of Nile Tilapia *Oreochromisniloticus* Fed Housefly Maggot Meal (Magmeal) Diets, *Turkish J. of Fisheries and Aquatic Sciences,* Vol.8: 141 -147.

Ridha, M.T. (2005): Preliminary Study on Growth, Feed Conversion and Production in Non-improved and Improved Strains of the Nile Tilapia *Oreochromisniloticus,* Aquaculture, Fisheries and Marine Environment Department, Kuwait Institute for Scientific Research, Kuwait.

Solomon, S.G., Ataguba, G.A. and Abeje, A. (2011): Water Stability and Floatation Test of Fish Pellets using Local Starch Sources and Yeast *(Saccahromycescerevisae), J. Latest Trends Agr. Food Sei.,*Vol. 1: 1 - 5.

Solomon, S.G., Tiamiyu, L.O. and Agaba, U.J. (2007): Effect of Feeding Different Grain Sources on the Growth Performance and Body Composition of Tilapia, *(Oreochromis niloticus)* Fingerlings Fed in Outdoor Hapas, Pakistan J, of *Nutrition*. Vol. 6(3): 271-275.

Somsued, P. (2004): Proten and Energy Requirement and Feeding of Fish, Island Feed Research Institute, Inland Fisheries Research and Development Bureau, Department of Fisheries.

Statistics-Ministryof Fisheries and Aquatic Resources Development, Sri Lanka, (2013): (http://www.fisheries.gov.lk/content.php?cnid=ststc, 15/06/2014).

Teshima, S., gonzalez, G.M.O. and Kanazawa , A. (1978): Nutritional Requirements of Tilapia: Utilization of Dietary Protein by *Tilapia zillii,* Mem. Fac. Fish., Kagoshima Univ., Vol. 27(1): 49-57.

Walker, G. (1980): Effects of Processing on the Nutritional Value of Feeds. *p. 321-324. In: Fish Feed Technology. FAO/UNDP, ADCP/REP/80/11.,* 3–6.

Watanabe, T. (2002): Strategies for Further Development of Aquatic Feeds. *Fisheries Science, 68*(2), 242–252. http://doi.org/10.1046/j.1444-2906.2002.00418.x

Weerakoon, D.E.M. (2007): Freshwater Fish Seed Resources in Sri Lanka, *Assessment of Freshwater Fish Seed Resources for Sustainable Aquaculture,* 425-440.

Wickins, J. (1998): Feeds and Feeding of Fish. *Aquaculture, 71*(1-2), 97–119.

Yang, Y., Xie S., Cui, Y., Lei, W., Zhu, X., Yang, Y. and Yu, Y. (2004): Effect of Replacement of Dietary Fish Meal by Meat and Bone Meal and Poultry by- Product Meal on Growth and Feed Utilization of Gibel Carp, *Carassius auratus gibelio. Aquac. Nutr.,* 10 (pp. 289-294).

Genetics and Bioengineering : *Concepts and Issues* Pages 98-115
Edited by: Dr. Ashok K. Rathoure and Dr. Pawan Kumar 'Bharti'
ISBN: 978-93-86841-92-6
Edition: 2019
Published by: Discovery Publishing House Pvt. Ltd., New Delhi (India)

6

RNA Binding and Inhibition of Function by Metal Complexes

[1]Prasann Kumar and [2]Shweta Pathak

ABSTRACT

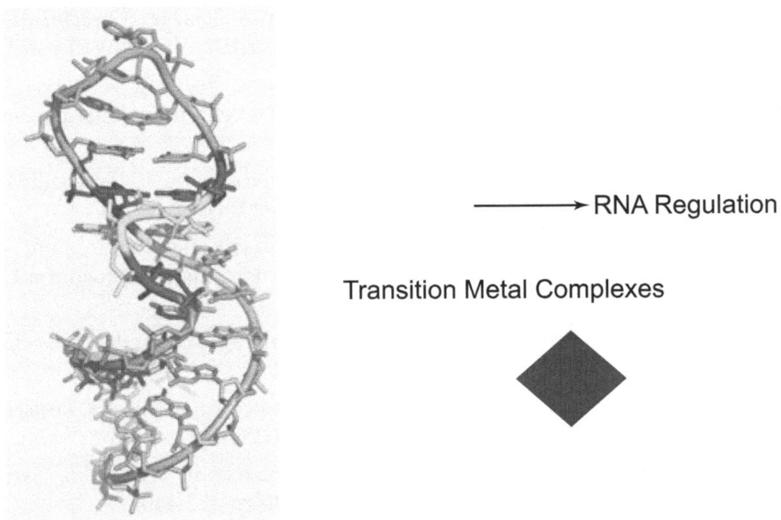

Keywords: Agriculture, Binding, Complexes, Density, Inhibition, Metal.

INTRODUCTION

Resistance to medicines: A Public Health Nuisance

Antibiotic resistance in the United States per year:

- $20 billion in extra health care costs
- $35 billion in societal costs
- 8 million additional days patients spend in hospitals

1 Division of Research and Development, Department of Agronomy, School of Agriculture, Lovely Professional University, Jalandhar, Punjab, 144411, India

2 Department of Plant Physiology, I.Ag. Sci., BHU., Varanasi, 221005, U.P., India

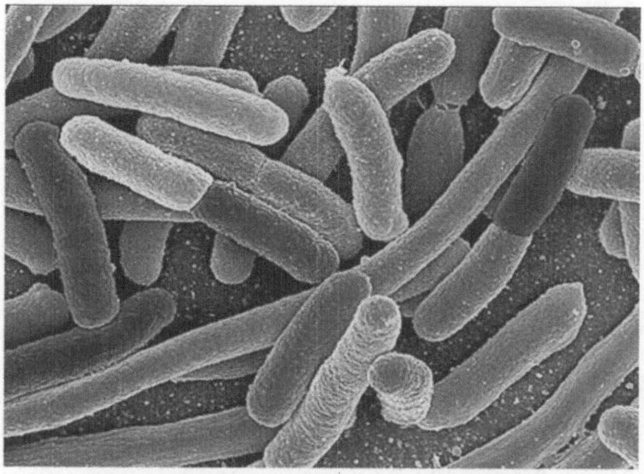

Fig. 6.1: Microbes for antibiotic production
(Source: Based on review of literature, 2018)

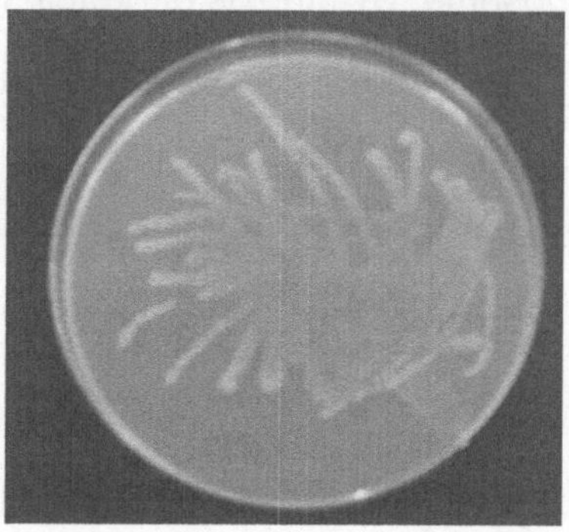

Fig. 6.2: Microbes for antibiotic production
(Source: Based on review of literature, 2018)

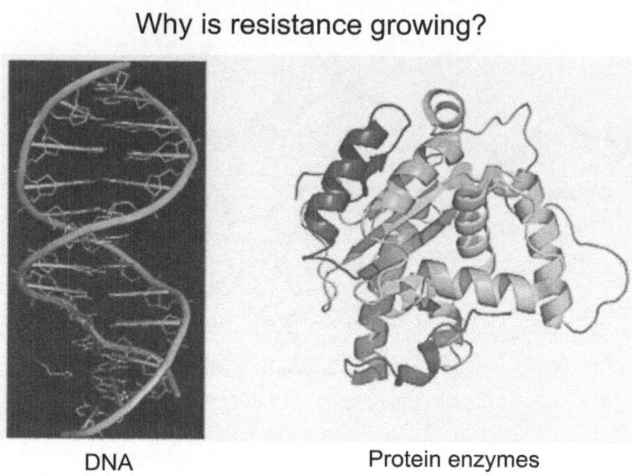

Fig. 6.3: Resistance and its cause
(Source: Based on review of literature, 2018)

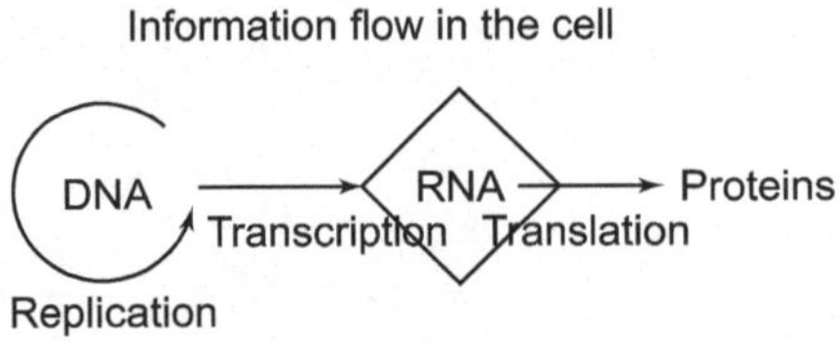

Fig. 6.4: Central dogma of molecular biology
(Source: based on review of literature, 2018)

THREE MAIN TYPES OF RNA

- Messenger RNA (mRNA)
- Transfer RNA (tRNA)
- Ribosomal RNA (rRNA)
- All three types of RNA are intricately involved in making proteins

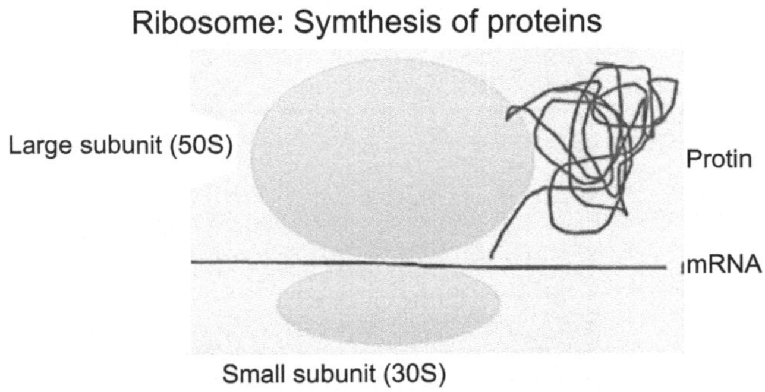

Fig. 6.5: Ribosome and synthesis of protein
(Source: Based on Review of Literature, 2018)

RNA: INFORMATION FLOW AND CATALYSIS

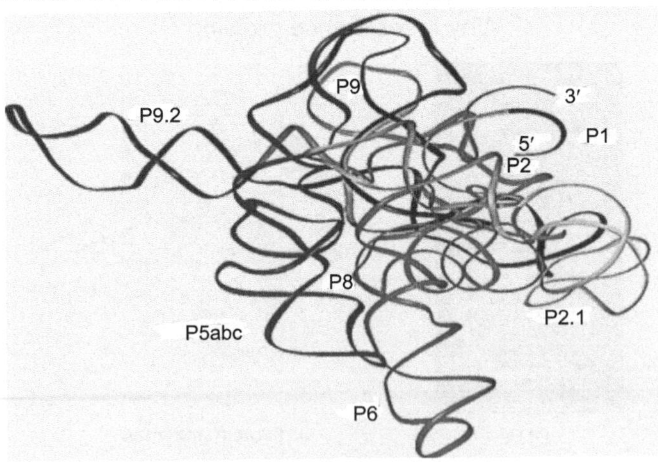

Fig. 6.6: RNA information flow
(Source: Based on review of literature, 2018)

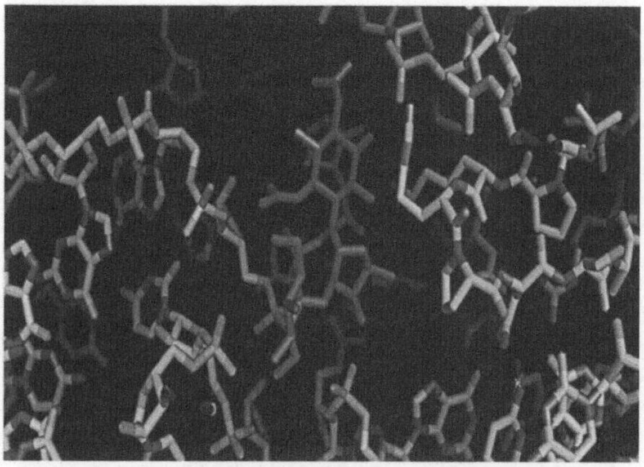

Fig. 6.7: RNA as a new target
(Source: Based on review of literature, 2018)

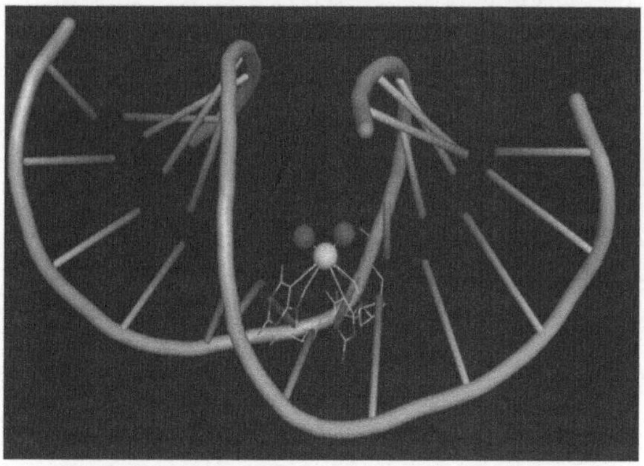

Fig. 6.8: Metal-based anticancer compounds
(Source: Based on review of literature, 2018)

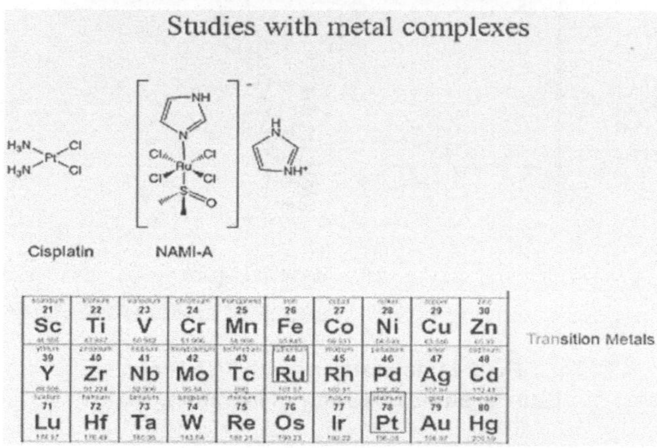

Fig. 6.9: Studies with metal complexes
(Source: Based on review of literature, 2018)

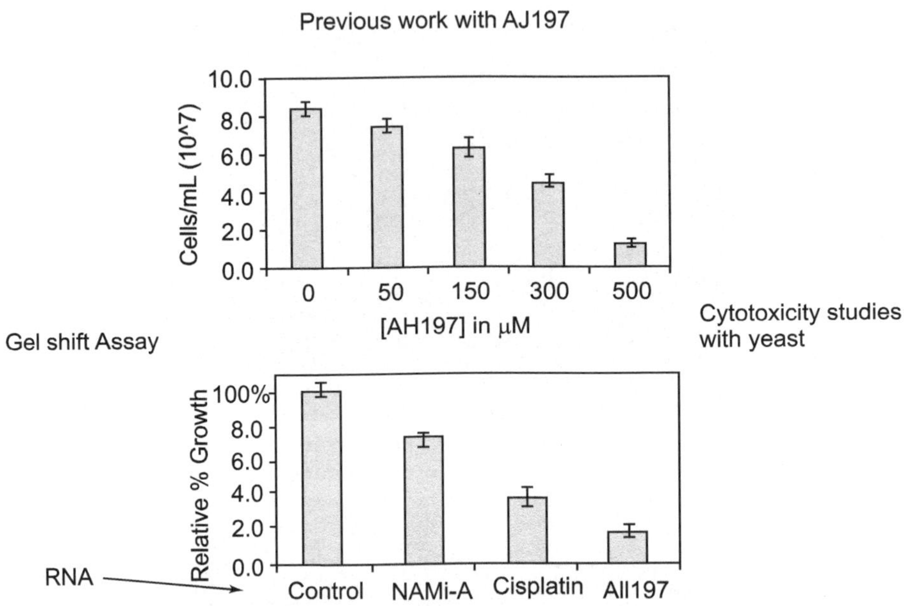

Fig. 6.10: Previous work with RNA
(Source: Based on review of Literature, 2018)

RNA Gel Mobility Shift Study

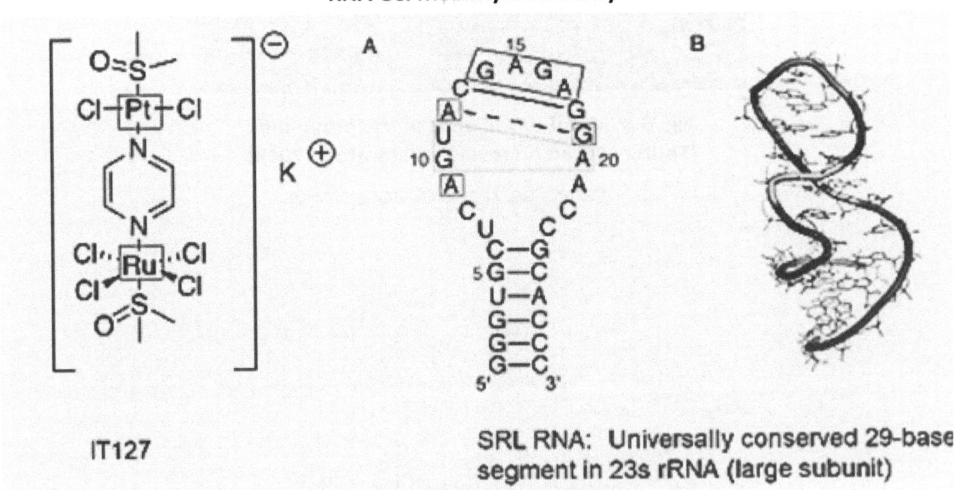

Fig. 6.11: Interactions with RNA Loop
(Source: Based on review of literature, 2018)

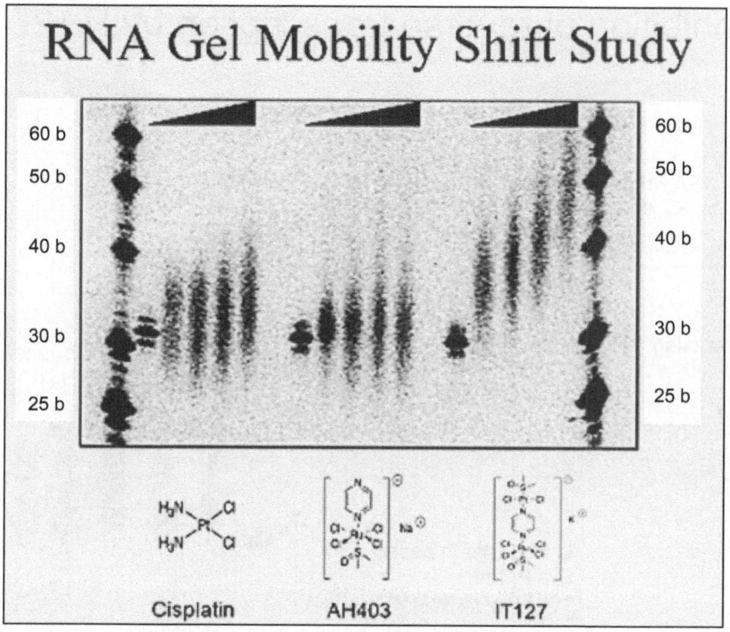

Fig. 6.12: RNA Gel Mobility shift study
(Source: Based on review of literature, 2018)

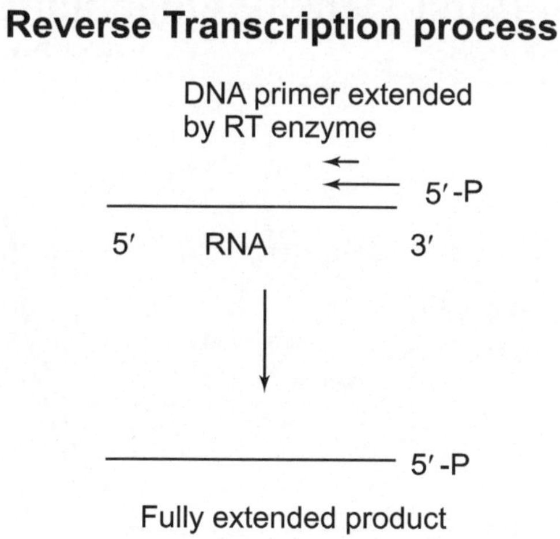

Fig. 6.13: Reverse transcription process
(Source: Based on review of literature, 2018)

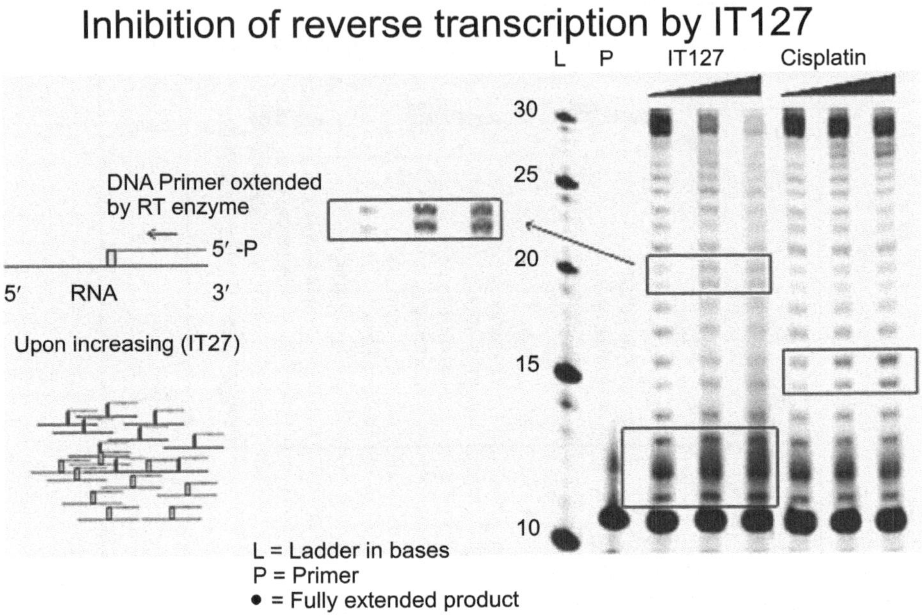

Fig. 6.14: Inhibition of reverse transcription
(Source: Based on review of literature, 2018)

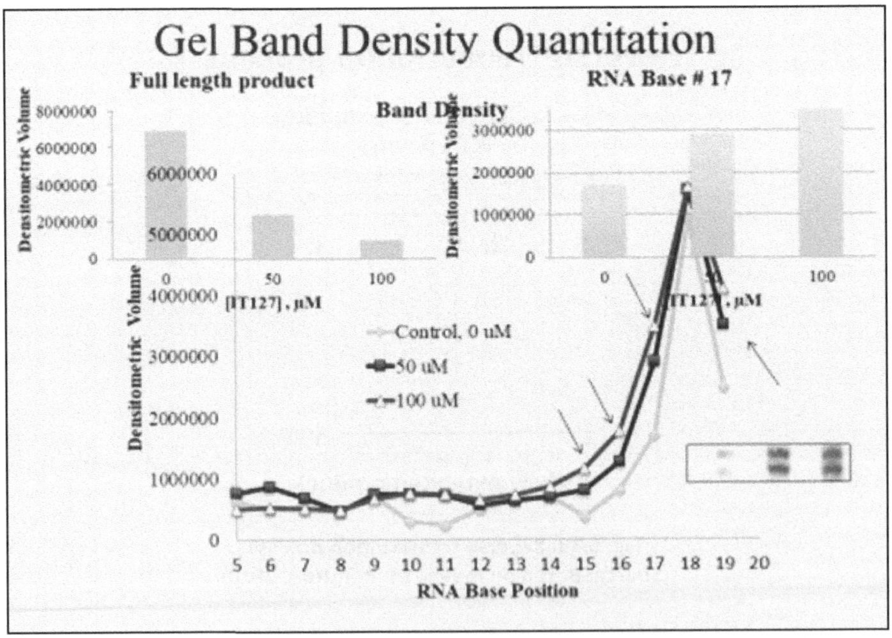

Fig. 6.15: Gel Band Density Quantitation
(Source: Based on review of Literature, 2018)

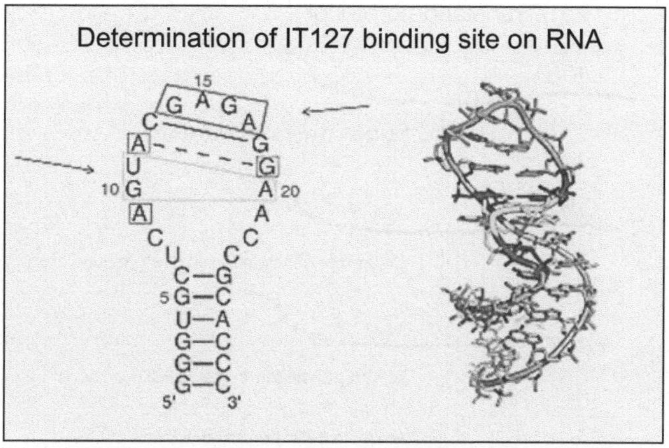

Fig. 6.16: Determination of IT127 binding site on RNA (Source: Based on review of literature, 2018)

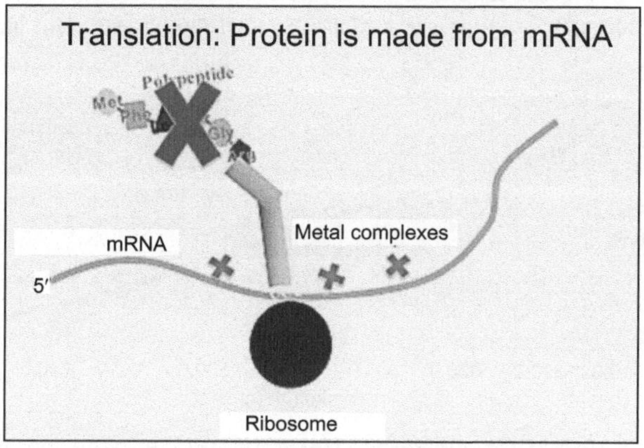

Fig. 6.17: Translation: protein is made from mRNA (Source: Based on review of literature, 2018)

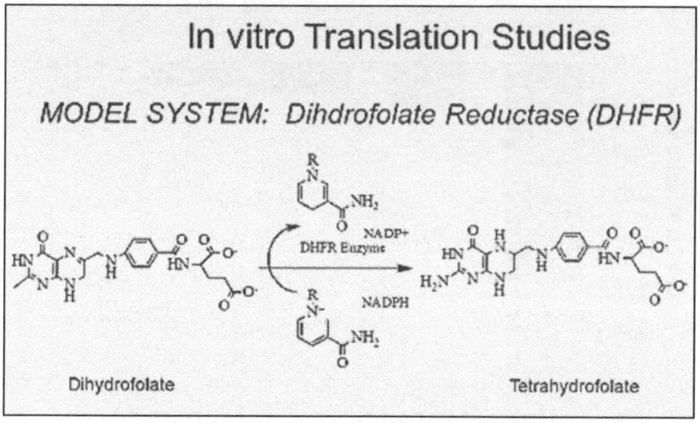

Fig. 6.18: In vitro translation study (Source: Based on review of literature, 2018)

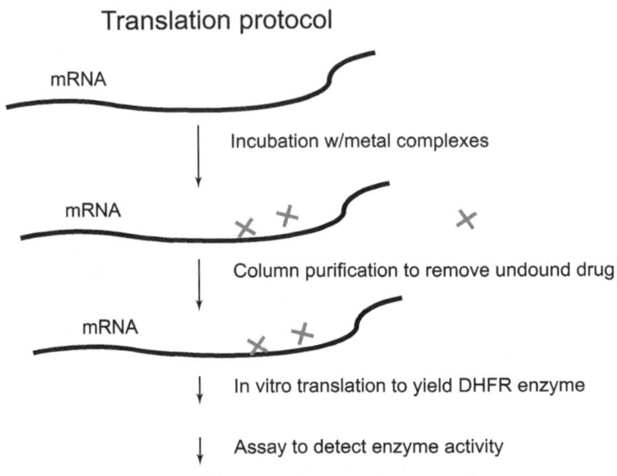

Fig. 6.19: Translational protocol
(Source: Based on review of literature, 2018)

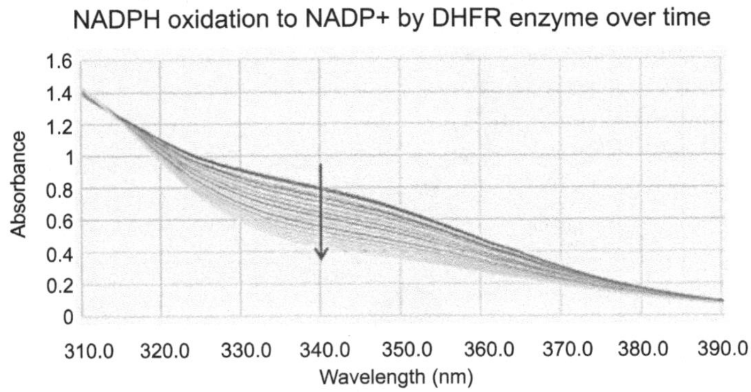

Fig. 6.20: NADPH oxidation to NADP$^+$ by DHFR enzyme over time
(Source: Based on review of literature, 2018)

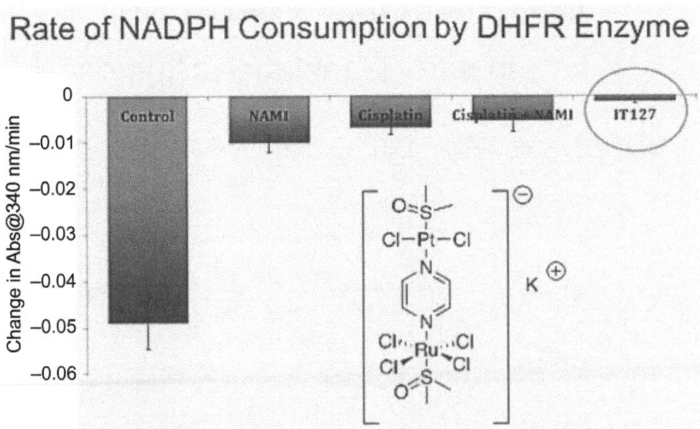

Fig. 6.21: Rate of NADPH Consumption by DHFR Enzyme
(Source: Based on review of literature, 2018)

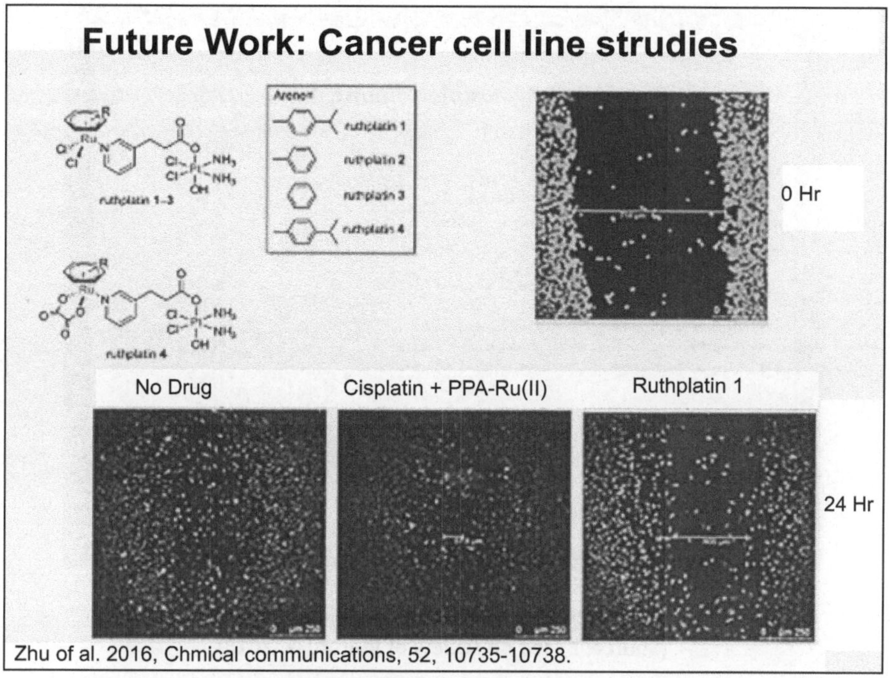

Fig. 6.22: Cancer cell line studies
(Source: Based on review of literature, 2018)

Efficient Conduct of Labs

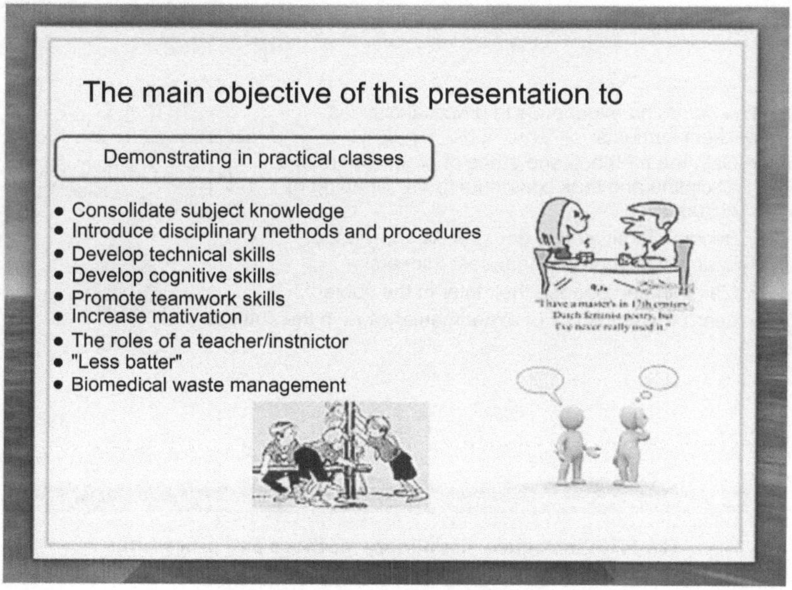

Fig. 6.23: Efficient conduct of labs
(Source: Based on review of literature, 2018)

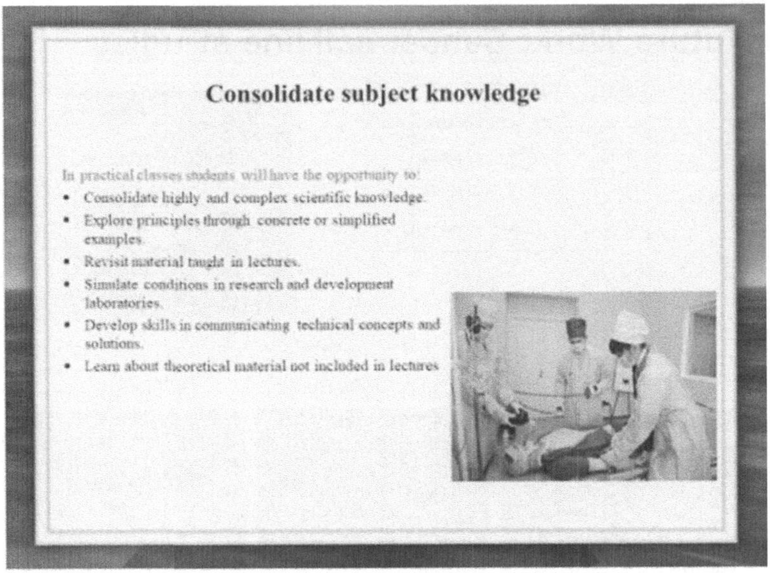

Fig. 6.24: Consolidate subject knowledge
(Source: Based on review of literature, 2018)

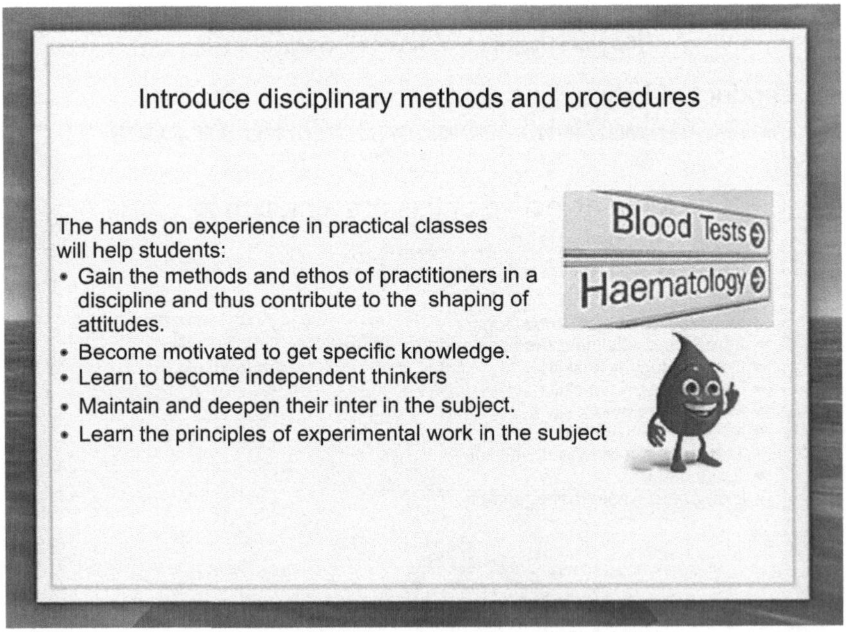

Fig. 6.25: Introduce disciplinary methods and procedures
(Source: based on review of literature, 2018)

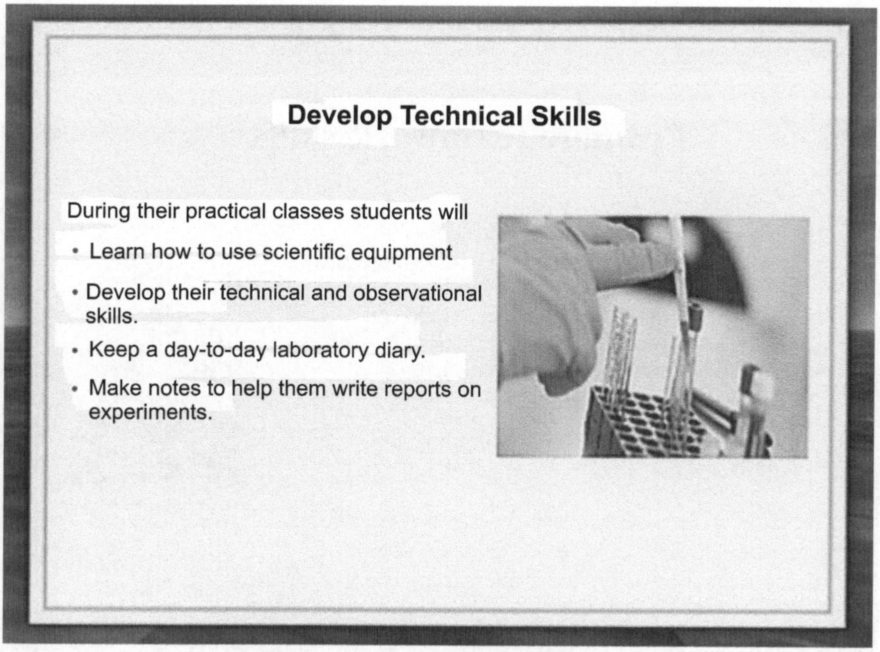

Fig. 6.26: Develop the technical skills
(Source: based on review of literature, 2018)

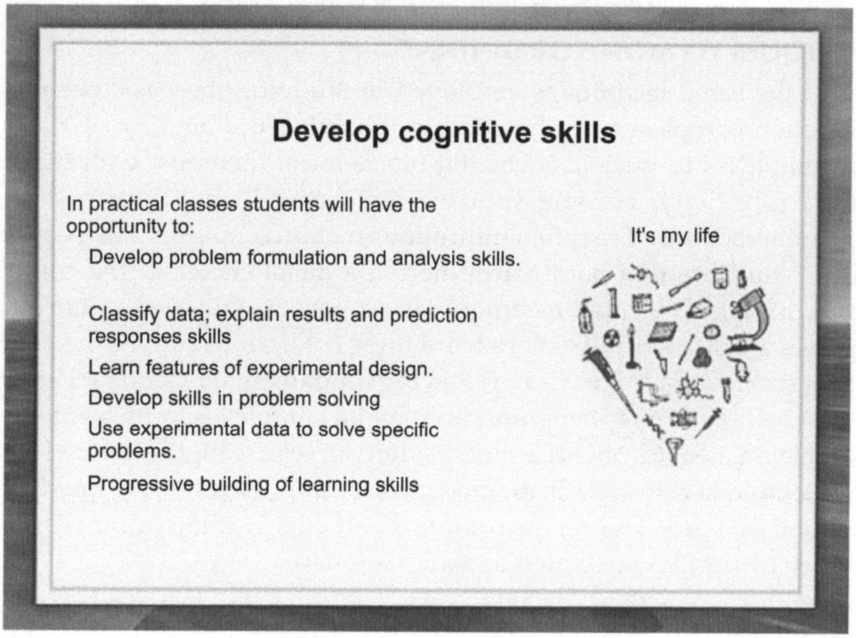

Fig. 6.27: Development of cognitive skill
(Source: Based on review of literature, 2018)

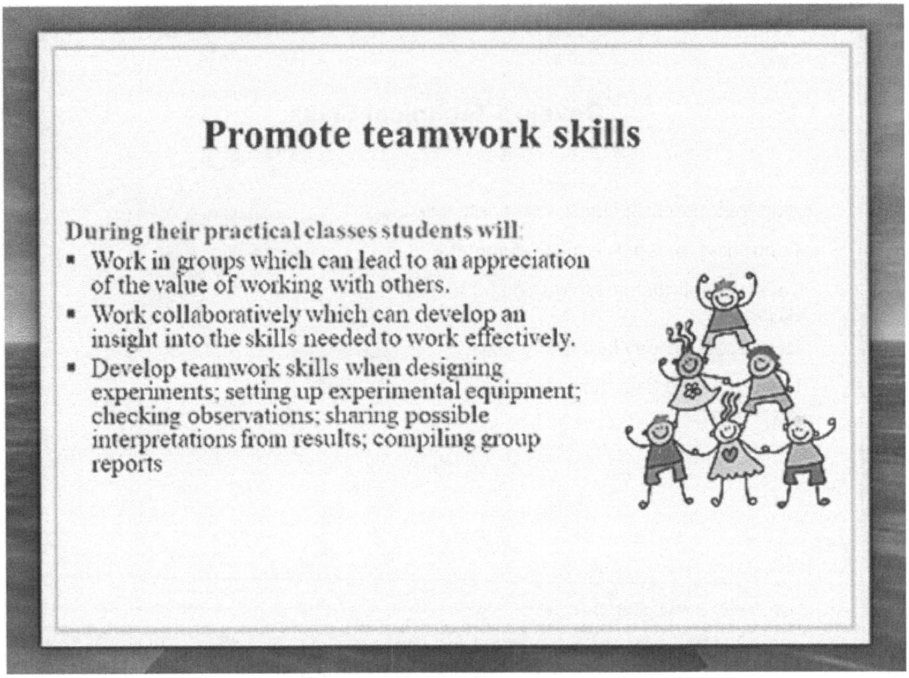

Fig. 6.28: Promote the team work
(Source: based on review of literature, 2018)

TECHNIQUES TO MONITOR BINDING

Many of the same techniques employed in studying the basic chemistry of coordination complexes can be used in following the binding of transition-metal complexes to nucleic acids, but biochemical methods, with their often exquisite sensitivity, become valuable aids as well in delineating specific binding interactions. Tris(phenanthroline) metal complexes are particularly useful to illustrate this point, since here the metal center in the complex is selected in terms of the technique used for examination. Coordination complexes are often visibly colored and these colorations provide a useful and sensitive spectroscopic handle in following fundamental reactions. This notion holds as well with tris (phenanthroline) metal complexes in their interactions with nucleic acids. Ru(phenh 2+ and its derivatives are highly colored because of an intense metal-to-ligand charge-transfer band (Amax = 447 nm, E = 1.9 X 104 M -Icm -I). Furthermore, the complexes are highly photoluminescent(Aem = 610 nm, *T* = 0.6 f.LS in aerated aqueous solution).

TRIS(phenanthrollnej metal complexes to nucleic acids these transitions are perturbed. Hypochromism is observed in the charge-transfer band, and intercalation leads to an increase in lifetime of the charge-transfer excited state.

43,46 Indeed, single-photon counting experiments show a biexponential decay in emission from Ru(phenh 2+ bound to double-helical DNA. The longer-lived component (T = 2 fLS) has been assigned as the intercalated component and the shorter-lived 0.6 fLScomponent has been attributed to a mixture of free and groove-bound species. These spectroscopic perturbations permit one to define equilibrium-binding affinities for the different components of the interaction as a function of metal-center chirality and under different solution conditions. One can also follow the polarization of emitted light from the complexes after excitation with polarized light and these studies have been helpful in describing the dynamics of association of the complexes on the helix. Mixed-ligand complexes of ruthenium (II) show similar spectroscopic perturbations, and these have been used to characterize binding affinities and chiral preferences, as well as the extent of intercalation versus groove binding as a function of ligand substitution on the metal center. The spectroscopic handle of the metal center therefore affords a range of experiments to monitor and characterize the binding of the metal complexes to polynucleotides. Binding interactions of metal complexes with oligonucleotides can also be followed by NMR and here as well the metal center offers some useful characteristics to exploit. As with organic DNA-binding molecules, shifts in the 1H_ NMR resonances of both the DNA-binding molecule and the oligonucleotide become apparent as a function of increased association with the helix. These shift variations can be used empirically to watch the dynamics of association and to gain some structural insights into the binding modes of the complexes on the helix. These kinds of experiments have been performed with tris(phenanthroline) complexes of ruthenium(II) and rhodium(III), where it was observed that the double-helical oligonucleotide is an exceedingly good chiralshiftreagent to separate resonances in an enantiomeric mixture of the tris(phenanthroline) complexes. For covalent binding molecules, such as *cis*diammineplatinum(II), furthermore, the lowering of the *pKa* of purine positions and therefore shifting of resonances as a function of coordination to an alternate site has been helpful as well in assigning the sites of covalent binding on the oligonucleotide. But also in NMR experiments, special advantage can be taken of the metal center. For tris(phenanthroline) metal complexes, 1H-NMR experiments were performed on the paramagnetic analogues, Ni(phenh 2+ and Cr(phenh 3+. It was reasonable to assume the binding characteristics would be identical with their respective diamagnetic analogues, Ru(II) and Rh(III); yet paramagnetic broadening by the metal complexes of nearby resonances on the oligonucleotide would allow one to deduce where along the helix the complexes associate. Using this method the groove-binding interaction of the complexeswas identified as occurring in the minor groove of the helix.

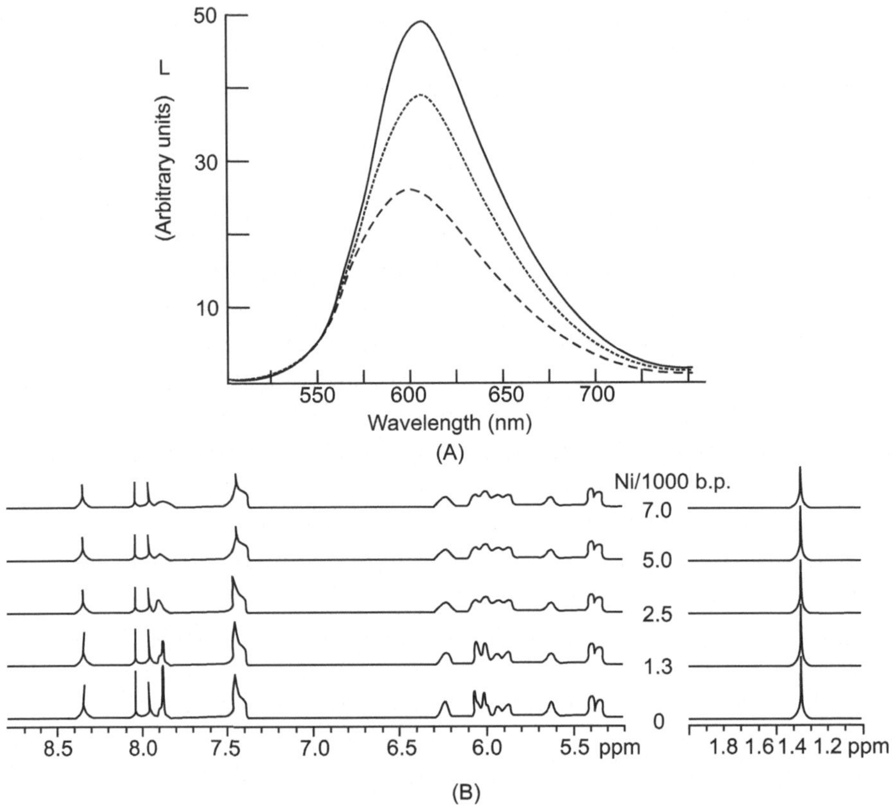

Fig. 6.29: Binding of DNA with Nickel and its illustration with Paramagnetic character of nickel
(Source: based on review of literature, 2018)

There are numerous other classic techniques of inorganic chemistry that havebeen or could be applied in studying the binding of metal complexes to nucleic acids. Coordination complexes have invariably been used in x-ray diffraction experiments because of the high electron density of the metal center. The tris(phenanthroline) metal complexes have not yet been applied in this context, but, as mentioned already, platinum metallointercalators were examined by fiberdiffraction to delineate intercalation requirements. In fact, many nucleic-acid crystal structures have required specific metal ion additions for isomorphousheavy-metal derivatives to solve the structure. Such has certainly been true for the crystal structure of tRNAPhe, where heavy-metal ions such as platinum, osmium and mercury were targeted to specific base positions, and lanthanide ions were used to label phosphate positions around the periphery of the molecule. Other techniques can also be exploited to monitor and characterize binding. A recent novel illustration is one from electrochemistry, which has been applied in monitoring the binding of Co(phenh^{3+} to DNA.Surely other techniques, from EXAFS to scanning tunnelling microscopy, will be exploited in the future.Metalloregulatory proteins, like the transcription factors, affectthe expression of genetic information through structural interactions that depend upon the metal ions, but unlike the zinc-finger proteins, metalloregulatory proteins act as triggers, repressing or activating transcription given the presence or absence of metal ion. In some respects, even more than zinc fingers, these systems resemble the Ca^{2+}-activated proteins.Consider the biological system that must respond to changing intracellularmetal concentrations. At high concentrations many metal ions become toxic to the cell; hence, a full system of proteins must be synthesized that will chelate and detoxify the bound-metal-ion pool. In order to actively engage these proteins, the genes that encode them must be rapidly transcribed. But at the sametime, the DNA itself must be protected from the high concentrations of metal ion.

Perhaps the best-characterized metalloregulatory system thus far is the MerRsystem, regulating mercury resistance in bacteria. An inducible set of genes arranged in a single operon is under the control of the metal-sensing MerRprotein, and it is this system that mediates mercury resistance. Mercury resistance depends upon the expression of these genes to import toxic Hg(lI), reduce Hg(II) to the volatile Hg(O) by NADPH, and often additionally to cleave organomercurialsto their corresponding hydrocarbon and Hg(II) species. The MerRprotein regulates mercury resistance both negatively and positively. MerR in the absence of Hg(II) binds tightly and sequencespecifically to the promoter. In so doing, MerR inhibits binding to the promoter by RNA polymerase. When Hg^{2+} is added at low concentrations, the metal ion binds specifically and with high affinity to the DNA-bound MerR and causes a DNA conformational change detectable by using other metal reagents as conformational probes. What are the structural requirements in the metal-binding site? Certainly onerequirement is Hg(II) specificity, so that other metal ions will not also trigger transcriptional activation. Another is high metal-binding affinity to protect the DNA from direct coordination of the Hg(lI). The MerR protein is dimeric, and contains four cysteine residues per monomer. Site-directed mutagenesis studies have indicated that three of these four cysteine residues are needed for Hg(II) binding, and EXAFS studies have been consistent with tricoordinate ligation, clearly a well-designed system for Hg(1I) specificity. Perhaps even more interesting, the site-directed mutagenesis studieson heterodimers (a mixture of mutant and wild-type monomers) have indicated that the coordinated Hg(II) bridges the dimer, ligating two cysteines of one monomer and one cysteine of the other. This scheme may provide the basis also for the kinetic lability needed in a rapidly responsive cellular system.

CONCLUSIONS

One system involves the assembly of two dipeptides linked by acentral acyclic metal-binding polyether ligand, with Fe(EDTAf tethered to one end to mark site-specific binding. In the presence of alkaline earth cations, which induce a conformational change that generates a central macrocycle, the linked peptides become oriented to promote sequence-specific binding in the minor groove. In the absence of the alkaline earth ion, no site-specific binding, or cleavage of DNA, is evident. One might consider this system as a simple, first-order synthetic model for the metalloregulatory proteins.

REFERENCES

W. Saenger, Principles of Nucleic Acid Structure, Springer-Verlag, 1984; J. K. Barton, Chem. Eng.News 66 (Sept. 26, 1988), 30.

M. McCall, T. Brown and O. Kennard, 1. Mol. Bioi. 183 (1985), 385.

R. Wing et al., Nature 287 (1980), 755.

A. H.-J. Wang et al., Nature 282 (1979), 680.

S. H. Kim et al., Proc. Nat!. Acad. Sci. USA 71 (1974), 4970.

E. N. Trifonov and J. L. Sussman, Proc. Natl. Acad. Sci USA 77 (1980), 3816; J. C. Marini et al., Proc. Natl. Acad. Sci. USA 79 (1982), 7664; H.-S. Koo, H.-M. Wu and D. M. Crothers, Nature 320 (1986),501.

M. Gellert et al., Cold Spring Harbor Symps. Quant. Bioi. 43 (1979),D. M. J. Lilley, Proc. Natl. Acad. Sci. USA 77 (1980), 6468.

J. S. Lee et al., Nucleic Acids Res. 12 (1984), 6603; V. I. Lyamichev, 1. Biomol. Struct. Dyn. 3 (1986),667; H. Htun and J. E. Dahlberg, Science 241 (1988), 1791.

R. D. Kornberg, Annu. Rev. Biochem. 46 (1977),931; A. Klug et al., Nature 287 (1980), 509.

T. R. Cech, Science 236 (1987), 1532.

(*a*) 1. K. Barton and S. J. Lippard, Metal Ions in Bioi. 1 (1980), 31;

(*b*) A. M. Pyle and 1. K. Barton, Prog. Inorg. Chem. 38 (1990), 413; (c) C. S. Chow and J. K. Barton, Meth. Enzym. 212 (1992),219.

S. E. Sherman et al., Science 230 (1985), 412.

D. Hodgson, Prog. Inarg. Chem. 23 (1977),211.

G. L. Eichhorn and Y. A. Shin, 1. Am. Chem. Soc. 90 (1968),7323.

L. G. Marzilli, Prog. Inarg. Chem. 23 (1977), 255.

C. H. Chang, M. Beer, and L. G. Marzilli, Biochemistry 16 (1977), 33; G. C. Glikinet 01, NucleicAcids Res. 12 (1984), 1725.

M. B. Fleisher, H. Y. Mei, and J. K. Barton, Nucleic Acids and Mol. Bioi. 2 (1988), 65.

S. J. Lippard, Acc. Chem. Res. 11 (1978), 211.

R. V. Gessner et 01, Biochemistry 24 (1985),237.

(*a*) K. W. Jennetteet 01., Proc. Nat!. Acad. Sci. USA 71 (1974), 3839; (b) A. H. Wang et 01.,Nature 276 (1978), 471.

H. Sigel, in T. D. Tullius, ed., Metal-DNA Chemistry, ACS Symposium 402 (1989), 159.

R. P. Hertzberg and P. B. Dervan, J. Am. Chem. Soc. 104 (1982), 313; R. P. Hertzberg and P. B. Dervan, Biochemistry 23 (1984),3934.

J. A. Latham and T. R. Cech, Science 245 (1989),276.

P. B. Dervan, Science 232 (1986), 464.

S. M. Hecht, ed., Bleomycin, Springer-Verlag, 1979.

D. S. Sigman, Acc. Chem. Res. 19 (1986), 180; S. Goldstein and G. Czapski, J. Am. Chem. Soc. 108 (1986), 2244.

For other Examples of Metal-mediated Redox Cleavage of DNA, see also: N. Grover and H. H. Thorp, J. Am. Chem. Soc. 113 (1991), 7030; X. Chen, S. E. Rokita, and C. J. Burrows, 1. Am. Chem. Soc.113 (1991),5884.

H. Y. Mei and J. K. Barton, J. Am. Chem. Soc. 108 (1986), 7414.

H. Y. Mei and J. K. Barton, Proc. Natl. Acad. Sci. USA 85 (1988), 1339.

A. M. Pyle, E. C. Long, and J. K. Barton, 1. Am. Chem. Soc. **111** (1989), 4520.

A. Sitlaniet 01., J. Am. Chem. Soc. **114** (1992),2303.

M. D. Purugganane t01., Science 241 (1988), 1645.

L. A. Basile and J. K. Barton, Metal Ions Bioi. Syst., 25 (1989), 31; J. K. Barton, in Frontiers of Chemistry: Biotechnology, Chern. Abstr. Serv., 5 (1989).

D. R. Jones, L. F. Lindoy, and A. M. Sargeson, 1. Am. Chem. Soc. 106 (1984),7807.

S. H. Gellman, R. Petter, and R. Breslow, 1. Am. Chem. Soc. 108 (1986),2388; J. Chin and X. Zhou, J. Am. Chem. Soc. 110 (1988), 223; J. R. Morrow and W. C. Trogler, Inorg. Chem. 27 (1988), 3387.

L. A. Basile, A. L. Raphael, and J. K. Barton, J. Am. Chem. Soc. 109 (1987), 7550.

G. L. Eichhorn and Y. A. Shin, J. Am. Chem. Soc. 90 (1968),7322.

R. S. Brown, J. C. Dewan, and A. Klug, Biochemistry 24 (1985),4785.

L. Behlenet 01., Biochemistry 29 (1990), 2515.

J. K. Barton, Science 233 (1986),727.

J. K. Barton et 01.,1. Am. Chem. Soc. 108 (1986), 2081.

A. M. Pyle et 01., J. Am. Chem. Soc. **111** (1989), 3051.

C. V. Kumar, J. K. Barton, and N. J. Turro, J. Am. Chem. Soc. 107 (1985), 5518.

S. J. Lippard et 01., Science 194 (1976), 726.

J. K. Barton, J. J. Dannenberg and A. L. Raphael, J. Am. Chem. Soc. 104 (1982), 4967.

J. K. Barton, A. T. Danishefsky and J. M. Goldberg, J. Am. Chem. Soc. 106 (1984), 2172.

R. F. Pasternack, E. J. Gibbs, and J. J. Villafranca, Biochemistry 22 (1983), 2406; R. F. Pasternackand E. J. Gibbs in T. D. Tullius, ed., Metal-DNA Chemistry, ACS Symposium 402 (1989), 59.

J. K. Barton and E. Lolis, J. Am. Chem. Soc. 107 (1985).

Genetics and Bioengineering : *Concepts and Issues* **Pages 116-147**
Edited by: **Dr. Ashok K. Rathoure and Dr. Pawan Kumar 'Bharti'**
ISBN: 978-93-86841-92-6
Edition: **2019**
Published by: **Discovery Publishing House Pvt. Ltd., New Delhi (India)**

7 Characterization, Assessment of Genetic Diversity, Screening for Protein Content and Bruchid Infestation in Cowpea

[1]Basavaraj Makanur, [2]V. K. Deshpane and [3]Esakkimuthu M.

ABSTRACT

Cowpea (*Vigna unguiculata* (L.) Walp.) is one of the most important pulse crops native to central Africa, belongs to family Fabaceae. Cowpea is called as vegetable meat due to its high amount of protein in grain with better biological value on dry weight basis. On dry weight basis, cowpea grain contains 23.4 per cent protein, 1.8 per cent fat and 60.3 per cent carbohydrate and it is rich source of calcium and iron. Apart from this, cowpea forms excellent forage and it gives a heavy vegetative growth and covers the ground, so well that it checks the soil erosion. As a leguminous crop, it fixes nitrogen about 70-240 kg per ha per year. Cowpea is mainly grown in tropical and sub-tropical regions of the world for vegetable and seed purpose and to lesser extent as a fodder crop. It is a most versatile pulse crop because of its smothering nature, drought tolerant characters, soil restoring properties and multi-purpose uses. As a pulse crop, cowpea fit well into most of the cropping systems. In India, the cowpea is grown in an area of about 3.9 million hectares with the productivity of 567 kg per ha. The productivity potential of the crop in Karnataka is low (420 kg/ha) as compared to national productivity (567 kg/ha). In this context, varietal description for identification of crop varieties has especially morphological description has assumed a critical importance in national and international seed programme and there is a considerable need for the development of reliable methods and identifiable characters for the purpose. Variety identification and varietal purity assessment are very important for varieties, hybrids and their parents. This is most essential for maintenance, multiplication and seed certification. The development of new and improved plant varieties or hybrids is a continuous process. It is of critical importance for sustained increase in agricultural productivity. Under the New Seed Policy 2001, all the new varieties have to be registered based on the criteria of novelty, distinctness, uniformity and stability (DUS). Cowpea is called poor man's meat due to its high protein

[1,2] University of Agricultural Sciences, Dharwad, Karnataka, India
[3] Kerala Agricultural University, RARS, Pilicode, Kerala, India

content. It is evident that all pulses in general and cowpea in particular are susceptible for storage pests especially the cowpea bruchid [C. maculatus (F.)]. Hence, there is a need to identify the morphological characters, assess, protein content and screening of cowpea genotypes for resistance to pulse beetle.

Index terms: Biological value, bruchid infestation, development, genetic diversity, productivity, protein and screening

Introduction

Cowpea [*Vigna unguiculata* (L.) Walp.] is one of the most important pulse crops, native of West Africa (Vavilov, 1951) but Steele (1976) suggested Ethiopia as the primary and Africa as the secondary centre of diversity. Cowpea belongs to the order *Rosale,* family *Legununosae,* sub family *Fabaceae* and the genus *Vigna.* It is a diploid species with somatic chromosome number $2n = 22$ (Darlington and Wylie, 1955). After successfully achieving the food security by way of increased production and comfortable levels of buffer stock nutritional security continue to be a cause for serious concern. Pulses occupy a unique position in the world agriculture by virtue of their high seed protein content. Cowpea is called as poor man's meat or vegetable meat due to its high amount of seed protein with better biological value on dry weight basis. Cowpea grain contains 23.4 per cent protein. 1.8 per cent fat and 60.3 per cent carbohydrates and also it is a good source of vitamins and phosphorus (Venkatesan *et al.*, 2003). It is widely adapted and capable of producing seeds even in low land and semi arid regions. However, grain yield of this legume varies widely when grown at different locations. It can be grown in a wide range of soil types and environmental conditions. As a pulse crop, it plays a key role in maintaining soil health and sustainability in the production from different cropping systems as they fix atmospheric nitrogen in their root nodules. On an average, the grain legumes fix 250-312 kg nitrogen per ha per year. In case of cowpea it fixes about 70-240 kg of nitrogen per ha per year. This ensures the soil fertility as well as reduces the financial burden on poor farmers. It is a most versatile pulse crop because of its smothering nature, drought tolerant characters and soil restoring properties. Inspite of much importance of pulses as per FAO (Anon., 2004), the per capita availability of pulses in India has decreased from 41 g in 1990 to 21 g in 2004. This is an alarming trend with respect to nutritional security is concerned, one of the possible ways to meet the needs of an ever increasing population is to go for modern method of plant breeding techniques which helps to evolve new varieties which could solve the above problem. Among the different pulses grown in the world, cowpea is grown in 10.1 million ha with a production of 4.99 million tonnes and the productivity of 494 kg per ha (Anon., 2008). In India, the cowpea is grown in an area of about 3.9 million ha with the production of 2.2 million tonnes having a productivity of 567 kg per ha, which is above the average productivity of world. In Karnataka, cowpea is grown in an area of 0.77 lakh ha with the production of 0.34 lakh tonnes (Anon., 2009a). The productivity potential of the crop in Karnataka is low (437 kg per ha) as compared to the national productivity of 567 kg per ha. This clearly indicates the necessity to identify the reasons for such a low productivity in Karnataka. In countries, having plant breeder's right in operation, a new variety is registered only if it is 'distinct' from other varieties, 'uniform' in its characteristics and genetically 'stable'. Therefore, description of characters for the assessment of varietal purity and identity are essential for seed production and certification programme of any given crop variety. In order to maintain genuineness (true to type) and quality of seed careful attention is needed at every stage of seed production of a variety. The proper variety identification serves the important goals of seed production. It ensures whether the seed being produced or offered for sale is of the variety ought to be; whether it is pure or any kind of nature; to know what to rogue out or what not to rogue out during seed production. Exchange of seeds is essential for plant breeder to improve genetic variability of available germplasm for recombination and selection of desired traits. Characterization and identification of plant varieties are thus, fundamental to the development, release and popularization of the crop varieties. In this context, varietal description for identification of crop variation has attained a critical importance in national and international seed programmes and there is considerable need for the development of reliable methods and identifiable characters for identification purpose. Hence, morphological descriptors have traditional significance and one immediately accessible on the spot without the need of equipment. All though this has been universally adopted as classical taxonomic approach, above to its limitations like environmental influence and time consuming. However, there is limited information on characterization of cowpea germplasm and also they are pre-requisite for the granting of plant variety protection and utility patents and therefore, it is necessary to allow seed technologists and breeders to identify germplasm and monitor for protection. National and international registration of the variety needs to pass the criteria of distinctness/uniformity/stability (DUS) tests. Varietal identification and purity are the critical elements in assessing seed entering factories and seed production *etc.*, for checking the sample to identify and investigate the origin of off types and distinguishing closely related species. In order to fulfill these requirements, variety description must be discriminatory free from environmental effects, interpretable in genetic terms and respective of pedigree and genetic constitution. The D^2 technique based on multivariate analysis developed by Mahalanobis (1936) is the most effective method for quantifying the degree of genetic diversity among genotypes, which helps in selecting the parents for hybridization. It is generally accepted that genetically diverse parents when crossed will show maximum heterosis and offer the maximum chance of isolating transgressive segregrants. It is an important source of protein in many tropical and subtropical countries and is a rich source of lysine. This compensates for low lysine content of cereals along with which they are usually eaten. Significant variability in seed protein exists among the varieties. Besides the yield potential, chemical composition from nutritional point of view is very important. It is necessary to assess the nutritional value, seed protein content of available cowpea germplasm lines/genotypes before they involved in breeding programme. Numbers of insects have been found to infest cowpea seed/grain both in the field as well as in the seed storages. Among the storage pests, bruchids are known to cause considerable loss. There are more than 100 species of bruchids belonging to 56 genera in five sub families (Southgate, 1979). In India, 117 species belongs to 11 genera have been recorded (Arora, 1977). The genus *Callosobruchus,* includes a number of economically important species that attack stored pulses throughout the world. But, *Callosobruchus maculatus* (Fabricus), *Callosobruchus chinensis* (Linnaeus) and *Callosobruchus analis* (Fabricus) are the important species in India. Among them *Callosobruchus maculatus (F)* is the most important and the common pest of cowpea. It is evident that all pulses in general and cowpea in particular are susceptible for storage pests due to which the qualitative and quantitative losses during storage are increased. Especially the cowpea bruchid (*Callosobruchus maculatus (F)*) cause considerable loss to cowpea seeds during storage. In the task of future breeding programmes of producing resistant varieties against insect pests can be made feasible primary by identifying various factors that elicit such resistance. In part considerable amount of work on relative susceptibility and extent of damage to different pulse varieties by bruchids has done in India. But practically, no information is available on susceptibility of different cowpea genotypes to true to combat it. Therefore, morphological characterization of germplasm lines of cowpea thus will be realized to the important tool towards identification of genotypes, maintenance of genetic purity, mitigating legal claims and confirming intellectual property rights.

According to Dabi *et al.* (1979) evaluated the relative susceptible of the seeds of 10 varieties of cowpea against *Collasobruches maculatus* (F) and found that RS-9 was the least susceptible and RS-118, PS-42 and NO-5-19-14-1 the most susceptible. The weight, volume, hardness and colour of the seed had no effect on susceptibility. Vir (1981) Studied that the mechanism of resistance to insect was not related to the morphological characteristics (weight, volume and colour of cowpea seeds) and he conducted that varieties with high protein content are susceptible to attack by *Collasobruches maculatus*. Singh *et al.* (1985) reported that the percentage of damaged seeds, 103 days after infestation was 25-26 per cent in Ife brown and it is concluded that the resistance is sufficient to provide reasonable protection against cowpea weevil during storage. Selvaraj *et al.* (1986) studied on a new high yielding drought tolerant cowpea varieties named CO-4. The protein content was highest in this variety. It was around 30.0 per cent (dry matter) as against the CO-3, C-152, KM.1 in which protein content was 28.59, 27.81 and 28.90 per cent (dry matter) respectively. Aghora *et al.* (1994) worked on evaluation of vegetable cowpea for protein content. The study showed that IIHR Sel-11 and IIHR Sel-16 were found to be superior genotypes in terms of protein content. Protein content ranges from 2.5-5.94 per cent indicating the wide variability among the genotypes. Suryawanshi *et al.* (2002) characterized seven soybean cultivates based on morphological characteristics and reported that the pigmentation on seedling, foliage colour, pubescence on leaf and stem. Flower colour, pod hairiness and pod colour at maturity were observed to be the most stable diagnostic characters and these are much helpful for identifying the genotypes at flowering and maturity stage. Among all characters at seed level, seed shape, hilum shape, seed coat colour and lusture on seed are most stable, uniform and distinguishing characters in green gram (Jain and Khare, 2002a). Jain and Khare (2002b) characterized fifteen green gram varieties based on morphological characteristics and reported that variation in pigmentation on hypocotyls, stem, petiole, leaf, leaf midrib and ventral suture of pod and immature and mature pod colour are most stable and uniform distinguishing characters. Density of hairiness on stem, raceme position, growth habit, pod constriction and pod curvature can be used to identify the mung bean varieties effectively. Days to flowering, days to maturity and plant height are the uniform characters but their expression is varied in different environments.

Morphological Characters

Seeds, seedlings and plants of various cultivars exhibit a wide range of morphological distinctness which is helpful in varietal identification and genetic purity testing. Continuous usage of morphological data to describe cultivars indicated that these data retain popularity as morphological descriptors.

Seed morphology: Morphological characters of seeds are useful traits for varietal identification of a number of crops based on seed coat colour, hilum colour, shape, size and test weight. Elsaeed (1967) reported varietal differences in Beladi and Rebaya-34 of broad beans, based on seed weight which was 192.7g and 317.1g, respectively per 500 seeds. Villalobos and Fournier (1978) studied 13 important characters *viz.*, colour of the seed coat, hilum and 100 seed weight *etc.*, for identification of soybean. Tiwari *et al.* (1978) grouped 21 soybean varieties based on 100 seed weight into three groups *viz.*, small, medium and bold. Payne and Koszykowski (1979) grouped 18 soybean cultivars based on seed size for cultivar differentiation. Srikantaradya (1980) classified 60 varieties of soybean based on the seed coat colour. Among them,

13 varieties were found black, three varieties were brown to brick red and rests of the 44 varieties were cream to dull white. Albina Musil (1980) reported that the seed coat colour varied from black, brown, yellow and green whereas hilum colour of the seed varied from yellow, black and grey or brown. Seed shape varied from round, oval oblong and flattened. Similarly seed size was also grouped into small, large and intermediate. Wagner and McDonald (1982) characterized 36 soybean cultivars based on hilum colour of the seed. Paramesh (1983) classified 24 soybean genotypes based on the number of seeds per pod, 100 seed weight and seed size. They were separated into small, medium and large seeded groups based on the test weight. Koszykowski and Burgoon (1983) grouped 64 soybean cultivars on the basis of hilum colour of the seed. Williams *et al.* (1984) recorded the platte soybean morphological characters as yellow seed coat with shiny luster and yellow hilum. Modesta and Cabral (1987) evaluated 11 soybean lines based on the seed coat colour, hilum colour, seed shape and 100 seed weight. Chakrabarthy and Agrawal (1989a) developed seed keys for the identification of 16 black gram varieties on the basis of seed size and colour of the seeds. Agrawal and Anil Pawar (1990) given seed keys for the identification of 13 soybean cultivars on the basis of seed size, colour and hilum colour. Sun and Chang (1990) analysed for the characteristics of green soybean in China based on 100 seed weight, seed shape and size. Charjan and Tarar (1991) reported the influence of soybean seed size on germination, seedling length, 100 seed weight and other seed quality parameters. All seed quality parameters were increased with seed size. Venkatareddy (1991) reported that 100 seed weight differed significantly among the soybean genotypes. Bragg recorded the highest 100 seed weight (20.35 g) followed by Hardee (19.53g) and PK471 (19.75 g) while the least (18.89 g) was recorded by Monetta. Fourty four chickpea cultivars collected from the different sites of Uttar Pradesh were grouped based on their variation in seed size (small, medium to large), seed shape (round and wrinkled), seed colour (light to dark brown, yellow, pink and white), (Anon., 1992a). Twenty two pea cultivars were grouped based on their variation in seed size (Small, medium and large) seed colour (white, pale green, mottled green and grey) and seed shape (round and flattened) (Anon., 1992b). Mohanrao (1993) reported that 100 seed weight was highest (20.50 g) in PK-472 followed by Bragg, KB-60 and Hardee soybean genotypes. Whereas, the lowest (14.24 g) was in KHSb-2. Copeland and McDonald (1997) identified soybean cultivars of chippewa-64 can easily distinguished from other varieties that do not have black hilum. Sophisticated techniques must be used for distinguishing the varieties with black hilum. Sridhara *et al.* (1997) grouped 10 soybean genotypes based on their seed coat colour and 100 seed weight. Among all characters at seed level, seed shape, hilum shape, seed coat colour and lusture on seed are most stable, uniform and distinguishing characters in green gram (Jain and Khare, 2002a). Arunkumar *et*

al. (2004) reported that 45 cultivars of pearl millet including 14 hybrids and their parental lines were characterized using qualitative morphological characters of seed (seed colour as green, grey, grey brown and brown), seedling characters and plant morphological characters. Karivartharaju (2005) presented a list of seed characters *viz.*, fuzz colour, seed size, 100 seed weight, density of fuzz and fibre characters like colour, strength, fineness, uniformity, maturity and ginning per cent in cotton for identification of varieties. Nkouannessi (2005) characterized 20 cowpea genotypes from different countries *viz.*, Cameroon, South Africa, Kenya and characterized them based on seed shape, seed testa texture, hundred seed weight. Ashok *et al.* (2008) grouped seven french bean varieties based on seed coat colour, hilum colour and seed shape. Naima *et al.* (2009) studied 20 landraces of cowpea and characterized based on seed morphological characters like seed colour, eye colour, shape, texture and weight of hundred seeds. Cupic *et al.* (2009) analyzed European pea (*Pisum sativum* L.) germplasm to estimate genetic variability using seed shape, colour of hilum and texta. Lingaraj (2009) assessed genetic diversity based on hundred seed weight in 80 cowpea genotypes.

Seedling characteristics: According to Lirindae (1986) and Terao (1986) classified the rice genotypes based on seedling characters *viz.*, seedling length, coleoptile and sheath colour and mesocotyl colour. Chakrabarthy and Agrawal (1989b) developed seed keys for identification of 16 blackgram genotypes using seedling characters like pigmentation (strong, moderate, weak), stem hairiness (glabrous, pubescent), leaflet shape (lanceolate, obovate), hypocotyl and radicle length. Eighteen soybean genotypes were classified based on morphological characters, pigmentation colour and presence of pubescence on seedling (Anon., 1995). Ashok *et al.* (2008) characterized seven french bean varieties based seedling characters *viz.*, hypocotyl colour, seedling cotyledon colour and pubescence on hypocotyl.

Plant morphological characteristics: According to Kooistra (1964) the morphological characters of plant *viz.*, shape of leaflets, leaf serration, and number of tendrils, shape of flower, pod size and pod shape could be used for distinguishing pea varieties. Edgar *et al.* (1970) studied the morphological characters for growth habit, nature of stem hairiness, flower colour and pubescence colour of soybean. Stahi and Pandey (1981) evaluated 21 soybean varieties and grouped them on the basis of nature of maturity and number of days to 50 per cent flowering. Agrawal (1984) classified soybean varieties based on spreading type, pubescence presence on stem, leaf shape and size, flower colour, pod colour at maturity, days to 50 per cent flowering and maturity. Bahrenfus and Fehr (1984) observed differences in two soybean cultivars *viz.*, Cumberland and Harper. Harper has purple flower, tawny pubescence, brown pods at maturity and higher seed yield compared to Cumberland. But both cultivars were similar in days to maturity and plant height. Bhagat *et al.* (1985)

evaluated groundnut germplasm collection of 4030 accessions for nine morphological characters. At maturity 191 accessions of var. vulgaris, 128 of var. fastigiata, 831 of var. hypogaea (bunch) and 1061 accessions of var. hypogaea (runner), had no stem pigmentation. While, 1099 accessions of var. vulgaris, 523 of var. fastigiata, 209 of var. hypogaea (bunch) and 33 of var. hypogaea (runner) showed stem pigmentation. From the french bean varietal trial, ten cultivars were grouped based on morphological characters *viz.*, plant height, number of branches and leaves per plant, seeds per pod, 100 seed weight and pod length (Anon., 1985). Tunwar and Singh (1985) recorded salient features of 31 improved soybean varieties based on seed and plant morphological characteristics. Diazcarrasco *et al.* (1986) grouped 17 soybean varieties based on days to maturity, plant height and seed yield per plant. Rasaily *et al.* (1986) tabulated 20 soybean genotype characters based on plant height, number of branches, pods per plant and seed yield per plant. Sisodia (1987) recorded influence of different size of large, medium and indeterminate seed sized gave seed yields of 2.87, 8.52, 2.04 t per ha, respectively. Harville *et a1.* (1988) compared soybean cultivar of Braxton with Gregg. Gregg has purple flower, tawny pubescence on pod, determinate growth habit, one day early maturity and 5 cm shorter in mature plant height than Braxton. Kenworthy (1988) compared soybean cultivars of Sparks with Morgan. Morgan has white flower, tawny pubescence on pod and 5 cm shorter in mature plant height than Sparks. Awasthi *et al.* (1989) studied on biochemical composition of ten important cowpea genotypes grown during summer. Freshly harvested edible immature pods of these cowpea genotypes were analysed for various physical parameters. Variability values for pod length, pod diameter, pod weight, pod yield were observed to range from 10.68-36.75 cm per pod, 0.18- 0.25 cm per pod, 2.2 1-3.80 g per pod, 65-98 g per plant, respectively. Faizabad and Sel-2 recorded highest pod yield. Observations recorded from 3175 soybean accessions with the help of following identification characters *viz.*, days to flowering, plant height, days to maturity and number of seeds per pod (Anon., 1989). Reddy *et al.* (1989) recorded 5 soybean cultivar variation for days to maturity, period from flower initiation to maturity, plant height, seeds per plant and yield per plant. Boerma *et al.* (1990) reported soybean cultivar of Colquitt based on morphological characters of determinate growth habit, purple flower, tawny pubescence on pod walls and matured 3 days later than Gorden and one day earlier than Thomas cultivar. Bowers *et al.* (1990) compared soybean cultivars of Dowling with Crockett. Crockett has purple flower, Tawny pubescence on pod walls at maturity, one day later maturity and 8cm taller than Dowling. From 150 soybean germplasm accessions based on useful characters *viz.*, plant height, days to flower, days to maturity, pods per plant, seeds per pod, number of branches per plant and seed yield per plant and other varietal identification characters were recorded (Anon., 1990). Vahab *et al.* (1991) studied on evaluation of selected varieties of vegetable cowpea with the objective of identifying high yielding good quality vegetable types suitable for both rainy and summer seasons. Seven selected varieties of cowpea *viz.*, IIHR 61-B (Bangalore) Sel-263 (Ludhiana), Kanakamani (Kerala), Pusakomal (IARI), VS-389 (Kerala), Sel-2-1 (Faizabad), VS-87 (Kerala) were taken for the study. Varieties differed significantly for plant height and spread in all the three seasons as well as the mean values pooled over the seasons. VS-389 was the tallest in all the seasons, with the mean value of 60 cm and Sel-263 the shortest with a mean value of 44 cm. The maximum spreading varieties were IIHR 61-B in rainy and Sel-2-l in summer season. Sel-263 had the minimum spread in both the seasons. In all the three seasons, IIHR 61-B had maximum pod weight. Sel-2-1 had the longest pods and seeds per pod were also maximum. From different locations of Utter Pradesh 44 chickpea cultivars were collected and all cultivars were exhibited variation for seeds per pod (1-3) foliage colour (green, purple and half green or half purple), plant height (20-55 cm) and branches per plant (4-10) were varied (Anon., 1992a). Aghora *et al.* (1994) studied an evaluation of vegetable cowpea for earliness and green pod yield. Nineteen diverse vegetable cowpea varieties were evaluated for their earliness and green pod yield. The study showed that IIHR Sel-l1 and IIHR Sel-16 were found to be superior genotypes in terms of earliness and green pod yield. Bonetti *et al.* (1995) reported that 17 bean cultivars were grouped based on leaf colour (very light green, light green, medium green, dark green, very dark green), pod length (very short, short, medium, long, very long), maturity (early, medium, late) and time of flowering (early, medium and late). Excellent work was done for the 18 soybean genotypes and classified based on diagnostic characteristics such as growth habit, plant height, stem pattern, leaf surface, foliage, pigmentation on stem, stem hairiness, colour of the hair, days to flowering, flower co1our, pod shape, pod hairiness, pod colour at maturity, pod hair colour at maturity and days to maturity (Anon., 1995). Mudzana *et al.* (1995) reported that the morphological characters such as plant height, foliage colour, number of days to 50 per cent flowering, flower length, pod length, pod breadth and number of seeds per pod could be used for variety identification of faba beans. Surendra Prakash and Singhal (1997) reported that seven grain and six vegetable pea cultivars were grouped based on plant height (short, medium, tall, very tall), leaf length (short, medium, long), time of flowering (early, medium) pod length (short, medium, long) and leaf colour (yellow green, blue green, green). Jain and Khare (2002b) characterized 15 green gram varieties based on morphological characteristics and reported that variation in pigmentation on hypocotyls, stem, petiole, leaf, leaf midrib and ventral suture of pod and immature and mature pod colour were most stable and uniform distinguishing characters. Density of hairiness on stem, raceme position, growth habit, pod constriction and pod curvature can be used to identify the mung bean varieties effectively. Days to flowering, days to maturity and plant height were the uniform characters but their expression is varied under different environments. Sankrapandian (2002) reported that four cowpea varieties were grouped based on pod shape, seed colour and leaf shape. Suryawanshi *et al.* (2002) characterized seven soybean cultivars based on morphological characteristics and reported that the pigmentation on seedling, foliage colour, pubescence on leaf and stem. Flower colour, pod hairiness and pod colour at maturity were observed to be the most stable diagnostic characters and these are much helpful for identifying the genotypes at flowering and maturity stage. Upadhyaya *et al.* (2002) evaluated 1956 chickpea accessions for flower colour (white, light flower), plant colour, seed colour (orange, yellow orange) and other characteristics. Yadav and Shrivasthava (2002) characterized chickpea varieties based on seed colour (brown, light brown, dark brown, reddish brown, light green), seed size (bold, medium, small), stem pigmentation (strong, medium and absent), flower colour (white, deep pink, pink, light pink), foliage colour (dark green, light green), plant height (tall, medium, dwarf), podding habit (single, double), pod number per plant (low, medium, high), number of locules per pod (one, two, three) and duration (early, medium and late). Tarasatyavathi *et al.* (2004) reported that 75 released soybean varieties were characterized based on leaf shape (lanceolate, pointed ovate, rounded ovate, triangular), leaf colour intensity (light, medium, dark), flower colour (white, violet), pod pubescence (absent, present), plant height (short, medium, tall), days to flowering (early, medium and late) and days to maturity (early, medium, late). Nkouannessi (2005) grouped 20 cowpea genotypes from different countries *viz.,* Cameroon, South Africa and Kenya. Based on plant morphological characteristics such as growth pattern, plant pigmentation, plant hairiness, raceme position, pod attachment to peduncle, immature pod pigmentation, leaf colour, flower colour, number of main branches, number of pods per peduncle, number of pods per plant, pod length, number of seeds per pod and plant height were employed for characterization. Mate and Shelar (2006) characterized 16 sorghum hybrids based on plant height (very short, very tall), days to 50 per cent flowering (early, late) anther colour, stigma anthocyanin, colour of straw and glume colour at maturity. Sarutayophat *et al.* (2007) characterized 13 cowpea accession based growth habit, days to 50 per cent flowering, pod colour, pod length, number of pods per plant, seed yield per plant. Ashok *et al.* (2008) grouped seven french bean varieties using flower colour and constriction on pod. Cupic *et al.* (2009) analysed European pea (*Pisum sativum* L.) germplasm, to determine differences between *P. sativum* var. *arvense* and *P. sativum* ssp. *sativum* groups, and to estimate genetic variability among and within 18 *P. sativum* accessions. Sixteen morphological traits (shape of seed, colour of hilum, shape of grain starch, unwrinkled seed and simple starch grain, colour of testa, colour of cotyledons, plant height, colour of foliage, anthocyanin, type of node, stipule length, colour of flower, maximum number of flowers per node, days to flowering, pod-shape of distal part, parchment of pod) were used to estimate genetic distances. Naima *et al.* (2009) studied 20 landraces of cowpea and characterized based on plant morphological characters such as flower colour, seed number per pod, pod purple pigmentation, pod length, number of seeds per pod and days to 50 per cent flowering. PPV and FRA (Anon., 2009b) published important morphological characters for the varietal identification of groundnut viz. Plant growth habit, leaflet colour, stem pubescence, inflorescence, pod construction, seed coat colour. Lingaraj (2009) assessed the genetic diversity based on plant height, days to 50 per cent flowering, number of pods per pant, pod length, number of seeds per pod and seed yield per plant characteristics in cowpea.

Genetic Divergence Studies

The magnitude of divergence between two groups under consideration is provided by D^2 statistic developed by Mahalanobis (1936). It considers the variation produced by any character and their consequent effect that it bears on other characters. The technique in the form of generalized distance was first used by Mahalanobis in an anthropometric survey of the united province in India. For the first time D^2 statistic was applied for biological population by Nair and Mukharjee (1960) to classify the natural and plantation teak tree types. Its application was extended later to taxonomic studies. Murthy and Pavate (1962) observed that D^2 analysis could be extended to the situations where overlapping species need to be discriminated and also when the discrimination at sub species level is needed. Dharmalingam and Kadambavanasundaram (1989) presented a data on 8 yield components measured in 40 genotypes was subjected to multivariate analysis (D^2). Wide genetic diversity was present among the 13 clusters formed. The genotypes Co2 and G5, belonging to the two most divergent clusters, were recommended as suitable for inclusion in heterosis breeding programmes. Renganayaki and Rangaswamy (1992) analyzed the mungbean, blackgram and cowpea using the Mahalanobis D^2 value and revealed that the genotypes of mungbean, blackgram and cowpea were grouped in seven, five and four clusters, respectively and also concluded that hundred seed weight, pod length and seed yield contributed most towards genetic divergence. Mahalanobis' D^2 statistic was used (Rewale *et al.*, 1996) to estimate genetic divergence of 12 yield related characters evaluated in 70 genotypes of *V. unguiculata subsp. cylendrica.* Multivariate analysis grouped the genotypes into 19 clusters, of which 11 had only one genotype each. Days to initiation of flowering, 50 per cent flowering and maturity, number of inflorescences and pods per plant, pod length, hundred seed weight, seed yield per plant and harvest index made the largest contribution to the total divergence. It is proposed that high yielding genotypes with early maturity and high harvest index could be selected as parents for hybridization. Santos *et al.* (1997) reported genetic divergence of cowpea under two different environments using Mahalanobis D^2 statistics that length of main branch, hundred seed weight and pod length were the most important characters to affect the divergence. Sharma and Mishra (1997) revealed that days to 50 per cent flowering, plant height, pods per peduncle and harvest index contributed the most towards the genetic divergence and seed yield had a high positive phenotypic correlation with pods per peduncle, number of seeds per pod and harvest index. Backiyarani *et al.* (2000) concluded that genetic divergence for physiological traits like single plant yield, harvest index and earliness in flowering together accounted for 80 per cent of the total divergence in cowpea. Usha Kumari *et al.* (2000) reported that contribution towards genetic divergence was recorded for plant height (22.69%), number of branches (16.82%), number of pods per cluster (15.27%) and pod length (13.47%) in cowpea. Borah and Khan (2002) revealed on genetic divergence in fodder cowpea, sixty fodder cowpea cultivars were grouped in to 10 clusters. Dry matter yield, green fodder yield and plant height were recorded the highest contribution to total genetic divergence. These traits could be good criterion for selection of parents in hybridization programme. Narayanankutty *et al.* (2003) Studied genetic variability and divergence on thirty seven genotypes of vegetable cowpea revealed significant differences for all the characters under study. The thirty-seven genotypes were grouped into eleven clusters using Mahalanobis D^2 statistics. In general, the intercluster distances were higher than intracluster distances. The maximum intercluster distance was between clusters VIII and X, followed by clusters VI and X and clusters VIII and IX, respectively. The intracluster distance was maximum in cluster VII. The nature of magnitude of genetic diversity was studied in a set of 45 cowpea (*Vigna unguiculata*) genotypes from indigenous and exotic sources (Nigude *et al.* 2004). The genotypes were grouped into five clusters using Mahalanohis D^2 statistics. Cluster-I was the largest with 28 genotypes followed by cluster-II with eleven genotypes and cluster-III with four genotypes. The clusters IV and V were monogenotypic. The maximum inter-cluster distance was observed between clusters III and V followed by distance between clusters II and III. Clusters I and III exhibited the minimum inter-cluster distance. The number of branches per plant, test weight, biomass (dry weight) at harvesting and number of pods per plant had contributed considerably toward divergence. Venkatesan *et al.* (2004) reported that clusters per plant, pods per cluster, and pods per plant and seed yield per plant had the maximum contribution towards total divergence. And in another report by Kumawat and Raje (2005) also showed seed yield per plant had the highest contribution towards the total genetic divergence; followed by seeds per pod, days to 50 per cent flowering, plant height and reproductive period. Sulnathi *et al.* (2007) assessed genetic divergence in 56 genotypes of cowpea using D^2 statistics for 13 yield contributing characters showed grouping of genotypes into 9 clusters. Cluster I had the maximum number of genotypes. The characters days to maturity, 100-seed weight and days to flowering were the highest contributors to D^2 values. Indradeo Pandey (2007) evaluated 44 grain cowpea for 13 characters to quantify the genetic diversity existing among them by using Mahalanobis D^2 statistics. The genotypes fell into 9 clusters. Cluster strength varied from single genotype (Cluster IV to IX) to 31 genotypes (cluster I). Cluster III had minimum days to first flower opening, days to 50 per cent flowering and seed yield per plant in addition to maximum number of pod per plant and primary branches. Cluster II, V, VII had maximum yield per plant, 100-seed weight; pod length and number of seeds per pod, respectively. Cluster II had minimum days to maturity, while cluster VII showed maximum days to maturity. Suganthi and Murugan (2007) evaluated 30 genotypes of cowpea for 10 characters to quantify the genetic diversity existing among them by using Mahalanobis D^2 statistics. These genotypes were grouped into 11 clusters. Cluster strength varied from single genotype (Cluster VI, IX and XI) to 7 genotypes (cluster III). Cluster VI had maximum seed yield per plant, number of pods per cluster, pod length, number of seeds per pod and number of pods per plant followed by cluster III. Cluster IX had maximum test weight.

Protein Content

According to Selvaraj *et al.* (1986) studied on a new high yielding drought tolerant cowpea varieties named CO-4. The protein content was highest in this variety. It was around 30.0 per cent (dry matter) as against the CO-3, C-152, KM.1 in which protein content was 28.59, 27.81 and 28.90 per cent (dry matter), respectively. Awasthi *et al.* (1989) studied biochemical composition and nutritional quality of ten important cowpea genotypes grown during summer, 1987. Freshly harvested edible immature pods of these cowpea genotypes were analyzed for various physical and biochemical parameters. Variability values for moisture, protein, reducing sugars, total sugars, crude fibre, ash, phosphorus, sulphur, iron, vitamin C and tannin content were observed in the range from 82.5-86.5 per cent, 2.5 mg per 100g, 14-22 mg per 100g and 47.4-65 mg per 100g, respectively. Genotypes L-1552, Barilobia and EC-4209 were found to be rich source of protein, while pod yield was recorded the highest in Faizabad Sel-2 having significantly less amount of tannins among various cowpea genotypes. Nevertheless on the basis of overall performance, Barilobia emerged to be the most promising genotype followed by IC20580, Chotilobia, Faizabad Sel-1 and Faizabad Sel-2 from nutritional stand point in particular. Aghora *et al.* (1994) studied on evaluation of vegetable cowpea for protein content: The study included the important nutritional factors responsible for the quality breeding programme of vegetable cowpea during rabi season. The study showed that IIHR Sel-11 and IIHR Sel-16 were found to be superior genotypes in terms of protein content. Protein content ranged from 2.5-5.94 per cent indicating the wide variability among the genotypes. IIHR-157, IIHR-345, IIHR-333, IIHR-353 were superior only for protein content and will be useful in breeding value added protein rich vegetable cowpea. Singh *et al.* (1997a) studied biochemical composition and nutritional quality of edible immature pods of broad bean. Wide variability in respect of moisture, protein, true protein, crude fat, crude fibre, carbohydrate, protein digestibility, phosphorus, sulphur, iron, tryptophan and methionine content was observed among 27 genotypes of broad bean grown under mid hill conditions of Himachal Pradesh at Palampur during 1995-96 ranging from 79.34 to 88.77 per cent, 3.98 to 6.25 per cent, 3.46 to 5.68 per cent, 0.73 to 1.07 per cent, 0.065 to 0.138 per cent, 1.10 to 2.75 per cent, 3.57 to 12.46 per cent, 48.90 to 56.80 per cent, 56.34 to 98.59 g per 100 g, 34.56 to 85.08 mg per 100g, 0.51 to 1.90 mg per 100 g 0.104 to 0.148 g per 100 g protein and 0.22 to 0.5 g per 100 g protein, respectively. Based on genotypic rating done in search of multipurpose genotypes the study indicated that genotypes JV-8, JV-7, JV-6, JV-5 and EC-284368, EC-284366, DPBB-l and Palampur Local-1emerged superior over others. Kamble *et al.* (1998) studied on nutritional quality evaluation of newly developed varieties of pigeon pea (*Cajanus cajan* (L.) Millsp.). Six varieties of pigeon pea were evaluated for nutritional quality. Significant difference was noticed in content of protein amongst the varieties tested. The varieties Dailhana Black, PBN-54 and C-11 recorded markedly low per cent of digestability of protein among the varieties of pigeon pea tested. Nirmal De *et al.* (2001) conducted a field experiment during the rainy season on 20 genotypes of cowpea on diet versatility in the field to study the protein content. The pod plus seed protein content was 21.2 per cent. High protein content in both foliage and pod or seed throughout the growth stage was recorded in Pusakomal. The protein content of IIHR Sel-11 and Sel-2-1 was also statistically on par with Pusakomal. In general higher protein content was recorded in local genotypes like 'Red seeded climbing', 'Cowpea Local-1' and 'Kalajhamla' compared to other tested groups. Naeem Ahmad and Mohammad Rahim (2007) Studies were carried out on cowpea variety Swat Kulat-1 (SK-1) at the Agriculture Research Institute (N) Mingora, Swat during the year 2002-03 and reported that the 23 per cent of seed protein content in the cowpea variety Swat Kulat-1 (SK-1). Sebetha *et al.* (2010) evaluated two different cowpea varieties from South Africa for seed protein content and results showed 24.25 and 25.35 per cent in Pan 311 and Red Caloona variety, respectively.

Screening of Cowpea Genotypes for their Relative Response to Bruchid Infestation and Seed Quality

Evaluation of cowpea genotypes for resistance* to *C. maculatus (F): According to Wadnerkar *et al.* (1978) studied the development of *Callosobruchus maculatus* (*F.*) on four varieties of Arhar and three varieties of gram. Arhar was more preferred to gram for oviposition and Arhar No. 148 was the most preferred variety. Development was significantly faster in white gram. Prabhat variety of Arhar showed maximum percentage loss in weight while, it was the lowest in white gram. Adult emergence did not differ significantly. Dabi *et al.* (1979) evaluated the relative susceptible of the seeds of 10 varieties of cowpea against *Callosobruchus maculatus* (F) and found that RS-9 was the least susceptible and RS-118, PS-42 and NO-5-19-14-1 were the most susceptible. The weight, volume, hardness and colour of the seed had no effect on susceptibility. Kameshwara Rao and Krishnamoorthy Rao (1982) reported life cycle of *Callosobruchus maculatus (F)* between 33 and 42 days in the pigeon pea varieties C-53 Hy-2 and PDM-1, while it extended to about 40 to 44 days in other varieties UPAS 120, ST1, Mukta and BDN- 1. Largest number (307) of adult developed in C-53, while only 50 adults developed in UPAS 120. Maximum egg laying was observed on C-53 followed by Hy-2. ST-1, BDN- 1, while on PDM-1, UPAS- 120 and Mukta significantly low number of eggs were deposited. The percentage of grain damage was the highest in C-53 while UPAS- 120 and Mukta showed least damage by the bruchid *C. maculatus*. Satya vir (1983) reported that 24 promising varieties of cowpea *Vigna unguiculata* (Linn.) were screened for their relative resistance to *C. maculatus* Fab. Among these genotypes V.C. 5, 25/8/2/2, R.S.9, C.G.28 and Sel-1476 proved to be relatively resistant, whereas Copusa-1, V-7, Copusa-2, 26/4/1, Culture-2, 5262 and P.T.B.1 were found to be most susceptible varieties. Varieties J.C.10, K-39, Culture-1, C.G.11, V-37, C-G.69, V-16, Copusa-3, PLS-382, H.G.22, C-152, C.G.5 showed as intermediate behaviour and none was found immune to attack of C. *maculatus (F)*. Katiyar and Khare (1983) while screening 20 genotypes of green gram for their relative susceptibility to pulse beetle *C. chinensis* observed a non significant difference in susceptibility due to variation in the seed size. Singh *et al.* (1985) screened over 8000 germplasm lines of cowpea. Three sources of resistance to cowpea weevil have been identified *viz.*, Tyul 2027, TVul 1952 and Tyul 1953. The per cent damaged seeds ranged from 25 to 26 per cent in the resistant lines and 95 per cent for Ife brown susceptible line. In AVRDC (Anon., 1986) one hundred and one mungbean breeding lines were tested for their susceptibility to bruchid in a laboratory screening. Five breeding lines *viz.*, VC1535-11-1B-1-3B, VC-2764-B-7-2Bm, VC-2764-B-7-1-B, VC- 1 209-3B-1-2-B and VC- 1482-C- 12-2-B were least damaged by the bruchids. The number of adults that emerged from these resistant entries was on par with no adult emergence from VM-2 164, the resistant cheek. At AVRDC (Anon., 1988) seeds of 500 mungbean accessions were screened for resistance to *C. chinensis*. Ten accessions were classified as highly resistant. Two entries, V-2802-G and V1128B-B2 were found free from bruchid infestation; V-2802BG is a selection from a resistant accession V8202. Ahmed *et al.* (1989) evaluated eighteen chickpea (*Cicer arietinum* L.) genotypes for their susceptibility pulse beetle, *Callosobruchus maculatus* F. (bruchidae) taking into account the number of undamaged seeds (resistance to bruchids), number of eggs oviposited (ovipositional preference) and number of emergence holes (Adult survival) per 50 seeds. Resistance to bruchids appeared to be a more heritable trait than the other two damage characters. The number of emergence holes is a better indicator of seed resistance than the number of eggs present on the seeds. Gobindan *et al.* (1989) screened seven legume species namely sweet peas, green gram (*V. radiata*), blackgram (*V. mungo*), bengalgram (*C. arietinum*), cowpea (*V. unguiculata*), pigeon pea (*C. cajan*) and wild mung (*V. vexillata*) against *C. chinensis*. They found *V. vexillata* to be the least susceptible. Kapila and Rajni (1989) screened seeds of 17 cultivars of *Phaseolus vulgaris* for resistance to *Zabrotus subfacicttus* in the laboratory and concluded that neither size nor colour of the seeds were important with regard to susceptibility. Manohar and Yadav (1990) studied the extent of damage on ten commonly cultivars of cowpea *viz.*, Udaipur-1, Udaipur-2, P-1309, P-1302, P-1414, P-454-157, IC-11325, CS-152, C0-1 and Kanpur black (141.23) to pulse beetle *C. maculatus (F)* , Udaipur-1 variety suffered maximum loss of 44.97 per cent in apparent weight, while, Co-1 variety had the least loss of 16.25 per cent. The respective real weight losses were 56.78 and 20.40 per cent. The loss in seed variability ranged from 9.0 to 49.34 per cent on CO-1 and Udaipur-1 varieties. Conclusively Co-1 was relatively resistant to *C. maculatus (F)* Fab. as compared to other varieties. Dushyant *et al.* (1991) studied comparative susceptibility of 33 genotypes of pigeon pea (*Cajanus cajan*) to pulse beetle tested in laboratory condition significant variation was found in the degree of resistance with none being completely immune. Laboratory study conducted at AVRDC (Anon., 1991) showed that *C. chinensis* resistant mungbean (*Vigna radiata*) accessions (V2709 and V2802) and one blackgram (*V. mungo*) accession (VM2 164) were equally resistant to *C. maculatus (F),* the second most important pest of *V. radiata* seeds in storage. AVRDC (Anon., 1992c) conducted genetic studies using a wild mungbean accession *Vigna radiate* sublobata (TC1966) and two mungbean accessions (V2709 and V12802) revealed that they were immune or highly resistant. Studies further showed that in each resistant line, resistance was controlled by a single dominant gene and these three resistance genes were not allelic. Talekar and Lin (1992) investigated on the characteristics of resistance to *Callosobruchus chinensis* in two mungbean and one blackgram accessions in a series of lab tests. They concluded that smaller seed size of the accessions was not responsible for the resistance. The results indicated the possible presence of antibiotic factors in the resistant accessions. Ahmed *et al.* (1993) evaluated seeds of 39 chickpea varieties infested with *C. chinensis* for number of damaged seeds, number of holed seed surface texture and seed coat thickness. They found that the varieties with a rough, hard, wrinkled and thick seed coat showed less damage and number of holes and therefore were more resistant than varieties with small, soft and thin seed coats. Correlation between the two damage parameters was positive and highly significant. Dogre *et al.* (1993) evaluated seeds of 24 accessions of pigeon pea (*Cajanus cajan* (L.) Millsp.) and four other species of *Cajanus* for their resistance to infestation by *Callosobruchus maculatus* (F.). None of pigeon pea accessions was resistant but resistance was evident in the three species of *Cajanus*. Relative susceptibility of 44 pigeon pea varieties attacked by *C. chinensis* and factors involved in their susceptibility were determined in a study by Modi *et al.* (1994). Based on number of eggs per 50 grains and grain damage, cultivars ICPL-89044, KM-9 and KPAS- 120 were found to be less susceptible than the other varieties and susceptibility was affected by size and shape of seed but not by seed colour. Kadoo and Rane (1995) used 12 commonly grown varieties of pigeon pea to study the extent of damage and varietal resistance and susceptibility to *C. chinensis*. None of the varieties were found to be immune to infestation by *C. chinensis*. However, there was a significant difference in the relative susceptibility of different varieties to bruchid attack. Sison *et al.* (1996) screened several mungbean varieties for resistance to *C. chinensis*, Results of both free choice and no choice tests showed that TC 1966 was highly resistant while pag-asa (1, 3, 5 and 7) were susceptible. Eight different varieties of mungbean (*Vigna radiata*) were evaluated for their susceptibility to *C. chinensis* by Muhammad Hussain *et al.* (1997) on the basis of number of eggs laid, duration of development of the immature stages, percentage adult emergence and weight loss due to damage by the pest. The varieties MB-2456 and Kanti were found to be highly susceptible with 13.6 and 13.0 per cent loss in the weight of seeds, respectively. The size, colour and protein content of the seeds had no influence on the susceptibility of mungbean seeds to *C. chinensis*. Both artificial and natural infestation of *C. chinensis* was used by Liu-xuming *et al.* (1998) in the identification of resistance source of mungbean (*Vigna radiata*). Among the tested germplasm, 17 lines from AVRDC showed moderate resistance to immunity, while only 3 land races from Gangxi showed moderate resistance. Lambrides and Imrie (2000) screened 26 mungbean (*Vigna radiata*) varieties and accessions for resistance to 4 bruchid species. On the basis of percentage of seed damage, all Australian commercial mungbean varieties tested were highly susceptible to strains of *C. chinensis* and *C. maculatus (F)*. Three accessions (TC1966, ACC23 arid ACC41) appeared to have bruchid resistance. All the three accessions had wild mungbean characteristics like small seed size and the presence of well formed texture layer on the seed. Bhalla *et al.* (2002) reported that seeds of 63 genotypes of cowpea, *Vigna unguiculata* (L.) were evaluated for their relative susceptibility to cowpea weevil, *C. maculatus (F)*. Genotype IC-58905, EC-240922A and Nic-1066 with growth indices of 0.96, 1.06 and 1.30, respectively were found to be superior to others in terms of bruchid resistance/tolerance. Mahgoub *et al.* (2005) conducted an experiment to study the infestation potential of *C. chinensis* and *C. maculatus (F)* on seeds of cowpea, mung bean, lentil, chick pea, kidney bean, peas and broad bean. The data were recorded for susceptibility index values, weight loss and some biological activities. The kidney bean seeds were completely resistant to infestation by both bruchids, while seeds of cowpea and mung bean were completely susceptible. The other 4 pulses showed varying degree of susceptibility. How ever, it was also found that, all studied crops were more susceptible to *C. chinensis* than to *C. maculatus (F).*Nagaraja (2006) evaluated different cowpea genotypes for bruchid resistance, reported that the genotypes KM-1, Goa local T-I and TV x 944 were least susceptible to *C. chinensis* and the genotypes DCP-2, V-118, T4, C-3 and KM4 were susceptible. Parameshwarappa *et al.* (2007) studied the comparative response of the seeds of 12 chickpea varieties against *Callosobruchus chinensis* L. and found that ICC-10 was the most susceptible and ICCV-0331 was least susceptible to attack by pulse beetle. Infestation studies were conducted to compare the susceptibility nature of the improved local varieties of pulses to the pulse beetle, *Callosobruchus maculatus* (Karthikeyan, *et al.*, 2008). The study confirmed that the varieties of pulses exhibit varied suitability to the life performance of *C. maculatus.* The varieties, Vamban-4 of *V. mungo,* Vamban-1 of *V. unguiculata* and Vamban-2 of *V. vadiata* possess complete resistance to antibiosis in terms of not supporting any adult emergence, which is the most important parameter in assessing the seeds resistance to insect infestation. The resistance status of the seed varieties among the infested seeds, Vamban-1 and Vamban-2 of *C. cajan* and Vamban-2 and Vamban-3 of *V. mungo* and Vamban-1 of *V. radiata* revealed poorer host suitability.

Quantitative losses: According to Chandola *et al.* (1969) have placed the loss at 20 per cent in cowpea infested with *C. chinensis.* Siddiqui (1972) reported that under artificial inoculation, percentages of the seeds infested by *C. chinensis* were 97.5, 81.68 and 30 per cent in cowpea, mungbean and chick pea, respectively. Studies carried out at ICRISAT, Hyderabad (Anon., 1976) on red gram revealed maximum bruchids infestation of 28 per cent with an average infestation of 5 per cent. Gupta *et al.* (1981) reported that 84 per cent damage in bengalgram is due to *C. maculatus (F)* after six months of storage. The loss caused by *C. maculatus (F)* in mung (T17) and cowpea (T171) was 63.2 and 31.3% according to Satya and Jindal (1981). Singh and Sharma (1984) reported that 42.53 to 57.33 per cent damage in mung and 7.97 to 10.27 per cent in mash due to *C. maculatus (F)* during 5 months storage. Venkategowda (1984) under forced infestation condition noticed the increase in apparent loss from 0.1 per cent (first month) to maximum of 12.31 per cent in 8 month after storage. He further recorded an actual loss of 45.45 per cent after 8 months of storage which did not increase further. Sukprakaran (1985) estimated 1 to 25 per cent damage in legume grains which was caused by *C. maculatus (F)* during storage period. Doharey *et al.* (1987) observed gradual increase in weight loss in green gram due to C. *maculatus (F)* with progressive increase in storage periods causing 1.15, 36.36, 48.84 and 51.91 per cent weight loss after 30, 60, 90 and 120 days after storage period, respectively. Singhal *et al.* (1989) studied the effect of initial infestation of chick pea seeds inoculated with 1, 2, 3, 4 and 5 pairs of male and female C. *chinensis* and 92 per cent of seed damage was noticed in F_1 and F_2 generation of insect. Ramzan *et al.* (1990) claimed that 69.2 per cent of seed damage was caused by C. *maculatus (F)* in cowpea (*Vigna unguiculuta*) under natural storage conditions. Ramesh (1993) studied the per cent soybean seeds inoculated with one and two pair of C. *maculatus (F)* and per cent actual loss was 45.36 and 100 after nine month of storage. Muhammad Shafique and Maqbool Ahmad (2005) screened the grains of 22 chick pea genotypes for resistance to pulse beetle C. *analis*. They were found that free choice oviposition by the beetle, adult progeny development, grain damage and weight loss varied significantly among the chick pea cultivars. The genotypes CM 3142-2/92, CM 88, CM 3142-3/92, CM 72 and PB91 harbored significantly lower number of eggs, adult progeny development, seed damage and weight loss indicating resistance to C. *analis*. Shaheen *et al.* (2006) screened grains of 15 chickpea cultivars against pulse beetle and reported that the minimum number of holes (0.80 per grain) made by pulse beetle was recorded in grains of Punjab-91 compared to the maximum of 1.77 holes per grain in Paidar-91. The minimum grain damage (24.35%) was recorded in Bittle-98 while the maximum of 54.46% damage was seen in Flip 97-192C.

Per cent loss in seed weight: According to Gujar and Yadav (1978) studied the feeding habits of grubs and observed the feeding progress in three stages corresponding to the early, mid and later stages of development. The percentage of seed weight loss was 55.6 to 60.0 in seed inoculated with C. *maculatus (F)* and 30.2 to 55.7 in seed inoculated with C. *chinensis*. According to Satya and Jindal (1981) C. *maculatus (F)* caused 63.2 and 31.3 per cent loss in seed weight in moong (G-2) and cowpea (T-17), respectively. Gupta *et al.* (1981) reported 55.2 per cent weight loss in bengalgram by C. *maculatus (F)* after six months of storage. Rustamani *et al.* (1985) studied four stored pulses in Pakistan for their resistance to the bruchid C. *maculatus (F)* and weight loss was 55.26, 46.70, 44.08 and 5.9 per cent in mash, mung, gram and pea, respectively. Doharey *et al.* (1987) observed gradual increase in weight loss in green gram due to C. *maculatus (F)* with progressive increase in storage period causing 1.15, 36.36, 48.84 and 51.91 per cent weight loss after 30, 60, 90 and 120 days after storage period, respectively. Ramzan *et al.* (1990) studied the damage caused by C. *maculatus (F)* on black eyed cowpea and reported 34.5 per cent of weight loss under natural storage conditions. Ramesh (1993) studied the per cent loss in weight of soybean inoculated with one, two, four and eight pairs of C. *maculatus (F)* and reported 0.08 to 12.57, 0.16 to 26.05, 0.34 to 58.29, 0.65 to 60.20 per cent weight loss during nine months of storage. Bhatnagar *et al.* (2001) studied the fifteen varieties of cowpea which were evaluated for their effect on orientation, oviposition, development and survival of *C. maculatus* (Fab.). varieties IFC 9907 and IFC 9909 were less preferred for orientation and oviposition, which resulted in less percentage of seed damage and weight loss, the survival percentage and food consumed per grub was also less in these varieties. Bhadauria and Jakhmola (2006) studied the oviposition preference and survival of the pulse beetle (*Callosobruchus maculatus*) and the effect of infestation intensity on the extent of losses and seed germination of different pulses (French bean, pigeon pea, chickpea, green gram, pea, black gram and cowpea) and reported that the loss within the damage seed was minimum in pea (8.8%) and chickpea (11.1%) and maximum in green gram (55.4%). These losses were inversely proportional to seed size, although such correlation was not significant. Parameshwarappa *et al.* (2007) reported that apparent weight and seed weight losses of grain were maximum in ICCV-03311 with 4.53 and 5.33 per cent, respectively and highest loss of 15.3 and 17.0 per cent in ICCV-10, respectively in chickpea against pulse beetle.

Qualitative losses in terms of seed germination: According to Pingale (1953) reported that the viability of grains was considerably affected by insects. He found in green gram the germination percentage was reduced to nil from 88 per cent due to infestation at the end of six months Storage. In another study Pingale *et al.* (1956) observed in greengram, the uninfested samples showed 88 per cent germination after six months, whereas in infested samples the germination had fallen by 6, 10, 44 and 100 per cent after 1, 2, 3 and 4 months of infestation. Jotwani *et al.* (1967) observed that the grubs of *C. maculatus (F)* during the first five days of their development did not cause much damage to cowpea, gram and greengram as the percentage of normal seedlings in the control and damaged lots were almost the same. As the development progressed the germination decreased. After 15 days of development the reduction in the germination was 46.2, 35.2 and 16.8 per cent in cowpea, gram and greengram, respectively. Shehnaz and Theophillus (1975) observed in bengal gram 97, 39 and 18 per cent viability in uninfested, modereately infested and highly infested samples, respectively, whereas in field bean 88, 29 and zero per cent viability in uninfested, moderately infested and highly infested samples, respectively. Yadav and Pant (1978) tested that germination of seven species of pulses infested with single egg of *C. maculatus (F)*. The germination of green gram seeds infested with different developmental stages of *C. maculatus (F)* was reduced to 98, 97, 33 and 0 per cent after 5, 10, 15 and 20 days of oviposition, respectively. In black gram there was no significant reduction in germination upto 20 days of oviposition. However, after 25, 30 and 35 days of oviposition the germination was reduced to 25, 22 and 0 per cent, respectively. Braich and Simwat (1984) recorded 96.3 to 59.3 per cent germination in mung bean seeds infested with 1, 2, 3 and 4 pairs of *C. chinensis* and *C. maculatus (F)*. Venkate

Gowda (1984) claimed that the seed germination declined from 92.5 per cent to zero per cent in seed infested with C *maculatus (F)* at the end of seven month of storage. Vimala and Pushpamma (1983a) found, progressive increase in the loss of viability with increase in level of infestation by C. *chinensis*. It was highest in red gram followed by black gram and bengalgram. Vimala and Pushpamma (1983b) from Andhra Pradesh claimed that bruchid infestation caused the reduction in viability of redgram seeds to the extent of 32.24, 26.03 and 22.02 per cent after 1.2 months of infestation in coastal, Thelangana and Rayalaseema regions, respectively. Singh and Sharma (1984) observed 47.53 to 70.6 and 14.13 to 19.7 per cent germination loss in mung and mash seeds after five months of storage. Doharey *et al*. (1987) reported that C. *maculatus (F)* caused cent per cent loss in viability in green gram after 90 days of storage. He also observed that the germination per cent gradually decreased with the increase in seed damage and storage period. In *Phaseolus vulgaris* increasing number of bruchid emergence holes per seed resulted in highly significant reduction in both germination and seedling vigour (Baiker and Webggster, 1992). Ramesh (1993) reported the germination per cent of soybean infested with C. *maculatus (F)* was 54 in one holed seeds and the viability was nil in two holed seeds compared to healthy seeds with 95 per cent germination. Lakshminarasimhaiah (1993) studied the reduction in germination percentage of pigeon pea seeds infested by C. *chinensis* and reported that 20, 4 and zero per cent germination in one, two and three holes seeds, respectively when compared to 86 per cent germination in uninfested seeds. Bhadauria and Jakhmola (2006) studied the oviposition preference and survival of the pulse beetle (*Callosobruchus maculatus*) and the effect of infestation intensity on the extent of losses and seed germination of different pulses (French bean, pigeon pea, chickpea, green gram, pea, black gram and cowpea) and reported that infested seeds of green gram, black gram and pigeon pea having only a single hole per seed failed to germinate, while only 20, 40 and 52% of the infected seeds of pea, chickpea and cowpea were able to germinate. Pulse beetle infestation generally reduced seed germination by 30% in cowpea to 72% in black gram. Germination of seeds having two holes was very much lower than those with only one hole. Shaheen *et al*. (2006) screened grains of 15 chickpea cultivars against pulse beetle and reported that the minimum grain weight loss of 25.66 per cet was recorded for Dasht compared to the maximum weight loss (39.48%) in CM-200. Chickpea cultivars of Punjab-91, Dasht, Bittle-98 and Parbat were resistant against pulse beetle while Paidar-91 and Flip 97-192C were found susceptible. Parameshwarappa *et al*. (2007) reported that highest loss in germination, seedling vigour index in ICCV-10 and lowest in ICCV-03311 after the infestation of 60 days by pulse beetle in chickpea varieties.

Conclusion

The findings of present investigation will benefit to all sectors of seed industry from ability to assess cultivar purity and identity. Well information on distinct characters of cowpea genotypes should be made available to the seed production and certification agencies in order to identify the off types, admixture, mutants and to ensure genetic purity during seed certification programme. Cowpea is called as vegetable meat due to high amount of protein in grain. Hence, present investigation helps to know the genotypes with better protein content. It will help to breeder to know which germplasm/genotypes are having high protein content. And also help to know is there any relation or effect of protein content on storability of cowpea genotypes. The present investigation helps to identify the relative susceptibility genotypes of cowpea against bruchid attack.

REFERENCES

Abdul-Baki, A. A. and Anderson, J. D. (1973): Vigour Determination in Soybean by Multiple Criteria, *Crop Sci.*, 13: 630-633.

Adams, J. M. and Schulten, G. G. M. (1978): Losses Caused by Insects, Mites and Micro Organisms in Post-harvest Grain Loss Assessment Methods, *An Assoc. Cereal Cheme., St.*, Paul Minnesota, USA., pp. 193.

Adjadi, O., Singh, B. B. and Singh, S. R. (1985): Inheritance of Bruchid Resistance in Cowpea, *Crop Sci.*, 25:740-742.

Adu-Dapaah, H., Singh, B. B. and Fatokun, C. A. (1988): Heterosis and Inbreeding Depression in Cowpea, *Tropical Grain Legume Bul.*, 35: 23-27.

Aghora, J. S., Mohan, N. and Somkumar, R. G. (1994): Evaluation of Vegetable Cowpea for Earliness, Protein Content and Green Pod Yield, *Legume Res.*, 17 (2): 138-140.

Agrawal, R. L. (1984): Identification of Crop Varieties, *Oxford and IBH Publishing Co.*, New Delhi, pp. 228.

Agrawal, R.L., Anil Pawar A. (1990): Identification of Soybean Varieties Based on Seed and Seedling Characteristics, *Seed Res.*, 18(1): 77-81.

Ahmed, K., Khalique, F., Afzal, M., Tahir, M. and Malik, B. A. (1989): Variability in Chickpea (*Cicer cirietinum* L.) Genotypes for Resistance to *Callosobruchus maculatus* (F.) Bruchidae. *J. of Stored Product Res.*, 25(2): 97-99.

Ahmed, K., Khalique, F., Khan, I. A. and Malik, B. A. (1993): Genetic Differences for Susceptibility of Chickpea to Bruchid Beetle, Callosobruchus Chinensis L. attack. *Pak. J. of Scientific and Industrial Res.*, 36: 96-98.

Albina, F., Musil. (1980): Identification of Crop and Weed Seeds, *Agril. Hand Book*, England (219), pp. 147.

Anonymous. (1954): Munsell Soil Colour Charts, Munsell Colour Macbesh Division of Kollmorgan Corporation, 2441, North Calvert Street, Baltimore.

Anonymous. (1976): ICRISAT, *Ann. Rep.*, pp. 136.

Anonymous. (1980): Official methods of analysis, 13th Ed., Association Official Agricultural Chemist, Washington, D. C., 20044.

Anonymous. (1983): IBPGR, Descriptors for Cowpea, Rome, J. Summerfield and A. H. Bunting), HMSO, London. pp. 183-185.

Anonymous. (1985): NBPGR, *Ann. Rep.*, New Delhi, pp. 133.

Anonymous. (1986): AVRDC, *Prog. Rep.*, Taiwan, pp. 79-82.

Anonymous. (1988): AVRDC, *Prog. Rep*, Taiwan, pp. 38-39.

Anonymous. (1989): NBPGR, *Ann. Rep.*, New Delhi, pp. 197.

Anonymous. (1990): NBPGR, *Ann. Rep.*, New Dehi, pp: 197.

Anonymous. 1991, AVRDC, *Prog. Rep*, Taiwan, pp: 70-72.

Anonymous. (1992a): NBPGR, *Ann. Rep.*, New Delhi, pp: 197.

Anonymous. (1992b): NBPGR, *Ann. Rep.*, New Delhi, pp:125.

Anonymous. (1992c): AVRDC, *Prog. Rep*, Taiwan pp: 91-94.

Anonymous. (1995): ICAR, *National Seed Projects (Crops)*, New Delhi, pp. 26.

Anonymous. (1999): International Rules for Seed Testing, *Seed Sci. Technol.*, 27: 25-30.

Anonymous. (2004): FAO, http://www.fao.stat.fao.org

Anonymous. (2008): FAO, http://www.fao.stat.fao.org

Anonymous. (2009a): Final Estimates of Area, Production and Yield of Important agricultural Crops in Karnataka, Directorate of Economics and Statistics, Govt. of Karnataka.

Anonymous. (2009b): Protection of Plant Varieties and Farmers Right Act, Government of India. (http://www.plantauthority.gov.in drafteropguide.htm.)

Arora, G. L. (1977): Bruchids of Northwest India. *Oriental Insects*, The Association for the Study of Oriental Insects, New Delhi, p. 132.

Arunkumar, M. B., Bherry, R. J., Malavika, D., Anuradha, V. and Sharma, S. P. (2004): Characterization of Pearl Millet Hybrids and Parental Lines using Morphological Characters, *Seed Res.*, 32 (1): 15 – 19.

Ashok S. Sajjan, Prashanth, N. D. and Hosmani, R. M. (2008): RAPD Markers and Morphological Characteristics for Identification of French Bean (*Phaseoous vulgaris* L.) Cultivars, *Seed Res.*, 36(1): 81-83.

Awasthi, P. C., Gutam, V. C., Kumar, S. and Kumar, S. (1989): Biochemical Composition and Nutritional Quality of Edible Pods of Promising Genotypes of Cowpea (*Vigna unguiculata* (L.) Walp.), *Prog. Hort.*, 21(3-4):203-207.

Backiyarani, S., Nadarajan, N., Rajendran, C. and Shanthi, S. (2000): Genetic Divergence for Physiological Traits in Cowpea, (*Vigna unguiculata.* (L.) Walp). *Legume. Res.*, 23(2): 114-117.

Bahrenfus, J.F. and Fehr, W.R. (1984): Registration of 'Harper' and 'Lakota' Soybean. *Crop Sci.*, 21: 385.

Baiker, K. A., and Webggster. (1992): Control of *Aganitho scelides obtectus* SAY (Coleaptera : Bruchidae) in *Phoseolus vulgaris* L. Seeds Stored on Small Farms-II. Germination and Cooking Time, *J. Stored Prod. Res.*, 28 (4): 295-299.

Bhadauria, N.S. and Jakhmola, S.S. (2006): Effect of Intensity of Infestation Caused by Pulse Beetle on Extent of Losses and Germination of Seeds in Different Pulses, *Indian J. Ent.*, 68(1): 92-94.

Bhagat, N. R., Taslim Ahmd, H. B., Lalwani and Harender Singh. (1985): Status of National Resource of Cultivated Groundnuts, *Indian J. Genetics and Plant Breeding*, 45 : 171 – 177.

Bhalla, S., Kapur, M. L. and Verma, B. R. (2002): Relative Suscsptibility of Cowpea Genotypes to Cowpea Weevil *C. maculatus.*, *Indian J. Ent.*, 64(1):63-67.

Bhatnagar, A., Bhadauria, N. S. and Jakhmola, S. S. (2001): Efficacy of Vegetable Oils Against Pulse Beetle, *Callosobruchus maculatus* in Cowpea, *Indian J. of Ent.*, 63(3):237-239.

Biradarpatil, N. K., Shekhargoud, M. and Giraddi, R. S. (1995): Viability of Bengal Gram Seeds Infested with Bruchids, *Seed Res.*, 23(1): 58-59.

Boerma, H. R., Hussey, R.S., Phillips, D.V., Wood, E.D. (1990): Registration of 'Colquitt' Soybean, *Crop Seed.*, 30(3): 748.

Bonetti, A., Miggiano, A., Dinelli, G. and Lovato, A. (1995): Identification of Bean (*Phaseolus vulgaris* L.) Cultivars Grown in Italy by Field and Electrophoresis Tests: A Comparative Study, *Seed Sci. Tech.*, 23: 69 – 84.

Borah, H. K. and Khan, A. K. F. (2002): Genetic Divergence in Fodder Cowpea (*Vigna unguiculata* (L.) Walp.), *Madras Agric. J.*, 88(10/12): 625-628.

Bowers, G. R., Hussey, R. S., Phillips, D. V. and Wood, E. D. (1990): Registration of 'Crockett' soybean, *Crop Sci.*, 30 (2): 427.

Braich, J. S. and Simwat, G. (1984): Effect of Different Levels of Initial Infestation of *C. chinensis* (L.) and *C. maculatus* (F.) on their Population Build up and Resultant Loss to Moong, *Bull. Grain Tech.*, 22 (3): 240-243.

Chakrabarthy, S. K. and Agrawal, R. L. (1989a): Identification of Blackgram Varieties-I Utilization of Seed Characteristics, *Seed Res.*, 17(1): 23-28.

Chakrabarthy, S. K. and Agrawal, R. L. (1989b): Identification of Blackgram Varieties-II Utilization of Morphological Characteristics of Seedlings, *Seed Res.*, 17(2): 139-142.

Chandola, R.P., Trechan, K. and Bagrecha, L.R. (1969): Varietal resistance of *Bruchus* sp. in cowpea under storage conditions, *Curr. Sci.*, 38: 370.

Chandrashekhar, S. S. (2005): Influence of the Age of the Seed on Plant Growth, Seed Yield and Quality and Characterization of French Bean Genotypes, *M.Sc. (Agri.) Thesis*, Univ. of Agric. Sci., Dharwad, Karnataka (India).

Chandrashekhar, S. S. (2008): Seed Technological Studies in French Bean. *Ph.D. Thesis*, Univ. of Agric. Sci., Dharwad, Karnataka (India).

Charjan, S. K. U., Tarar, J. L. (1991): Influence of Seed Size on Germination and Seedling Vigour in Soybean Varieties, *Bioved*, 7(2): 165-168.

Copeland, L. O. and McDonald, M. B. (1997): Principles of Seed Science and Technology, III Edition, Pub., New York, pp. 393.

Cupic, T., Tucak , M., Popovic, S., Bolaric, S., Grijusic, S. and Kozumplik, V. (2009): Genetic Diversity of Pea (*Pisum sativum* L.) Genotypes Assessed by Pedigree, Morphological and Molecular Data, *J. Food Agric. Environ.*, 7 (3&4): 343-348.

Dabi, R. K., Gupta, H. C. and Sharma, S. K. (1979): Relative Susceptibility of Some Cowpea Varieties to Pulse Beetle (*Collosobruchus maculatus*), *Indian J. Agril. Sci,.* 49(1): 48-50.

Darlington, C. D. and Wylie, A. P. (1955): Chromosome Atlas of Flowering Plants, George Allen and Unwin., London, pp: 132-134.

Dharmalingam, V. and Kadambavanasundaram, M. (1989): Genetic Divergence in Cowpea (*Vigna unguiculata* (L.) Walp.), *Madras Agric. J.*, 76(7): 394-399.

Diazcarrasco, H., Abreuferrer, S., Velazquez. O., Garcia, O. (1986): Similarities between Some Agronomic Characters in Soybean, *Ciencias de la Agricultura*, 27: 108-113.

Dogre, T. K., Pawar, S. E. and Harwalkar, M. R., (1993): Resistance to *Callosobruchus maculatus* (F.) (Caleoptera : Bruchidae) in Pigeonpea (*Cajanus cajan* L. Millsp.) and other *Cajanus* Species, *J. of Stored Product Res.*, 29(4): 319-322.

Doharey, R. B., Katiyar, R. N. and Singh, K.M. (1987): Ecotoxicological Studies on Pulse Beetles Infesting Green Gram, *Bull. Grain Tech.*, 25 (1): 12-15.

Drabo, I., T. A. O., Ladeinde and Reden, R. (1988): Inheritance of Eye Pattern and Seed Coat Colour in Cowpea [*Vigna unguiculata* (L.) Walp], *Plant Breeding,*100 : 119-123.

Dushyant, S., Khokhar, K. S. and Singh, D. (1991): Susceptibility of Pigeon Pea Genotypes to Pulse Beetle *Callosobruchus chinensis* (L.) Incidence, *Int. J. of Tropical Agril.*, 9:78-50.

Edgar, E., Hartwig and Calton, J., Edwards, J. R. (1970): Effects of Morphological Characteristics Upon Seed Yield in Soybean, *Agron. J.*, 62: 64-65.

Elsaeed, E. A. K. (1967): Seed Size as a Varietal Differences in Broad Beans (*Vicia faba* L.), *J. Agric. Sci., Camb.*, 68 : 69-73.

Girish, G. K., Jain, S. K., Ashok Kumar and Agrawal, N. S. (1975): Assessment of Storage Losses Quality and Particular Concentration in Wheat Availability in the Marker of Western UP, Punjab and Haryana, *Bull. Grain Tech.*, 13: 8-18.

Gnyandev, B. (2009): Seed Technological Studies in Chickpea Varieties (*Cicer arietinum* L.), Ph. D., *Thesis*, Univ. of Agric. Sci., Dharwad, Karnataka, (India).

Gobindan, R., Narayanaswamy, T. K., Rao, M. R. G. and Munirajappa, R. (1989): Relative Susceptibility of Wild Mung and Other Pulse Seeds for *Callosobruchus chinensis, Env. and Eco.*, 7 : 469-471.

Gujar, G.T. and Yadav, T.D., (1978): Feeding of *Callosobruchus maculatus* (F.) and *Callosobruchus chinensis* L. in green gram, *Indian J. Ent.*, 40 (2): 108-112.

Gupta, S. K., Singaal and Doharey, R.B. (1981): Studies on he Chemical and Nutritional Changes in Bengal Gram (*Cicer arietinum*) during storage Caused by the Attack of Pulse Beetle *Callosobruchus maculatus* F, *Bull. Grain Tech.*, 19 (3): 185-190.

Gupta, V.K. and Gupta, Y.K. (1977): Variability, Interrelationship and Path Coefficient Analysis for Some Qualitative Characters in Sesame (*Sesamum indicum* L.) cultivars, *Indian J. of Heredity*, 9 : 31 – 37.

Hanamantappa, R. (1996): Screening of Horse Gram and Efficacy of Different Seed Treatments against Bruchids (*Callosobruchus chinensis* L.) during Storage. *M.Sc.(Agri.) Thesis*, Univ. Agric. Sci.., Bangalore, Karnataka, (India).

Harville, B. G., Elkins, W. M., Hall, W. and Green, M. A. (1988): Registration of 'Gregg' Soybean, *Crop Sci.*, 28: 196.

Henshaw, F. O., (2008): Varietal Differences in Physical Characteristics and Proximate Composition of Cowpea (*Vigna unguiculata*), *World J. Agric. Sci.*, 4 (3): 302-306.

Indradeo Pandey (2007): Genetic Diversity in Grain Cowpea [*Vigna unguiculata* (L.) Walp], *Legume Res.*, 30(2): 92-97.

International Board for Plant Genetic Resources. (1983): Cowpea Descriptors. IBPGR, Rome. J. Summerfield and A. H. Bunting), HMSO, London, pp. 183-185.

Jackson, M. L. (1967): Soil Chemical Analysis, *Prentice Hall of India Pvt. Ltd.*, New Delhi, pp. 183-192.

Jain, S. and Khare, D. (2002a): Characterization of Mung Bean Varieties for Verification of Genetic Purity at Seed Level, *JNKVV Res. J.*, 36 (1&2) : 35-37.

Jain, S. and Khare, D. (2002b): Characterization of Mung Bean Varieties for Verification of Genetic Purity at Plant Level, *JNKVV Res. J.*, 36 (1&2) : 38-43.

Jotwani, M. G., Sircar, P. and Yadav, T. D. (1967): Studies on the Extent of Damage and Germination of Seeds. I. Germination of Pea Seeds Damaged by *C. maculatus* (F.), *Indian J. Ent.*, 29 (3) : 309 – 311.

Kachare, D. P., Chavan, J.K. and Kadam S. S. (1988): Nutritional Quality of Some Improved Cultivars of Cowpea, *Plant Foods for Human Nutrition*, 38 : 155-162.

Kadoo, S. and Rane, A. E. (1995): Relative Susceptibility of Some Pigeon Pea Varieties to Pulse Beetle *Callosobruchus chinensis* L. in storage. *J. of Soils and Crops*, 5: 49-52.

Kamble, R. M., Khan, T.N. and Reddy, N. S. (1998): Nutritional Quality Evaluation of Newly Developed Varieties of Pigeonpea. *Legume Res.*, 21(2): 67-73.

Kameshwara Rao, P. and Krjshnamorthy Rao, B. H. (1982): Studies on the Relative Resistance to Certain Pigeon Pea Varieties to *Callosobruchus maculatus* (F.), *The Andhra Agril. J.*, 29(1): 51-54.

Kapila, R. and Rajni, H. R.(1989): Screening of Different Cultivars of *Phaseolus vulgaris* to the attack of *Zabrotes subfasciatus*, *Bulletin of Entomology*, 28: 138-144.

Karivartharaju, T. V. (2005): Physiological and Biochemical Techniques for Crop Variety Identification, Training Manual, DUS Test in Cotton with Reference to PPV and FR Legislation, 2001, pp. 101-115.

Karkannavar, J. C., Venugopal, R. and Goud, J. V. (1991): Inheritance and Linkage Studies in Cowpea [*Vigna unguiculata* (L.) Walp.], *Indian J. Gen.*, 51: 203-207.

Karthikeyan, K. A. M., Vijayakumar, I., Suresh, P. and Janarthanan, S. (2008): Susceptibility of Genetically Improved Varieties of Indian Pulses to the Pulse Beetle, *Callosobruchus maculatus* (Fab.), *Indian J. Ent.*, 70(1): 64-67.

Katiyar, P. N. and Khare, B. P. (1983): Relative Susceptibility of Twenty Germplasms of Gram to Pulse Beetle *C. Chinensis* (Linnaeus), *Bull. Grain Techl.*, 21(1) : 31-36.

Kenworthy, W. J. (1988): Registration of 'Morgan' Soybean, *Crop. Sci.*, 28: 196.

Khairnar, G. P., Adsule, V. M. and Thakur, S. G. (1996): Quantitative and Qualitative Losses Caused by *Callosobruchus chinensis* L. in Pigeonpea Over Different Period of Storage, *Seed Res.*, 24(1): 42-44.

Khare, D., Shukla, S.S., Nair, P. and Bhale, M.S. (2009): Characterisation of Linseed Varieties Based on Seed Coat Colour, *Seed Res.*, 37 (1 & 2): 62-67.

Kooistra, E. (1964): Identification Research on Pulses, *Proceedings of Intl. Seed Testing Assoc.*, 29 (4): 937 – 947.

Koszykowski, W. J. and Burgoon, A. C. (1983): Soybean Cultivar Testing Update, *Newslett. AOSA*, 57(2): 32-39.

Kumawat, K. C. and Raje, R. S. (2005): Association Analysis in Cowpea [*Vigna unguiculata* (L.) Waip.], *J. Arid Legunes*, 2(1): 47-49.

Lakshminarasimhaiah, M. N. (1993): Bio—Efficacy of Non-edible Plant Oils as Seed Protectants against *Callosobruchus chinensis* L. and their Effect on Seed Quality of Pigeon Pea (*Cajanus cajan* L.) during Storage, *M.Sc.(Agri) Thesis*, Univ. of Agric. Sci., Bangalore, Karnataka (India).

Lambrides, C. J. and Imrie, B. C. (2000): Susceptibility of Mungbean Varieties to the Bruchid Species *Callosobruchus maculatus* (F.), *C. phaseoli* (Gyll), *C. chinensis* (L.) and *Achenthoscelides obtectus* (Say) (Coleoptera: Chroysomelidae). *Aust. Agric. Res.*, 50 : 85 – 89.

Lingaraj, C., Halemani. (2009): Assessment of Genetic Diversity in Cowpea (*Vigna unguiculata* L. Walp.) Germplasm, *M.Sc. (Agri) Thesis*, Univ. of Agric. Sci., Dharwad, Karnataka (India).

Lirindae, M. A. (1986): Laboratory Methodology for Cultivar Purity Testing in US Rices, *Dissertation Abstracts Int.*, B (Sciences and Engg.), 47 (4) : 1336B – 1337B.

Liu-xuming, Jin-Dasheng,. Cheng-Xuzhen and Wu-Xiaofei. (1998): Preliminary Evaluation on their Resistance to *Callosobruchus chinensis* L. in Mungbean Germplasm, *Crop Genetic Resources*, 2: 35-37.

Mahalanobis, P. C. (1936): On the generalized distance in statistics. Proc. *Natl. Acad. Sci.*, 2: 55-79.

Mahgoub, S. M., Hamed, M. S., Ali, S. M. and Gharib, M. S. A. (2005): Susceptibility of some Egyptian Pulses to Infestation by *Callosobruchus Chinensis* (L.) and *Callosobruchus maculatus*(F.). *Egyptian J. Agric. Res.*, 83(4): 1601-1612.

Manjaya, J.G. and Bapat, V.A. (2008): Studies on Genetic Divergence in Soybean, *Glycine max* (L). *J. Oilseeds Res.*, 25 (2): 178-180.

Manohar, S. S. and Yadav, S. R. S. (1990): Laboratory Observation on Relative Resistance and Susceptibility of Some Cowpea Cultivars to Pulse Beetle *Callosobruchus maculatus* F. (Bruchidae:Coleoptera), *Indian J. of Ento.*, 52(2): 180-186.

Mate, S. N. and Shelar, V. R. (2006): Morphological Characterization of Sorghum Hybrids and their Parental Lines, *Abstract XII National Seed Seminar*, 24-26 February, ANGRAU, Hyderabad, pp: 175 – 176.

Modesta, R. C. D. and Cabral, L. C. (1987): Characteristics of Seeds of Some Soybean Lines with Coloured Testas, EMBRAPA, *News lett. Brazil*: (17). Pp: 17.

Modi, B. N., Papasai, S. K., Verma, R. S. and Singh, C. B. (1994): The Reaction of Pulse Beetle *C. chinensis* L. on Grains of 44 Varieties of Pigeon Pea, *Bhartiya Krishi Anusandhan Patrika*, 9:283-288.

Mohanrao. (1993): Influence of Genotypes and Seed Size on Seed Quality, Storability and Field Performance in Soybean, *M. Sc. (Agri) Thesis*, Univ. Agric. Sci., Bangalore, Karnataka, (India).

Mudzana, G., Pickett, A. A., Jarman, R. J. and Cooke, R. J. (1995): Variety Discrimination in Faba Beans: An Integrated Approach. *Plant Verities and Seed*, 8 : 135 – 145.

Muhammad Arshad, Naazar Ali and Abdul Ghafoor. (2006): Character Correlation and Path Coefficient In Soybean *Glycine max* (l.) Merrill, *Pak. J. Bot.*, 38(1): 121-130.

Muhammad Hussain, Roy, G. C. and Husain, M. (1997): Laboratory Evaluation of Some Rnungbean Strains for Susceptibility to Pulse Beetle, *Callosobruchus chinensis* L., *Bangladesh J. of Ento.*, 7: 21-26.

Muhammad Shafique and Maqbool Ahmad. (2005): Chickpea Grains Resistance to Pulse Beetle, *Callosobruchus analis* (F.) (Coleoptera: Bruchidae), *Pakistan J. Zoology*, 37 (2):123-126.

Murthy, G. S. and Pavate, M. Y. (1962): Studies on Quantitative inheritance in *Nicotiana tobaccum* L. I. Varietal Classification and Selection by Multivariate Analysis, *Indian J. Genet.*, 22: 68.

Muthaiah, A.R. (2006): Morphological Varietal Characterization in Pulses. In: Advance in Seed Science and Technology., Vol. I. Recent trends in Seed Technology and Management, (Ed) Vanangamudi, K., Agrobios, Jodhapure.

Naeem Ahmad and Mohammad Rahim. (2007): 'Swat Kulat-1' A High Yielding and Semi Erect Cowpea Variety For Irrigated Areas Of Malakand Division, *Gomal Univ. J. Res.*, 23 (2): 13-17.

Nagalakshmi, R. M., Usha Kumari, U. and Anandha Kumar, C. R. (2009): Cowpea, The Unexploited pulse, *Agribios News Letter*, 7 (9) : p. 41.

Nagaraj, M. M. (2002): Genetics Variation for Productivity and Bruchid Resistance in Greengram (*Vigna radiata* (L.) Wiczek), *M.Sc.(Agri.) Thesis*, Univ. of Agric. Sci., Dharwad, Karnataka, India.

Nagaraja, M. (2006): Evaluation of Pigeon Pea and Cowpea Genotypes for Bruchid Resistance (bruchids), *M.Sc.(Agri.) Thesis*, Univ. of Agric. Sci., Dharwad, Karnataka, India.

Naima Ghalmi, Marie Malice, Jean-Marie Jacquemin, Sidi-Mohamed Ounane, Leila Mekliche and Jean-Pierre Baudoin. (2009): Morphological and Molecular Diversity within Algerian

Cowpea (*Vigna unguiculata* (L.) Walp.) Landraces, *Genet. Resour. Crop Evol.*, 4: 22-24. *springerlink.com.*

Nair, K. R. and Mukherjee, H. K. (1960): Classification of Natural Plantation Teak (*Teetona grandis*) Grown at Different Location of India and Burma with Respect to Its Mechanical and Physiological Properties, *Sankhya*, 22:11-20.

Narayanankutty, C., Mili, R. and Jaikumaran, U. (2003): Variability and Genetic Divergence in Vegetable Cowpea, *J. Maharashtra Agric. Univ.*, 28(1): 26-29.

Nigude. A. D., Dumbre, A. D. and Lad, D. B. (2004): Genetic Diversity Studies in Cowpea, *J Maharashtra Agric. Univ.*, 29(3): 250-252.

Nirmal de, Rajkumar and Kallo, G. (2001): Diet Versatility in Cowpea Genotypes, *Indian J. Agric. Sci.*, 71(9): 598-601.

Nkouannessi Magloire. (2005): The Genetic, Morphologicl and Physiological Evaluation of African Cowpea Genotypes, *M.Sc. (Agri) Thesis, Univ. of* Free State, Bioemrontein, South Africa.

Ogunbodede, B. A. and Fatunla, T. (1985): Quantitative Studies of Some Cowpea [*Vigna unguiculata* (L.) Walp.] Traits, *East African Agril. and Forestry J.*, 50 : 89-100.

Paramesh, R. (1983): Screening of Soybean Cultivars for Seed Size, Seed Vigour and Establishment of the Relationship with Yield and Yield Components, *M. Sc. (Agri) Thesis*, Univ. Agric. Sci.., Bangalore, Karnataka, (India).

Parameshwarappa, S. G., Deshpande, V. K. and Salimath, P. M. (2007): Studies on Comparative Response and Seed Quality Attributes of Certain Chickpea Varieties to Pulse Beetle (*Callosobruchus chinensis* L.) in storage, *Karnataka J. Agric. Sci.*, 20 (3) : 492-495.

Parameshwarappa, S.G., Palakshappa, M.G., Salimath, P.M. and Parameshwarappa, K.G. (2009): Studies on Genetic Variability and Character Association in Germplasm Collection of Sesame (*S. indicum* L.), *Karnataka J. Agric. Sci.*, 22(2): 252-254.

Patil, S. K., Tanpure, S. V. and Mate, S. N. (2003): Effect of Different Levels of Pulse Beetle [*Callosobruchus maculatus* (Fab.)] Infestation on Chickpea during Storage, *Seed Res.*, 31(1) : 119-120.

Payne, R.C. and Koszykowski, T.J. (1979): The Effect of Seed Size on Hypocotyl Length of Soybean Cultivars, *Seed Sci. Technol.*, 7 : 109-115.

Pingale, S. V. (1953): Effect of damage by Some Insects on the Viability and Weight of Stored Grain, *Bull. Cent. Fd. Technol. Res. Inst.*, Mysore. 2 : 153.

Piper, C. S. (1966): Soil and Plant Analysis, *Academic Press*, New York, pp: 368.

Purnima, Jharia, A.N., Shrivastava, K.M.S., Raghuwanshi and Shrivastava, M.K. (2008): Genetic Variability in Induced Mutants of Soybean, *Glycin max* (L.), *J. Oilseeds Res.*, 25 (2):175-177.

Ramamoorthy, K., Ponnuswamy, A. S. and Sundareshwaran. (2010): Varietal Deterioration and Reference Variety Maintenance, Training Manual on "Vareital Purity Testing-Testing of Specified Traits, 4th to 8th January, 2010, Coimbatore, Tamilnadu.

Ramesh, C. V. (1993): Effectiveness of Edible Oils and Chemicals as Seed Protectants on Bruchid Infestation in Soybean and their Effects on Seed Quality and Storability, *M.Sc. (Agri) Thesis*, Univ. of Agric. Sci., Bangalore, Karnataka (India).

Ramzan, M., Chahal, B.S. and Judge, B.K. (1990): Storage Losses to Some Commonly Used Pulses Caused by Pulse Beetle, *J. Insect Sci.*, 3 (1) : 106 - 108.

Rao, C. R. (1952): Advanced Statistical Methods in Biometrical Research, *John Wiley and Sons*, New York.

Rasaily, S.K., Desai, N.D. and Kukadia, M.U. (1986): Genetic Variability in Soybean (*Glycine max* (L.) Merrill), *Gujarat Agril. Uni. Res. J.*, 11(2) 57-60.

Ravikumar. (1999): Identification of Soybean Varieties Based on Seed, Seedling and Plant Characters, *M. Sc. (Agri.) Thesis*, Univ. Agric. Sci.., Bangalore, Karnataka, (India).

Reddy, P.N., Reddy, K.N. and Singh, S.P. (1989): Effect of Seed Size on Qualitative and Quantitative Traits in Soybean, *Seed Sci. and Technol.*, 17: 289-295.

Renganayaki, K. and Rengasamy, S. R. (1992): Path Co-efficient Analysis in Cowpea [*Vigna unguiculata* (L.) Walp.], *Madras Agric. J.*, 79: 476-481.

Rewale, A. P., Birari, S. P. and Apte. U. B. (1996): Genetic Divergence in Cowpea [*Vigna unguiculata* (L.) Walp.], *Indian .J. Agric. Res.*, 30 (2): 73-79.

Richard and Payne, R.C. (1979): Sonic New Test and Procedures for Determining Variety (soybeans), *J. Seed Technol.*, 3(2): 61-77.

Roopa Anantareddy. (2008): Varietal Characterization and Identification of Soybean Genotypes Through Morphological and Molecular Markers, *Ph. D Thesis*, Univ. Agric. Sci.., Bangalore, Karnataka, (India).

Rustamani, M.A., Naqui, S.M.S.H., Munshi, G.H. and Abbo, G.H. (1985): Relative Resistance/ Susceptibility of Different Pulses Against Pulse Beetle *Callosobruchus chinensis* L., *Pak. J. Zool.*, 17 (1) : 99-100.

Sankrapandian, R. (2002): Identifying Some Pulse Cultivars Based on Key Characters Alone Among Popular Varieties of Tamil Nadu, *Seed Tech News*, 32 (1): 146.

Santos, C. A. F., Menezes, E. A. and Araujo, F.de. (1997): Genetic Diversity in Genotypes of Cowpea Under 2 Different Environments, *Revista Ceres*, 44 (25 1): 35-42.

Sarutayophat, T., Nualsri, C., Santipracha, Q. and Saereeprasert, V. (2007): Characterization and Genetic Relatedness Among 37 Yard Long Bean and Cowpea Accessions Based on Morphological Characters and RAPD Analysis, *Songklanakarin J. Sci. Technol.*, 29 (3): 591-600.

Satya Vir. (1983): Varietal Resistance and Susceptibility of Cowpea to *Callsobruchus maculatus* Fab, *Indian J. Ent.*, 45(3): 213-217.

Satya, V. and Jindal, S.K. (1981): Oviposition and Development of *C. maculatus* (Fab.) on Different Host Species, *Bull. Grain Tech.*, 19 : 180-184.

Sebetha, E. T., Ayodele, V. I., Kutu, F. R. and Mariga, I. K. (2010): Yields and Protein Content of Two Cowpea Varieties Grown Under Different Production Practices in Limpopo Province, South Africa., *Afr. J. Biotechnol.*9 (5): 628-634.

Selvaraj, V., Annappan, R. S. and Giridharran, S. (1986): CO-4, A New High Yielding Drought Tolerant Cowpea Variety, *Madras Agril. J.*, 73 (3) : 125-128.

Shaheen, F. A. Khaliq, A. and Aslam, M. (2006): Resistance of Chickpea (*Cicer arietinum* L.) Cultivars Against Pulse Beetle, *Pak. J. Bot.*, 38(4): 1237-1244

Sharma, S. K., Teckchandani, C. K. and Nakhotore, C. L. (1991): Physical Characteristics of Greengram Varieties, *JNKVV Res. J.*, 25: 1-4.

Sharma, T.R. and Mishra, S.N. (1997): Genetic Divergence and Character Association Studies in Cowpea, *Crop Res. Hissar.*, 13: 109- 114.

Shehnaz, A. and Theophillus, F. (1975): Effect of Insect Infestation on Chemical Composition and Nutritive Value of Bengal Gram (*Cicer arientium*) and Field Bean (*Doilchos lablab*), *J. Food Sci. and Tech.*, 12 : 29.

Siddique, A. K. and Gupta, S. N. (1991): Genotypic and Phenotypic Variability for Seed Yield and Other Traits in Cowpea [*Vigna unguiculata* (L.) Walp.], *Int. J. Tropical Agric.*, 9 : 144-148.

Siddiqui, P.M. (1972): Studies on Longevity, Oviposition, Fecundity and Development of *Callosobruchus chinensis* L. (Coleoptera:Bruchidae) *Zeitschrift fur Angewandte Entomologie,* 72 (1) : 66-72. (Abstr. Rev. Applied Ent.., 1974, 62: 536).

Singh, A. B., Awasthi, C. P. and Singh, N. (1997a): Biochemical Composition and Nutrition Quality of Edible Immature Pods of Broad Bean (*Vicia faba* L.), *Prog. Hort.,* 29(3-4) : 147-154.

Singh, B. B., Mohan, D. R., Dashiell, K. E., and Jackai, L. E. N. (1997b): *Advances in Cowpea Research,* Copublication of Int. Inst. of Tropical Agril. (IITA) and Japan Int. Res. Centre for Agric. Sci., (JIRCAS), IITA, Ibadan, Nigeria.

Singh, B. B., Singh, S. R. and Adjadi, V. (1985): Bruchid Resistance in Cowpea. *Crop Sci.,* 25 (5) : 736-739.

Singh, D. P. and Sharma, S. S. (1984): Studies on Grain Damage and Germination Loss Caused by *Callosobruchus maculatus* Fab. in Different Varieties of Moong and Mash During Storage, *Bull. Grain Tech.,* 20 (1): 20 - 24.

Singh, R. P. and Choudhary, B. D. (1977): Biometrical Methods in Quantitative Genetic Analysis, *Kalyani Publishers,* New Dehli.

Singhal, S.K., Singh, Z. and Jaglan, R.S. (1989): Effect of Different Levels of Bruchid *Callosobruchus chinensis* L. Infestation on Chickpea *Cicer arietinum* (L.) in India, *Trop. Pest Management,* 35 (2): 187—189.

Sisodia, G. S. (1987): Effect of Seed Size on Yield in Soybean, *Seeds and Farms,* 13(4): 30-31.

Sison, M. L. J., Adalla, C. B. and Mantala, J. P. (1996): Life History of *Callosobruchus chinensis* L. and New Sources of Mungbean Resistance to this Storage Pest, *Philippine Entomologist,* 10:175-187.

Southgate, B. J. (1979): Biology of Bruchidae, *Ann. Rev. Ent.,* pp: 449 – 473.

Sridhara, S., Thimmegowda, S. and Chalapathi, M. V. (1997): Nutritional Values, Physical and Phsico-chemical Characteristics and Cooking Quality of Soybean Genotypes, *Crop Res.,* 13(2) : 259-266.

Srikantaradya, M.G. (1980): Genetic Variability with Respect to Different Seed Characters in Relation to Viability and Vigour in Soybean (*Glycinc max* (L.) Merrill), *M. Sc. (Agri) Thesis,* Univ. Agric. Sci.., Bangalore, Karnataka, (India).

Stahi, J. P. and Pandey, M. P. (1981): Association of Seed Impermeability with Flowering and Maturity Duration in Soybean, *Tropical Grain Legume Bull.,* 22 : 119 – 121.

Steele, W. M. (1976): Cowpeas, *Vigna unguiculata.* In: *Evolution of crop plants,* (Eds. R. Summerfield and A. H.Bunting), HMSO, London, pp. 183 – 185.

Stoilova, T. and Berova, M., Morphological and Agrobiological Study on Local Germplasm of Common Beans (*Phaseolus vulgaris* L.) and Cowpea (*V. unguiculata* L.). *XI Anniversary Scientific Conference,* Special Edition: 385-388.

Sudhakar, N., Shridevi, O. and Salimath, P.M. (2007): Variability and Character Association Analysis in Sesame (*Sesamum indicum* L.), *J. Oilseeds Res.,* 24 (1): 56-58.

Suganthi, S and Murugan, S. (2007): Variability Studies in Cowpea [*Vigna unguiculata* (L) Walp.], *Crop Res. Hissar.,* 33(1/3): 195-197.

Suhasini, K.S. (2006): Characterization of Sesame Genotypes Through Morphological, Chemical and RAPD Markers, *M. Sc. (Agri.) Thesis,* Univ. Agric. Sci., Dharwad, Karnataka, India.

Sukprakaran, C. (1985): Pest Problems and the Use of Pesticides in Grain Storage in Thailand, ACIAR Proceedings Series, Australian Centre for *Int. Agric. Res.,* No. 14, 31-35.

Sulnathi, G., Prasanthi, L. and Sekhar, M. R. (2007): Character Contribution to Diversity in Cowpea, *Legume Res.*, 31 (1) : 70 -72.

Sun, J. and Chang, R. (1990): Analysis of the Characteristics of Green Soybean in China, *Crop Genetic Resources*, (3): 4-6.

Sundarraj, N., Nagaraju, S., Venkataram, M. N. and Jagannath, M. K. (1972): Design and Analysis of Field Experiments. Univ. Agric. Sci., Bangalore, Karnataka, India.

Surendra Prakash and Singhal, N. C. (1997): Characterization of Some Indian Pea (*Pisum sativum* L.) cultivars, *Seed Res.*, 25 (1) : 53 – 58.

Suryawanshi, V. B., Patil, R. B., Mata, S. N., Gagare, K. C. and Manjare, M. R. (2002): Morphological Characterization of Soybean Cultivars, *Seed Tech. News*, 32 (1) : 211.

Talekar, N. S. and Lin, C. L. (1992): Characterization of *Callosobruchus chinensis*, Resistance in Mungbean, *J. of Eco. Ento.*, 85: 1150-1153.

Tarasatyavathi, C., Bharadwaj, C. H., Husain, S. M., Karmakar, P. G. and Yogendra Mohan. (2004): Identification Key for Soybean (*Glycine max*) Varieties Released or Notified in (India), *Indian J. Agric. Sci.*, 74 (4): 215-218.

Terao, H. (1986): Studies on the Mesocotyl Elongation of Seedling in Japanese Paddy Rice Cultivars. *Oryza sativa* L., *Bull. Institutional Tropical Agril.*,9 : 77 – 87.

Tiwari, D. K., Tiwari, J. P. and Agarwal, V. K. (1978): Evaluation of Soybeans for High Germinability and Field Emergence, *Seed Res.*, 6(2): 125-128.

185. Tunwar, N.S. and Singh, S.V. (1985): *Handbook of Cultivars*, India, pp. 302.

Umoren , U.E., Tewe O.O., Bokanga, M. and Jackai, L.E.N. (1997): Protein Quality of Raw and Autoclaved Cowpeas: Comparison Between Some Insect Resistant and Susceptible Varieties, *Plant Foods for Human Nutrition*, 50: 301-315.

Upadhyaya, M. D., Roomiroortiz, Daula, I., Bramel and Sube Singh. (2002): Phenotypic Diversity for Morphological and Agronomic Characteristics in Chickpea Core Collection, *Emiphytica*, 12(3): 333-342.

Usha Kumari, R., Backiyarani, S. and Dhanakodi. (2000): Character Contribution to Diversity in Cowpea, *Legume Res.*, 23: 122-125.

Vahab, M. A., Joseph, S., Mathe, S.K., Devadas, V. S. and Peter, K. V. (1991): Evaluation of Selected Varieties of Vegetable Cowpea, *Veg. Sci.*, 18(2): 222-224.

Vavilov, N. I. (1951): The Origin, Variation, Immunity and Plant Breeding of Cultivated plants, *Ronald Press Co.*, New York, pp. 256-257.

Venkatareddy, D. M. (1991): Investigations on Seed Technology of Soybean, *Ph.D Thesis*, Univ. Agric. Sci., Bangalore, Karnataka, (India).

Venkategowda, N. (1984): Estimation of Loss of Stored Soybean Due to Bruchid, *Callosobruchus maculatus* (Fabricius) and Its Biology, Ecology and Control, *M.Sc. (Agri) Thesis*. Univ. of Agric. Sci., Bangalore, Karnataka (India).

Venkatesan, M., Prakash, M. and Ganesan, J. (2003): Correlation and Path Analysis in Cowpea (*Vigna unguiculata* (L.) Walp.), *Legume Res.*, 26: 105-108.

Venkatesan, M., Veeramani, P., Thangavel and Ganeshan, J. (2004): Genetic Divergence in Cowpea (*Vigna unguiculata* (L.) Walp.), *Legume Res.*, 27(3): 223-225.

Villalobos, E. and Fournier, L. A. (1978): Morphological Identification of Some Soybean Selections Introduced Into Costa Rica, *Agronomia Costarricense*, 2(10): 23-27.

Vimala, V. and Pushpamma, P. (1983a): Storage Quality of Pulses Studied in Three Agro-climatic Regions of Andra Pradesh I Qualitative Changes, *Bull. Grain Tech.*, 21 (1) : 54 – 62.

Vimala, V. and Pushpamma, P. (1983b). Storage Quality of Pulses Studied in Three Agro-climatic Regions of Andra Pradesh II Viability Changes, *Bull. Grain Tech.*, 21 (3) : 217 – 222.

Wadnerkar, D. W., Kaunsale, P. P. and Pawar, V. M. (1978): Studies on Preference of Pulse Beetle (*Callosobruchus maculatus* F.) to Some Varieties of Arhar and Gram, *Bulletin of Grain Technology*, 16(2) : 122-124.

Wagner, C.K. and McDonald, M.B. (1982): Rapid Laboratory Tests Useful for Differentiation of Soybean (*Glycine max* L.) Cultivars, *Seed Sci. Technol.*, 10: 431-449.

Weiss, E. A. (1971): Caster, Sesame and Safflower, *Leonard Hill Books*, London, 311 – 355.

Williams, J.H., Specht, J.E., Dreier, A.F, Moomaw, R.S. and Elmore, R.W. (1984): Registration of 'Platte' Soybean, *Crop Sci.*, 24: 334.

Yadav, R. D. S. and Srivastava, J.P. (2002): DUS Characteristics of Chickpea Varieties, *Seed Tech News*, 32(32): 29-30.

Yadav, T.D. and Pant, N. C. (1978): Development Response of *C. maculatus* and *C. chinensis* on Different Pulses, *Indian J. Ent.*, 40 (1) : 7 – 15.

Genetics and Bioengineering : ***Concepts and Issues*** **Pages 148-166**
Edited by: **Dr. Ashok K. Rathoure and Dr. Pawan Kumar 'Bharti'**
ISBN: 978-93-86841-92-6
Edition: **2019**
Published by: **Discovery Publishing House Pvt. Ltd., New Delhi (India)**

8

Bioinformatics Tools in Microbial Biotechnology

[1]Prasann Kumar, [2]Shweta Pathak M.

GRAPHICAL ABSTRACT

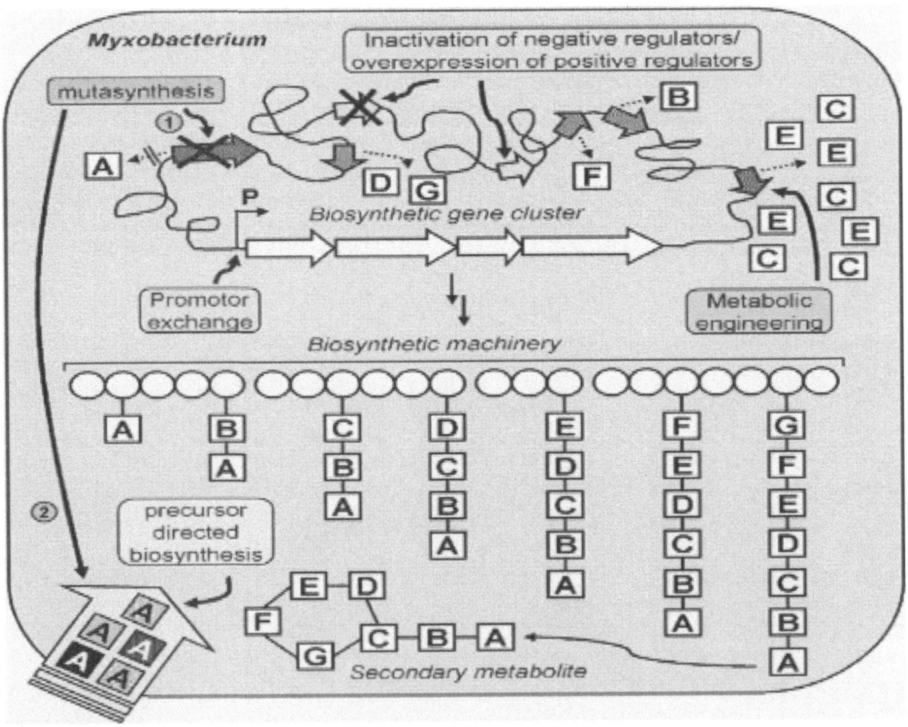

Keywords: Agriculture, Bioinformatics, Crop, Microbes

INTRODUCTION

- Microorganisms are important for us in many reasons, especially because they produce things that are of value to us. Produced things

[1] Division of Research and Development Department of Agronomy, School of Agriculture, Lovely Professional University, Jalandhar, Punjab, 144411, India
[2] Department of Plant Physiology, I. Ag. Sci., BHU., Varanasi, 221005, U.P., India

can be very large materials (e.g. proteins, nucleic acids, carbohydrate polymers) or smaller molecules.

- Microbes usually produce compounds which are in small amounts and are needed for their own.
- Regulatory mechanisms facilitate a strain to avoid unnecessary production of its metabolites so that it can compete proficiently with other forms of life and survive in nature.
- Whereas the industrial microbiologist screens for a 'wasteful' strain that will overproduce a particular compound that can be isolated and marketed
- After a desired strain has been found, a development program is initiated to improve strains through modification of culture conditions using mutation and recombinant DNA techniques.

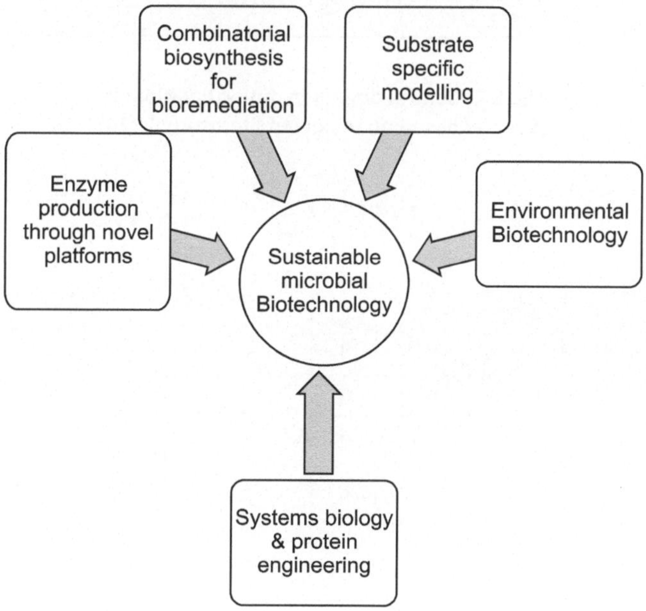

Fig. 8.1: Sustainable microbial biotechnology
(Source: Based on review of literature, 2018)

What is Bioinformatics?

"The field of science in which biology, computer science, and information technology merge to form a single discipline". Ultimate goal: to enable the discovery of new biological insights as well as to create a global perspective from which unifying principles in biology can be discerned.

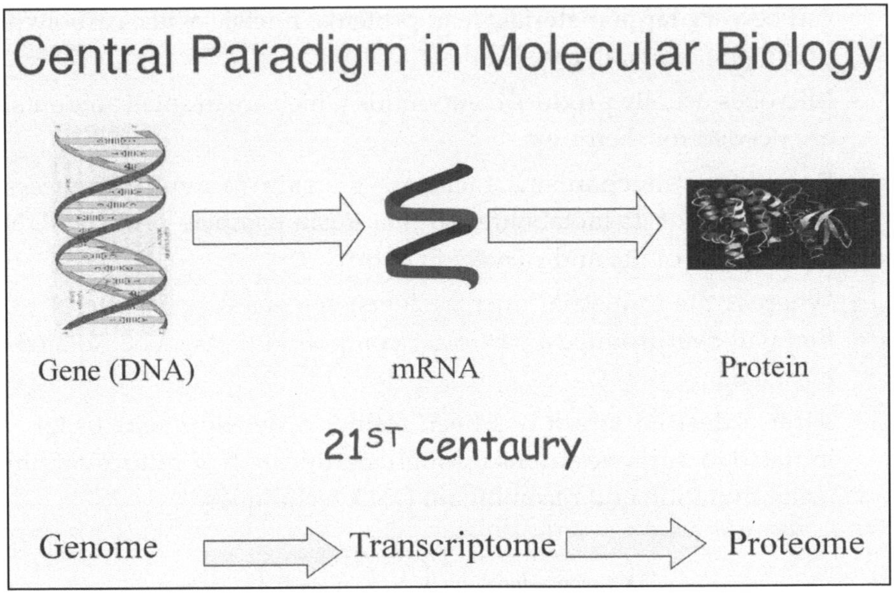

Fig. 8.2: Central dogma in molecular biology
(Source: based on review of literature, 2018)

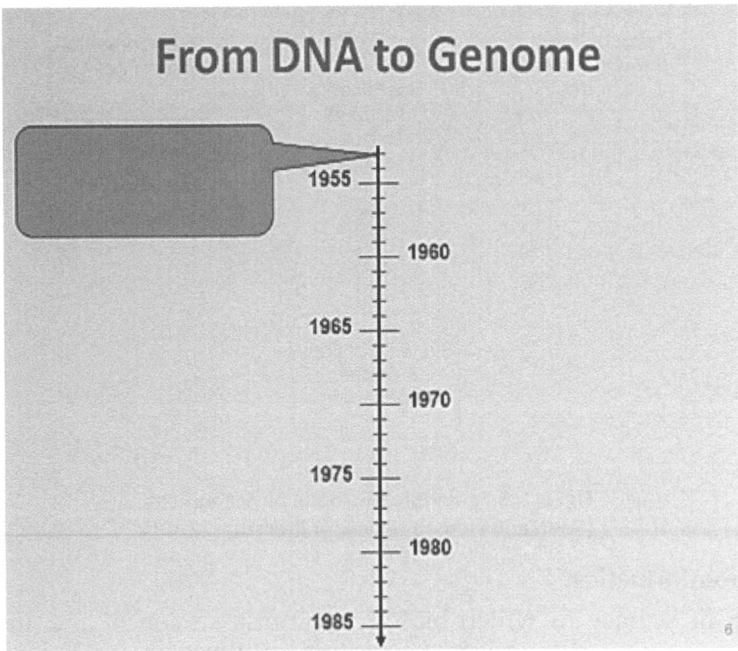

Fig. 8.3: From DNA to genome
(Source: based on review of literature, 2018)

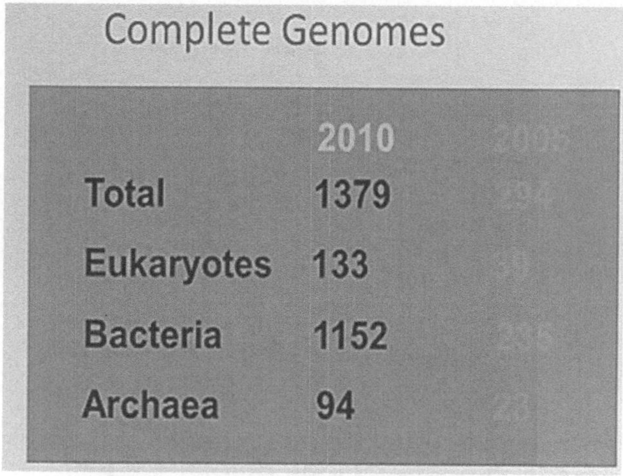

Fig. 8.4: Complete Genome
(Source: based on review of literature, 2018)

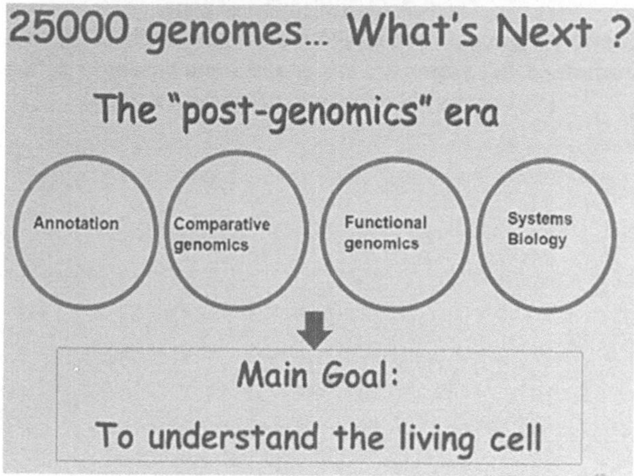

Fig. 8.5: Post Genomics Era
(Source: based on review of literature, 2018)

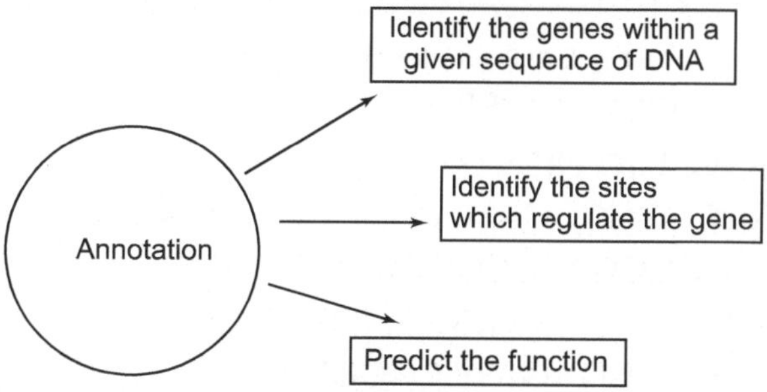

Fig. 8.6: Annotation
(Source: based on review of literature, 2018)

Fig. 8.7: Identification of gene
How do we identify a genein a genome?A gene is characterized by several features (promoter, ORF...)some are easier and some harder to detect...
(Source: based on review of literature, 2018)

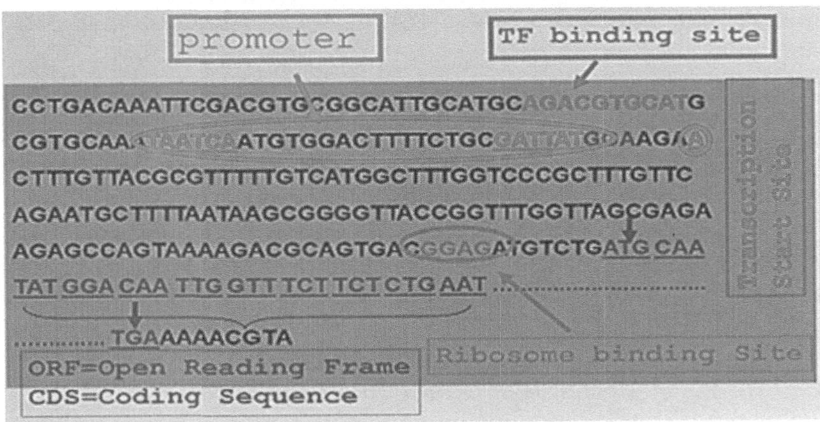

Fig. 8.8: Promoter and TF binding site
(Source: based on review of literature, 2018)

SO WHERE ARE WE DIFFERENT??

Human ATAGCGGGGGATGCGGGCCCTATACCC
Chimp ATAGGGGGGATGCGGGCCCTATACCC
Mouse ATAGCGGGATGCGGCGCTATACCA
Human ATAGCGGGGGATGCGGGCCCTATACCC
Chimp ATAGGGG—GGATGCGGGCCCTATACCC
Mouse ATAGCG—GGATGCGGCGC-TATACC-A

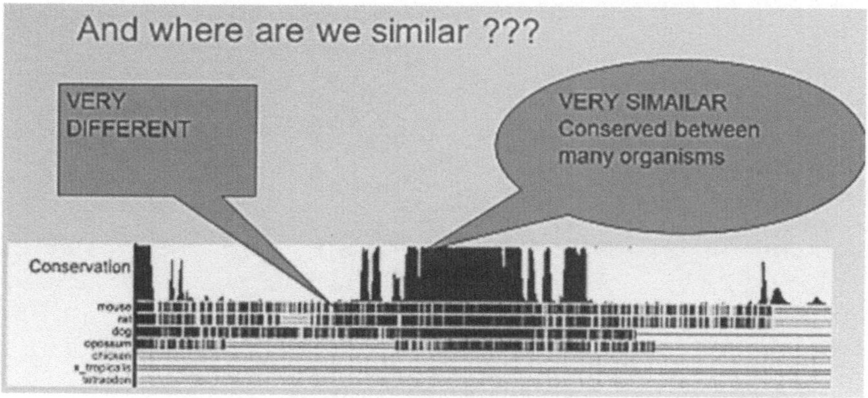

Fig. 8.9: where we are different
(Source: based on review of literature, 2018)

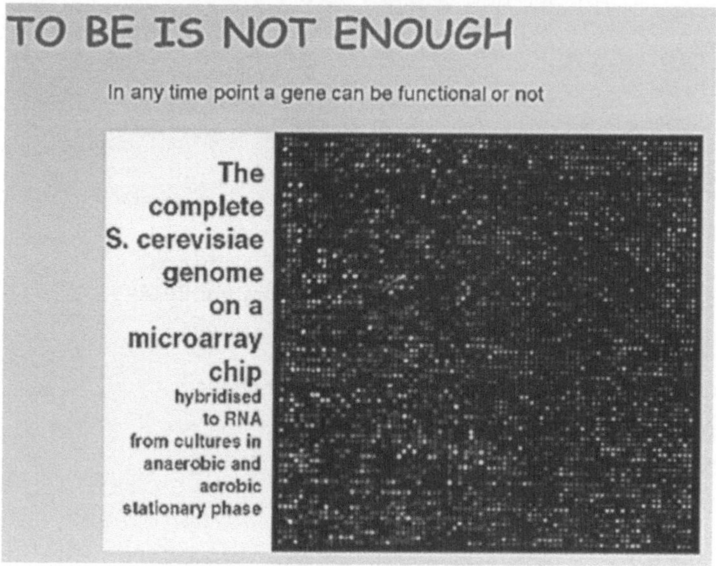

Fig. 8.10: Functional genomics
(Source: based on review of literature, 2018)

From the gene expression pattern we can lean:

What does the gene do?

When is it needed?

What other genes or proteins interact with it?

.....

What's wrong??

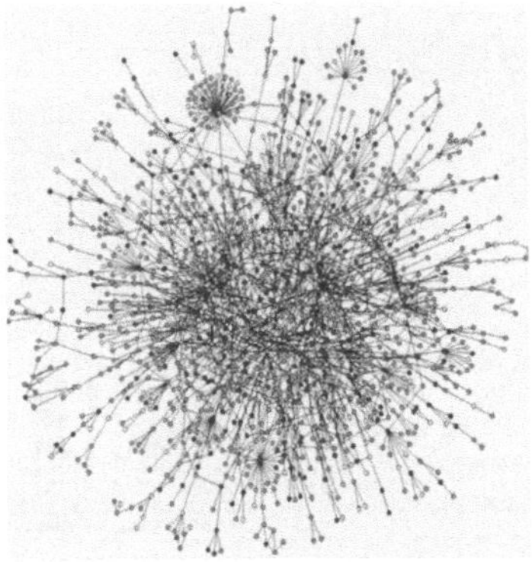

Fig. 8.11: Biological network
(Source: based on review of literature, 2018)

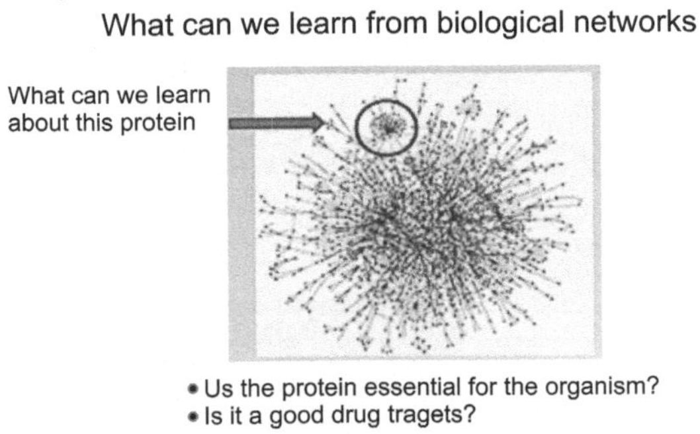

Fig. 8.12: Learn from biological network
(Source: based on review of literature, 2018)

Biological Data Base

The different types of data are collected in **database**

- Sequence databases
- Structural databases
- Databases of Experimental Results

All databases are connected

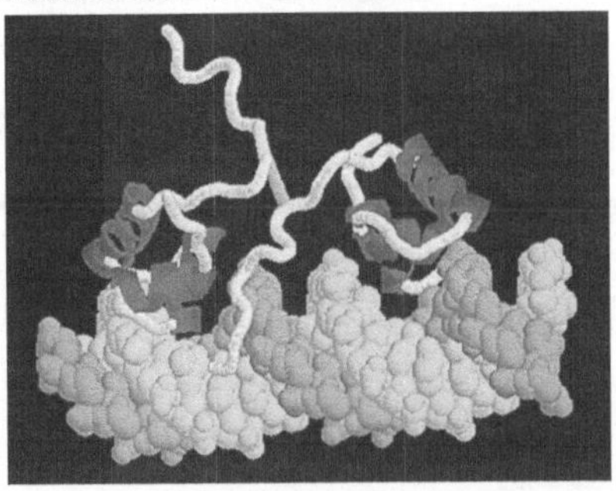

Fig. 8.13: Biological data base
(Source: based on review of literature, 2018)

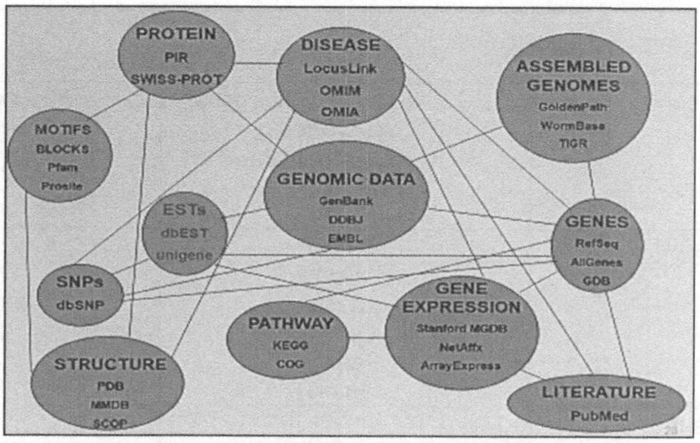

Fig. 8.14: Biological network
(Source: based on review of literature, 2018)

Use of Molecular Dynamics Simulation

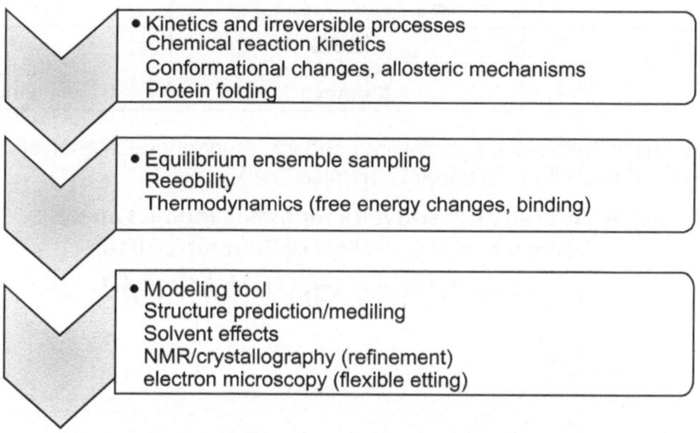

Fig. 8.15: Use of molecular Dynamic System
(Source: based on the review of literature, 2018)

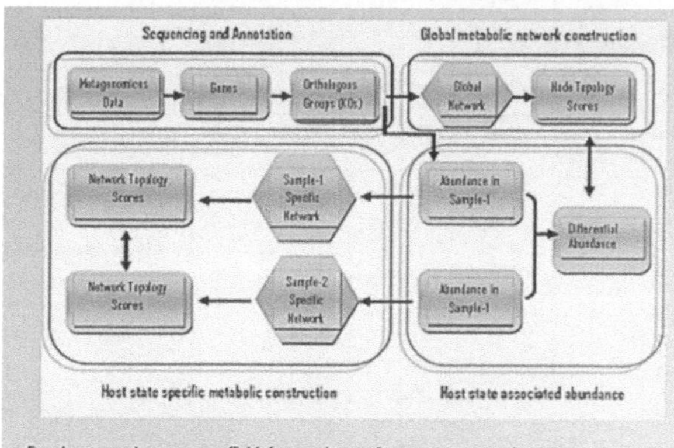

Fig: A comprehensive scaffold for analysis of metagenomics data
(Singh and Shukla, Briefings in Functional Genomics 2014;)

Fig. 8.16: Sequencing of Annotation
(Source: based on review of literature, 2018)

Analysis		Software
Functional Category	COG (Clusters of Orthologous) KO (KEGG Orthology) NOG (Non Superviaed orthologous group) Subsystem	MEGAN METAREP MG-RAST
Taxonomic Analysis	Domain Phylumn Class Order Family Gemis	QIIME MOTHUR MLST
Clustering	Out (Operational Taxonomic unit) table Tree Building Alpha-diveraity Beta-diveraity Taxonomic composition Rank-A bundance	Galaxy IMGM MEGAN
Pathways	KEGG SEED Metacys	CAMERA MetaLook Unifrae

Table: sophisticated techniques and software used for metagenomics analysis (Sing and Shukla, Briefings in Functional Genomics 2014)

Fig. 8.17: Statistical software for metagenomics analysis
(Source: based on review of literature, 2018)

Case study on HMGCR

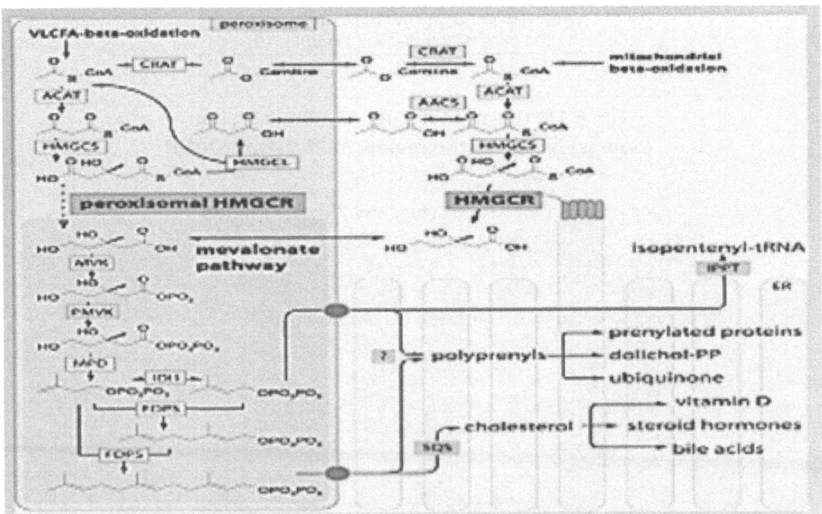

Figure showing the involvement of peroxisomal HMGCR in mevalonate pathway (Reproduced from krisans et al. 2002 with his kind permission)

Fig. 8.18: Case study of peroxisomal HMGCR
(Source: based on review of literature, 2018)

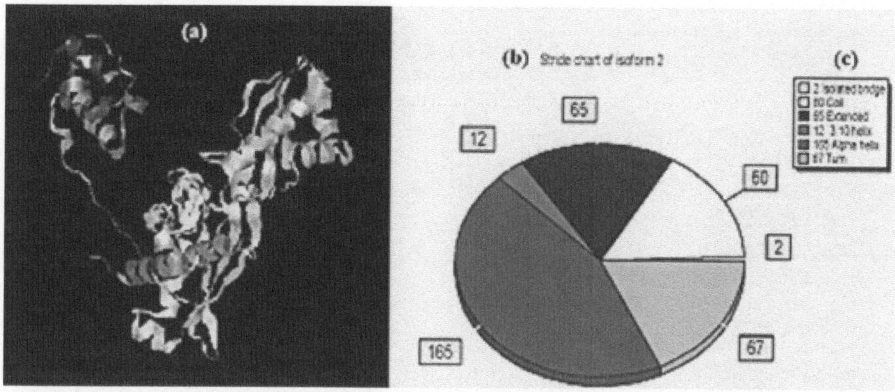

(a) Systematic ribbon view representation of 30 structure of HMGCR isoform 2 of H. sapiens. (b) Structure composition of modeled HMGCR isofrom 2 showing different specifications in a form of pie chart. (c) Detailed structure composition where different color represents different type of strucuter.

Fig. 8.19: Systematic ribbon view
(Source: based on review of literature, 2018)

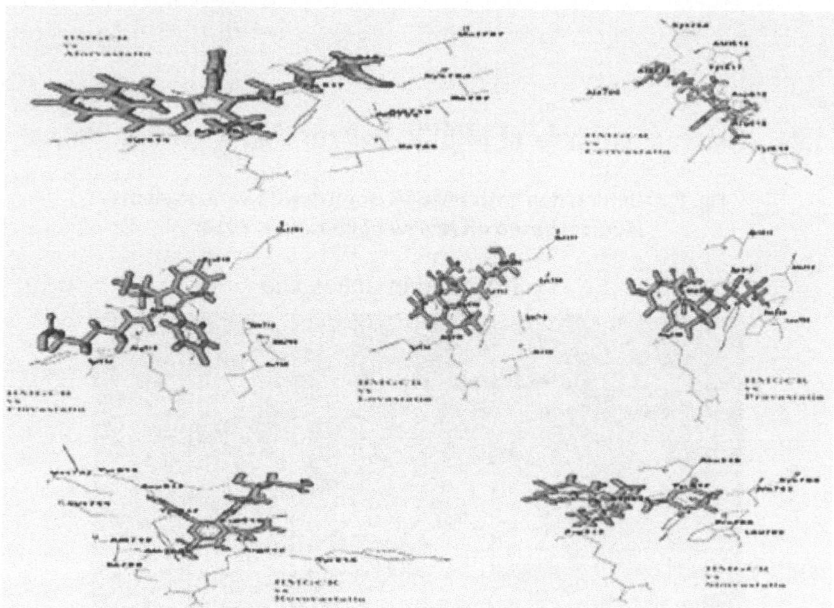

Systematic representation of binding site of HMGCR isform 2 with various statins generated by discovery stodio 2.5.

Fig. 8.20: Systematic representation of binding site
(Source: based on review of literature, 2018)

Atorvastatin	Cerivastatin	Fluvastatin	Lovastatin	Pravastatin	Rosuvastatin	Simvastatin
Tyr514	Tyr514	Tyr514	Tyr514		Tyr514	Tyr514
Arg515	Arg515	Arg515	Arg515	Arg515	Arg515	Arg515
Asp516	Asp516	Asp516	Asp516	Asp516	Asp516	Asp516
Tyr517	Tyr517	Tyr517	Tyr517	Tyr517	Tyr517	Tyr517
Asn518	Asn518	Asn518	Asn518	Asn518	Asn518	Asn518
					Tyr519	
Ala706	Ala706	Ala706				
Ile707						
Ile709		Ile709	Ile709		Ile709	
Ala710	Ala710	Ala710	Ala710		Ala710	
				Leu759		Leu759
				Pro760		Pro760
				Ala763		Ala763
Cys764			Cys764		Cys764	Cys764
Met767		Met767	Met767		Met767	

Table : Interaction table of HMGCR isoform 2 with various statins

Fig. 8.21:Interaction with HMGCR isoform with various stains
(Source: based on review of literature, 2018)

Tyr77 found in active site

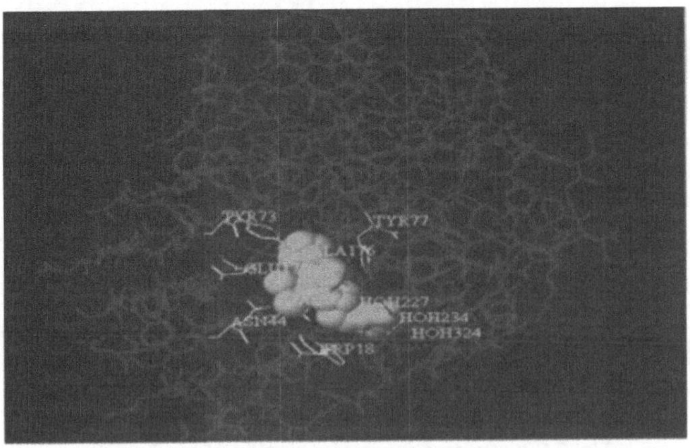

Fig. 8.22: TYR77 found in active site
(Source: based on TYR77)

Systematic representation of binding site of endo-1,4-beta-xylanase (IYNA) with xylobiose and beta-D-xylopyranose. Green dotted lines represent hydrogen bonding interaction between amino acids.

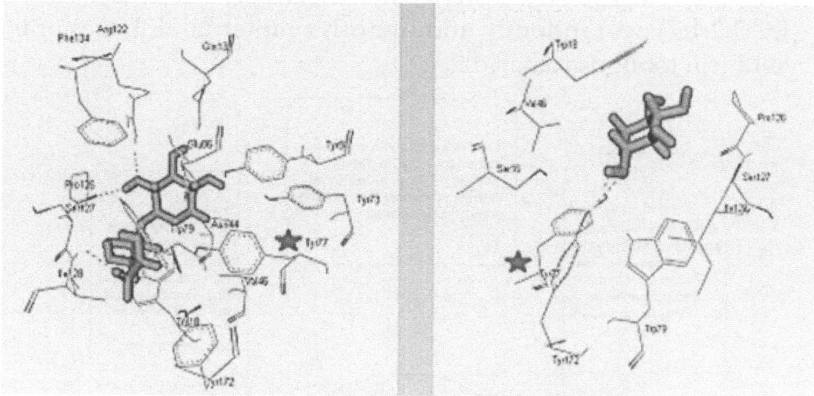

Fig. 8.23: Systematic representation of binding site (Source: based on review of literature, 2018)

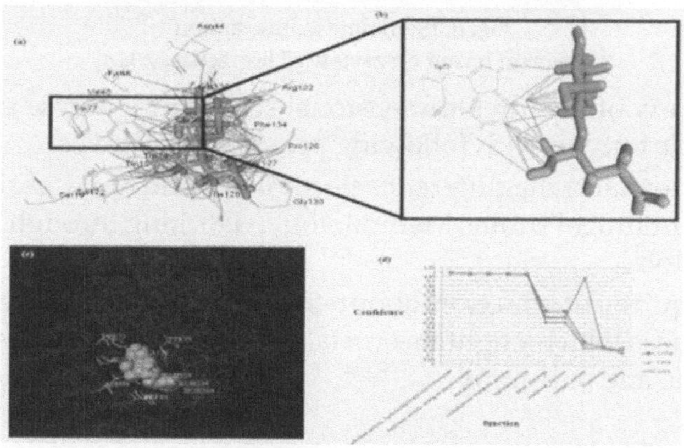

Fig. 8.24: Interaction studies (Source: based on review of literature, 2018)

CASE STUDY OF INULINASE

- Inulin is a non digestible carbohydrate that is found in many plants as a storage carbohydrate which is part of man's daily diet.
- It is a polyfructan consisting of linear β-2,1-linked polyfructose chains, terminated by a glucose residue attached through a sucrose-type linkage, it is present in many regularly consumed vegetables, fruits and cereals, including leek, onion, garlic, wheat, chicory, artichoke and banana.
- Fructose is having more sweetening capacity than table suger, has beneficial effect in diabetic patient and increase iron absorption in children.
- Inulinase is the enzyme which hydrolyzes inulin to produce fructooligosaccharides. Inulinases are of type exo and endo inulinases.

Exoinulinases (EC 3.2.1.80) cleave β-2,1 linkages sequentially starting from the non-reducing end of inulin and split off terminal fructosyl units, releasing fructose with a molecule of glucose, whereasendoinulinases (EC 3.2.1.7) act randomly and hydrolyze internal linkages of inulin to yield fructooligosaccharides.

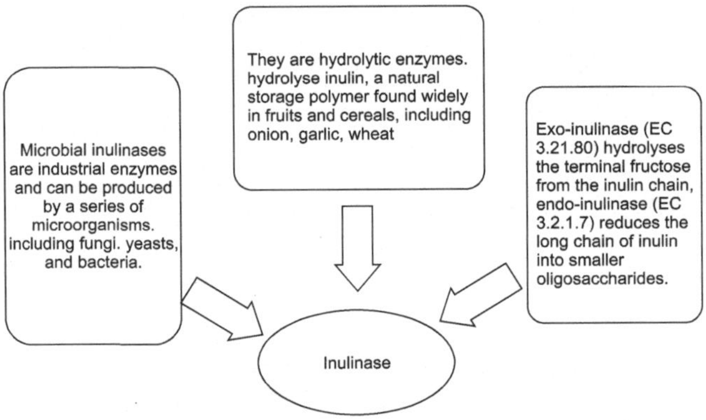

Fig. 8.25: Inulinase interaction
(Source: based on review of literature, 2018)

- The study of the three-dimensional structures of these two enzymes is to be performed with following principal objectives:
- To understand the different selectivity of endo and exoinulinase from different fungal strains Methodology:- Docking through AutoDock and Swissdock
- To acquire information about the energetics of the endo- andexo-inulinases which might be crucial for understanding the interaction of enzyme and substrate.

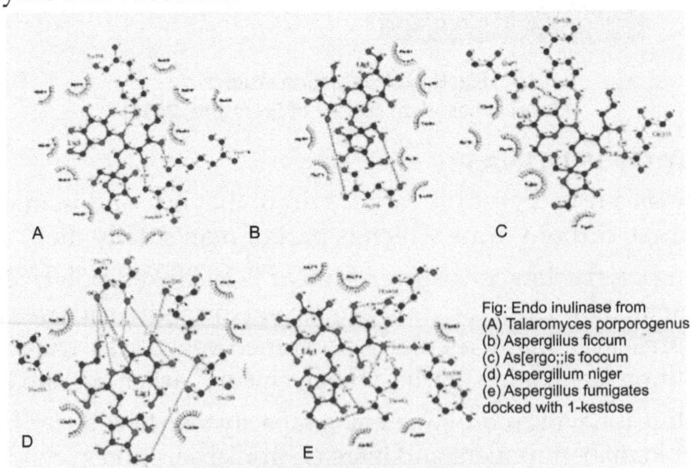

Fig. 8.26: Endo inluinase
(Source: based on review of literature, 2018)

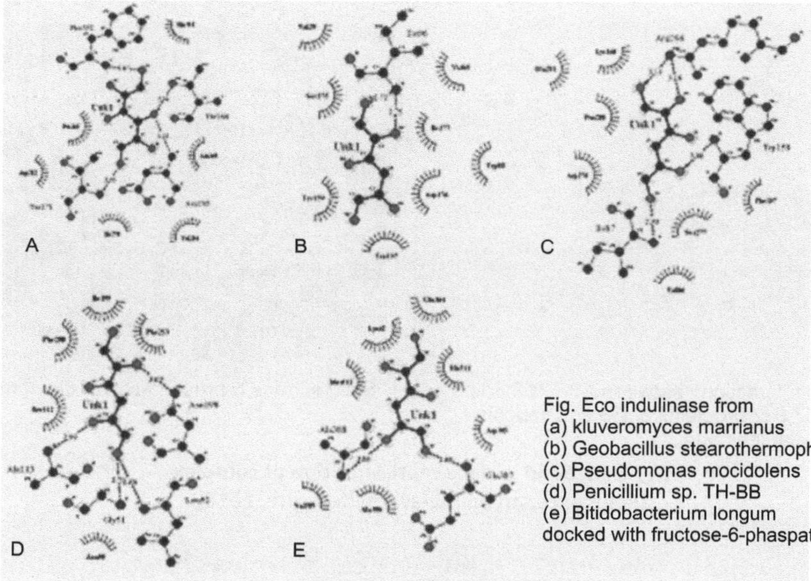

Fig. 8.27: Exoinulinase
(Source: based on review of literature, 2018)

- Study of interaction for both exo- and endo- Inulinase revealed the effective interaction between enzyme and substrate.
- Exo- inulinase binds to its substrate with greater efficiency and with greater stability.
- One of the important thing observed in exo- Inulinase that it forms a pocket size active site which is rich in Asp and Asn, it binds the substrate and is involved in the selection of the substrate.

Structures of saponins

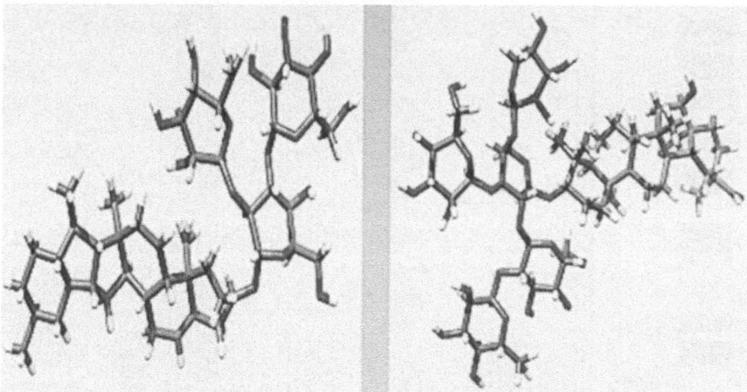

Saponins from solanum tuberosum | Pentacyclic triterpencid saponin from cyclamen coum

Fig. 8.27: Structure of saponins
(Source: based on review of literature, 2018)

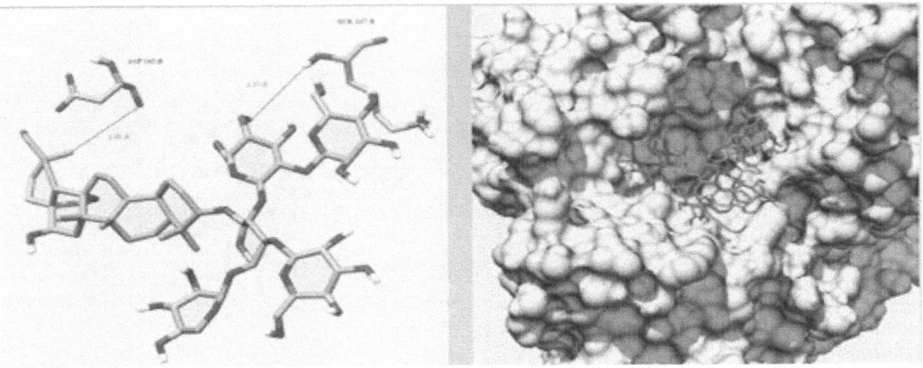

H-bond interactions between ASP 163.8 and SET 167.8 of procteins 3H38 and saponin from cyclamen coun

Solid surface representation of the complex

Fig. 8.28: Solid surface representation of complex (Source: based on review of literature, 2018)

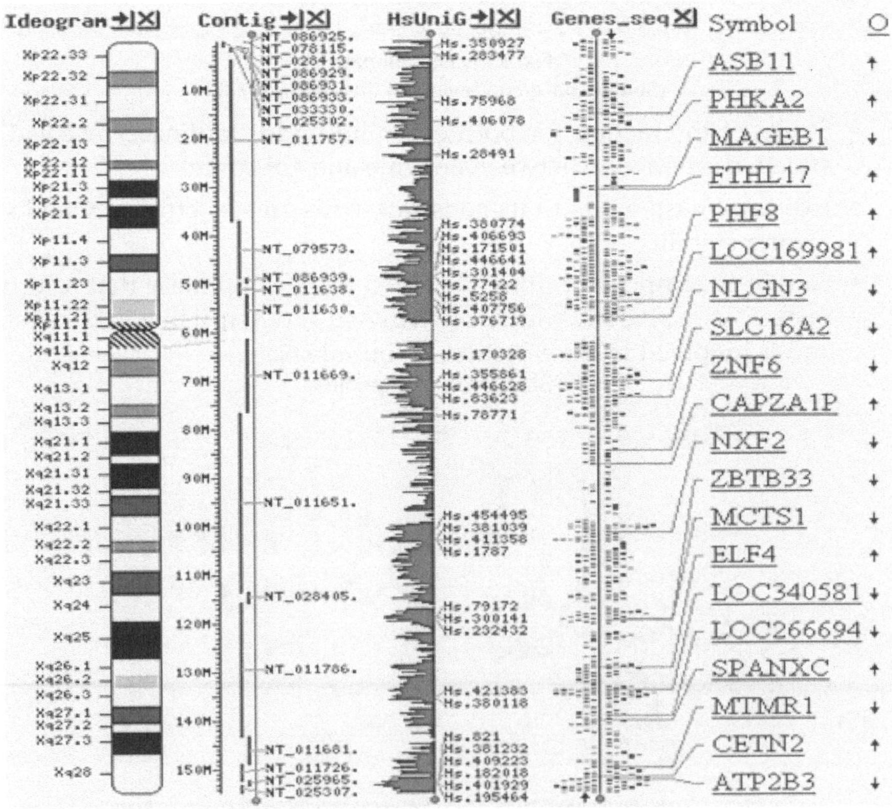

Fig. 8.29: Map of the human X-chromosome (Source: based on review of literature, 2018)

Bioinformatics has become an important part of many areas of biology. In experimental molecular biology, bioinformatics techniques such as image and signal processing allow extraction of useful results from large amounts of raw data. In the field of genetics and genomics, it aids in sequencing and annotating genomes and their observed mutations. It plays a role in the text mining of biological literature and the development of biological and gene ontologies to organize and query biological data. It also plays a role in the analysis of gene and protein expression and regulation. Bioinformatics tools aid in the comparison of genetic and genomic data and more generally in the understanding of evolutionary aspects of molecular biology. At a more integrative level, it helps analyze and catalogue the biological pathways and networks that are an important part of systems biology. In structural biology, it aids in the simulation and modeling of DNA, RNA, proteins as well as biomolecular interactions.Computers became essential in molecular biology when protein sequences became available after Frederick Sanger determined the sequence of insulin in the early 1950s. Comparing multiple sequences manually turned out to be impractical. A pioneer in the field was Margaret Oakley Dayhoff. She compiled one of the first protein sequence databases, initially published as books and pioneered methods of sequence alignment and molecular evolution. Another early contributor to bioinformatics was Elvin A. Kabat, who pioneered biological sequence analysis in 1970 with his comprehensive volumes of antibody sequences released with Tai Te Wu between 1980 and 1991.To study how normal cellular activities are altered in different disease states, the biological data must be combined to form a comprehensive picture of these activities. Therefore, the field of bioinformatics has evolved such that the most pressing task now involves the analysis and interpretation of various types of data. This includes nucleotide and amino acid sequences, protein domains, and protein structures.[16] The actual process of analyzing and interpreting data is referred to as computational biology. Important sub-disciplines within bioinformatics and computational biology include:

- Development and implementation of computer programs that enable efficient access to, use and management of, various types of information
- Development of new algorithms (mathematical formulas) and statistical measures that assess relationships among members of large data sets. For example, there are methods to locate a gene within a sequence, to predict protein structure and/or function, and to cluster protein sequences into families of related sequences.

The primary goal of bioinformatics is to increase the understanding of biological processes. What sets it apart from other approaches, however, is its focus on developing and applying computationally intensive techniques to achieve this goal. Examples include: pattern recognition, data mining, machine learning algorithms, and visualization. Major research efforts in the field include sequence alignment, gene finding, genome assembly, drug design, drug discovery, protein structure alignment, protein structure prediction, prediction of gene expression and protein–protein interactions, genome-wide association studies, the modeling of evolution and cell division/mitosis.Bioinformatics now entails the creation and advancement of databases, algorithms, computational and statistical techniques, and theory to solve formal and practical problems arising from the management and analysis of biological data.Over the past few decades, rapid developments in genomic and other molecular research technologies and developments in information technologies have combined to produce a tremendous amount of information related to molecular biology. Bioinformatics is the name given to these mathematical and computing approaches used to glean understanding of biological processes.Common activities in bioinformatics include mapping and analysing DNA and protein sequences, aligning DNA and protein sequences to compare them, and creating and viewing 3-D models of protein structures.

Fig. 8.30: Sequence mapping
(Source: based on review of literature, 2018)

CONCLUSION

Since the Phage Ö-X174 was sequenced in 1977, the DNA sequences of thousands of organisms have been decoded and stored in databases. This sequence information is analyzed to determine genes that encode proteins, RNA genes, regulatory sequences, structural motifs, and repetitive sequences. A comparison of genes within a species or between different species can show similarities between protein functions, or relations between species (the use of molecular systematics to construct phylogenetic trees). With the growing amount of data, it long ago became impractical to analyze DNA sequences manually. Today, computer programs such as BLAST are used daily to search sequences from more than 260 000 organisms, containing over 190 billion nucleotides. These programs can compensate for mutations (exchanged, deleted or inserted bases) in the DNA sequence, to identify sequences that are related, but not identical. A variant of this sequence alignment is used in the sequencing process itself.

REFERENCES

Lesk, A. M. (26 July 2013). "Bioinformatics". Encyclopaedia Britannica. Retrieved 17 April 2017.

Sim, A. Y. L.; Minary, P.; Levitt, M. (2012). "Modeling Nucleic Acids". Current Opinion in Structural Biology. 22 (3): 273–278. doi:10.1016/j.sbi.2012.03.012. PMC 4028509/. PMID 22538125.

Dawson, W. K.; Maciejczyk, M.; Jankowska, E. J.; Bujnicki, J. M. (2016). "Coarse-grained Modeling of RNA 3D Structure" (PDF). Methods. 103: 138–156. doi:10.1016/j.ymeth.2016.04.026/.

Kmiecik, S.; Gront, D.; Kolinski, M.; Wieteska, L.; Dawid, A. E.; Kolinski, A. (2016). "Coarse-Grained Protein Models and Their Applications". Chemical Reviews. 116: 7898–936. doi:10.1021/acs.chemrev.6b00163/. PMID 27333362.

Wong, K. C. (2016). Computational Biology and Bioinformatics: Gene Regulation. CRC Press/Taylor & Francis Group. ISBN 9781498724975.

Joyce, A. P.; Zhang, C.; Bradley, P.; Havranek, J. J. (2015). "Structure-Based Modeling of Protein: DNA specificity". Briefings in Functional Genomics. 14 (1): 39–49. doi:10.1093/bfgp/elu044/. PMC 4366589/. PMID 25414269.

Spiga, E.; Degiacomi, M. T.; Dal Peraro, M. (2014). "New Strategies for Integrative Dynamic Modeling of Macromolecular Assembly". In Karabencheva-Christova, T. Biomolecular Modelling and Simulations. Advances in Protein Chemistry and Structural Biology. 96. Academic Press. pp. 77–111. doi:10.1016/bs.apcsb.2014.06.008.

"Protein–peptide Docking: Opportunities and Challenges". Drug Discovery Today. 2018-05-04. doi:10.1016/j.drudis.2018.05.006. ISSN 1359-6446.

Hogeweg P (2011). Searls, David B., ed. "The Roots of Bioinformatics in Theoretical Biology". PLoS Computational Biology. 7 (3): e1002021. Bibcode:2011PLSCB...7E2021H. doi:10.1371/journal.pcbi.1002021. PMC 3068925/. PMID 21483479.

Hesper B, Hogeweg P (1970). "Bioinformatica: eenwerkconcept". 1 (6). Kameleon: 28–29.

Hogeweg P (1978). "Simulating the Growth of Cellular Forms". Simulation. 31 (3): 90–96. doi:10.1177/003754977803100305.

Moody, Glyn (2004). Digital Code of Life: How Bioinformatics is Revolu-tionizing Science, Medicine and Business. ISBN 978-0-471-32788-2.

Dayhoff, M.O. (1966) Atlas of Protein Sequence and Structure. National Biomedical Research Foundation, 215 pp.

Eck RV, Dayhoff MO (1966). "Evolution of the Structure of Ferredoxin Based on Living Relics of Primitive Amino Acid Sequences". Science. 152 (3720): 363–6. Bibcode: 1966Sci...152.363E. doi:10.1126/science.152.3720.363. PMID 17775169.

Johnson G, Wu TT (January 2000). "Kabat Database and Its Applications: 30 Years After the First Variability Plot". Nucleic Acids Res. 28 (1): 214–218. doi:10.1093/nar/28.1.214. PMC 102431/. PMID 10592229.

Attwood TK, Gisel A, Eriksson NE, Bongcam-Rudloff E (2011). "Concepts, Historical Milestones and the Central Place of Bioinformatics in Modern Biology: A European Perspective". Bioinformatics – Trends and Methodologies. InTech. Retrieved 8 Jan 2012.

Sanger F, Air GM, Barrell BG, Brown NL, Coulson AR, Fiddes CA, Hutchison CA, Slocombe PM, Smith M (February 1977). "Nucleotide Sequence of Bacteriophage phi X174 DNA". Nature. 265 (5596): 687–95. Bibcode:1977Natur.265..687S. doi:10.1038/265687a0. PMID 870828.

Benson DA, Karsch-Mizrachi I, Lipman DJ, Ostell J, Wheeler DL (January 2008). "GenBank". Nucleic Acids Res. 36 (Database issue): D25–30. doi:10.1093/nar/gkm929. PMC 2238942/. PMID 18073190.

Fleischmann RD, Adams MD, White O, Clayton RA, Kirkness EF, Kerlavage AR, Bult CJ, Tomb JF, Dougherty BA, Merrick JM (July 1995). "Whole-genome Random Sequencing and Assembly of Haemophilus Influenzae Rd". Science. 269 (5223): 496–512. Bibcode:1995Sci...269..496F. doi:10.1126/science.7542800. PMID 7542800.

Carvajal-Rodríguez A (2012). "Simulation of Genes and Genomes Forward in Time". Current Genomics. Bentham Science Publishers Ltd. 11 (1): 58–61. doi:10.2174/138920210790218007. PMC 2851118/. PMID 20808525.

Brown, TA (2002). "Mutation, Repair and Recombination". Genomes (2nd ed.). Manchester (UK): Oxford.

Carter, N. P.; Fiegler, H.; Piper, J. (2002). "Comparative Analysis of Comparative Genomic Hybridization Microarray Technologies: Report of a Workshop Sponsored by the Wellcome trust". Cytometry, Part A. 49 (2): 43–8. doi:10.1002/cyto.10153.

Chaudhari Narendrakumar M., Kumar Gupta Vinod, Dutta Chitra (2016). "BPGA-an Ultra-fast pan-genome Analysis Pipeline". Scientific Reports. 6. Bibcode: 2016NatSR...624373C. doi:10.1038/srep24373.

Ionescu-Tîrgovi°te, Constantin; Gagniuc, Paul Aurelian; Guja, Cristian. "Structural Properties of Gene Promoters Highlight More than Two Phenotypes of Diabetes". PLOS ONE. 10 (9): e0137950. Bibcode: 2015PLoSO..1037950I. doi:10.1371/journal.pone. 0137950. PMC 4574929. PMID 26379145.

Aston KI (2014). "Genetic Susceptibility to Male Infertility: News from Genome-wide Association Studies". Andrology. 2 (3): 315–21. doi:10.1111/j.2047-2927.2014.00188.x. PMID 24574159.

Véron A, Blein S, Cox DG (2014). "Genome-wide Association Studies and the Clinic: A Focus on Breast Cancer". Biomarkers in Medicine. 8 (2): 287–96. doi:10.2217/bmm.13.121. PMID 24521025.

Tosto G, Reitz C (2013). "Genome-wide Association Studies in Alzheimer's Disease: A Review". Current Neurology and Neuroscience Reports. 13 (10): 381. doi:10.1007/s11910-013-0381-0. PMC 3809844. PMID 23954969.

Genetics and Bioengineering : *Concepts and Issues* **Pages 167-188**
Edited by: **Dr. Ashok K. Rathoure and Dr. Pawan Kumar 'Bharti'**
ISBN: 978-93-86841-92-6
Edition: **2019**
Published by: **Discovery Publishing House Pvt. Ltd., New Delhi (India)**

9

Tools for Recombinant Antibody Production

[1]Prasann Kumar, [2]Shweta Pathak

ABSTARCT

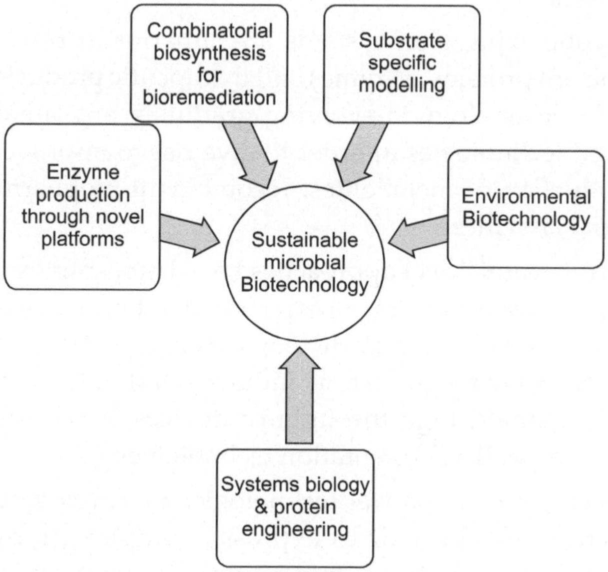

Keywords: Antibody, Biotic,Crop, Disease, Tool

INTRODUCTION

- Recombinant bio-therapeutic proteins such as hormones, growth factors, cytokines and monoclonal antibodies play an important role in modern medicine.

[1] Division of Research and Development Department of Agronomy, School of Agriculture, Lovely Professional University, Jalandhar, Punjab, 144411, India
[2] Department of Plant Physiology, I. Ag. Sci., BHU., Varanasi, 221005, U.P., India

- Continuously cultured animal cells (CHO) are unable to completely oxidize glucose to CO_2 and H_2O due to low activity/absence of the key enzyme pyruvate carboxylase (PC).
- PC connects glycolysis to the tricarboxylic acid (TCA) cycle in metabolic pathway of the recombinant cells and generates energy in the form of ATP.
- Low enzyme activity leads to acidification of the medium, due to accumulation of high concentration of Lactate.
- Lactate accumulation can be reduced by Cell Engineering & Process optimization.

Advanced Technologies for Improved Expression of Recombinant Proteins in Bacteria

- Prokaryotic expression systems are superior in producing valuable recombinant proteins, enzymes and therapeutic products. Conventional microbial technology is evolving gradually and amalgamated with advanced technologies in order to give rise to improved processes for the production of metabolites, recombinant biopharmaceuticals and industrial enzymes.
- Recently, several novel approaches have been employed in a bacterial expression platform to improve recombinant protein expression. These approaches involve metabolic engineering, use of strong promoters, novel vector elements such as inducers and enhancers, protein tags, secretion signals, high-throughput devices for cloning and process screening as well asfermentation technologies.
- Advancement of the novel technologies in *E. coli* systems led to the production of "difficult to express" complex products including small peptides, antibody fragments, few proteins and full-length aglycosylated monoclonal antibodies in considerable large quantity. Wacker's secretion technologies, Pfenex system, inducers, cell-free systems, strain engineering for post-translational modification, such as disulfide bridging and bacterial N-glycosylation, are still under evaluation for the production of complex proteins and peptidesin E. coli in an efficient manner.
- Here, we will discuss expression technologies developed in recent times for enhanced production of heterologous proteins in *E. coli* which are of foremost importance for diverse applications in microbiology and biopharmaceutical production.

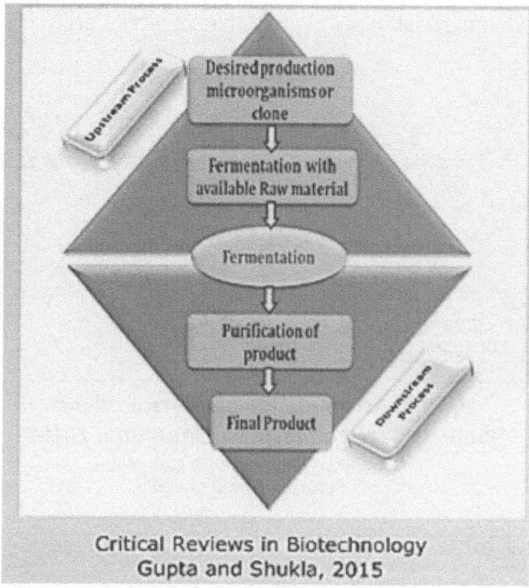

Fig. 9.1: A customary protein production process (Source: Gupta and Shukla, 2015)

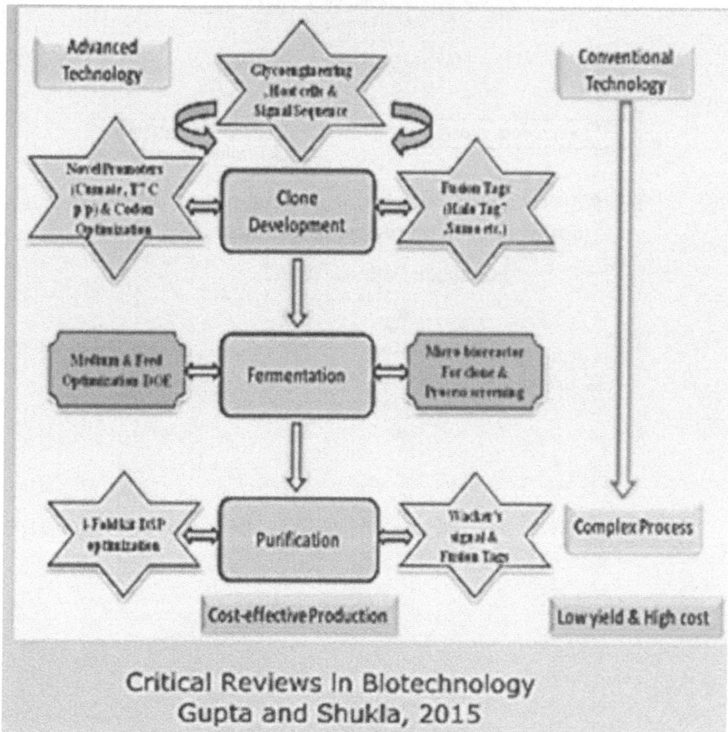

Fig. 9.2: An outline of proposed technology innovation in E.coli (Source: Gupta and Shukla, 2015)

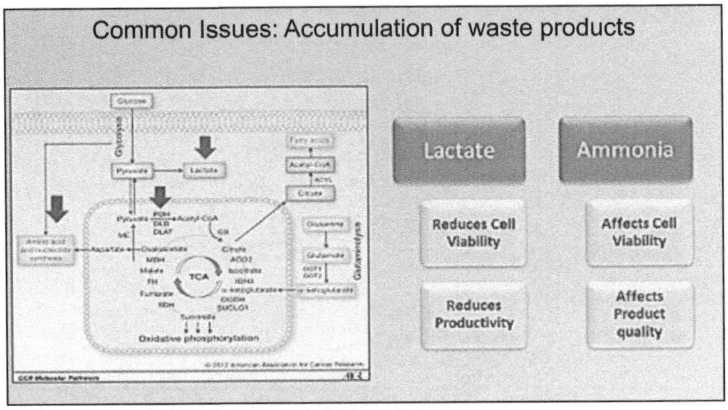

Fig. 9.3: Accumulation of waste products
(Source: based on review of literature, 2018)

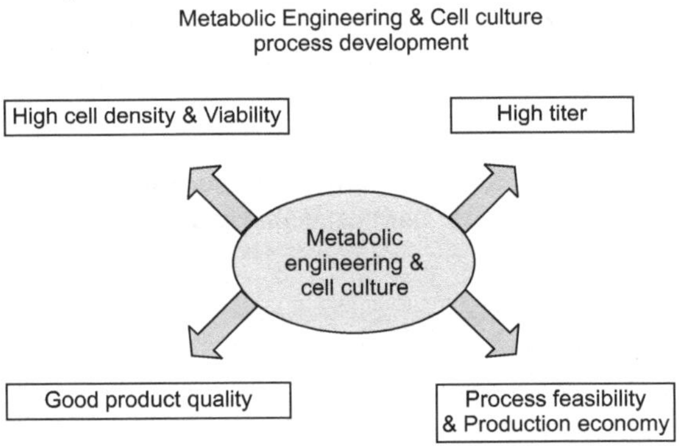

Fig. 9.4: Metabolic engineering and cell culture process
(Source: based on review of literature, 2018)

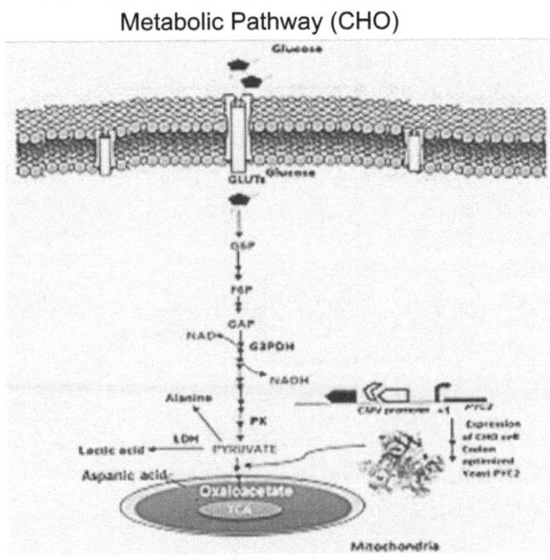

Fig. 9.5: Metabolic pathway CHO
(Source: based on review of literature, 2018)

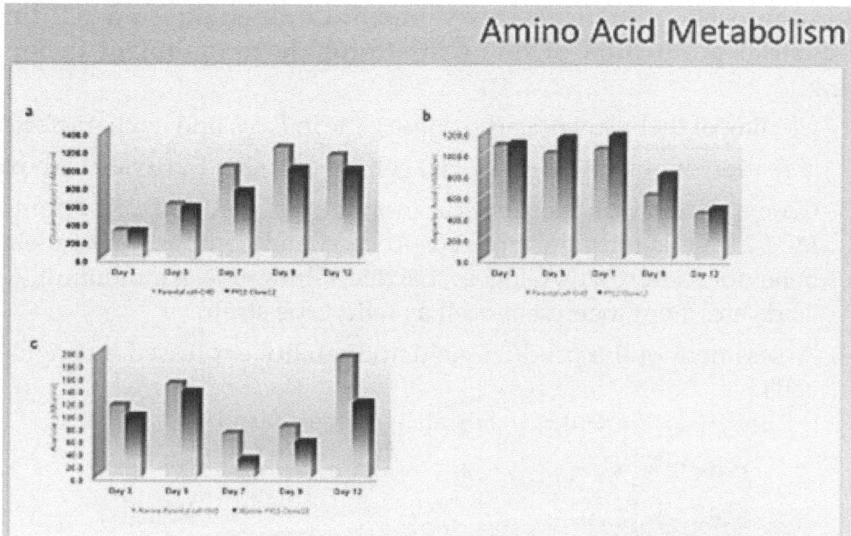

Amino acid analysis of spent medium, concentration of the ghtanic acid, and alanine profile of parental CHO cells and cloe# 12 grown in a fed-batch culture cuture at different time interval. (a) Glutamic acid (b) Aspartic acid (e) Alnine

Fig. 9.6: Amino acid metabolism
(Source: based on review of literature, 2018)

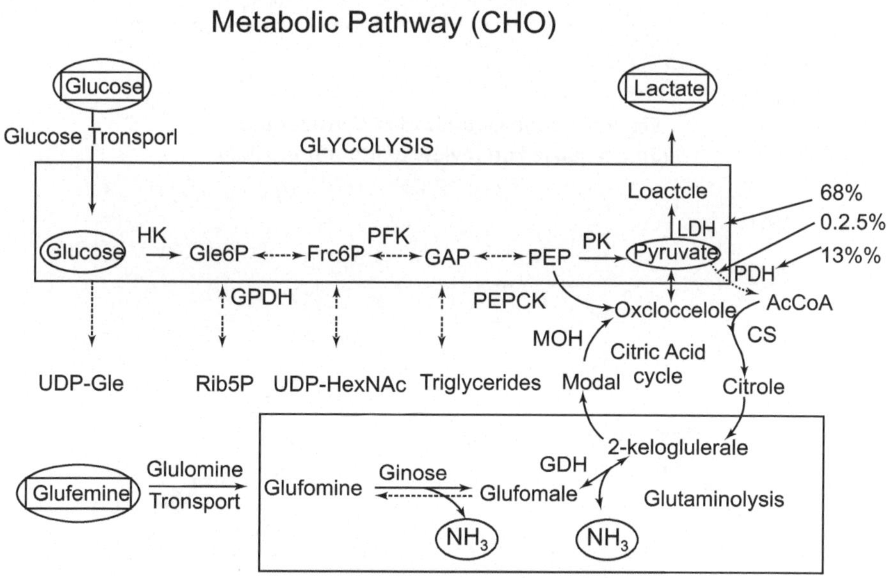

Fig. 9.7: Metabolic pathways CHO
(Source: based on review of literature, 2018)

Our approach & strategy -Development of an engineered cell line for the industrial production of low cost affordable recombinant therapeutic proteins

1. Cloning of thePyruvate carboxylase gene in *E.coli* and its characterization
2. Creation of an engineered CHO cells expressing Pyruvate carboxylase
3. Co-expression of therapeutic monoclonal antibody in engineered PC-CHOcells for an optimized process, and comparison of metabolic behavior (cellgrowth, Glucose, Lactate, Glutamine, Ammonium, Amino acids etc.of engineered as well as wild type strain
4. Assessment of the product yield and quality expressed by engineered cells

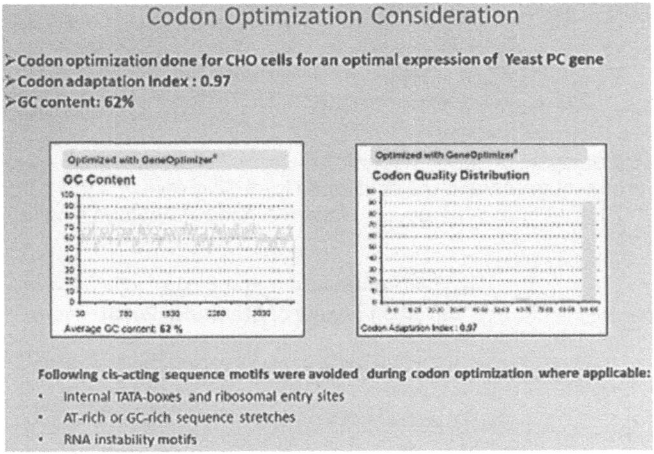

Fig. 9.8: Codon Optimization Consideration
(Source: Based on review of literature, 2018)

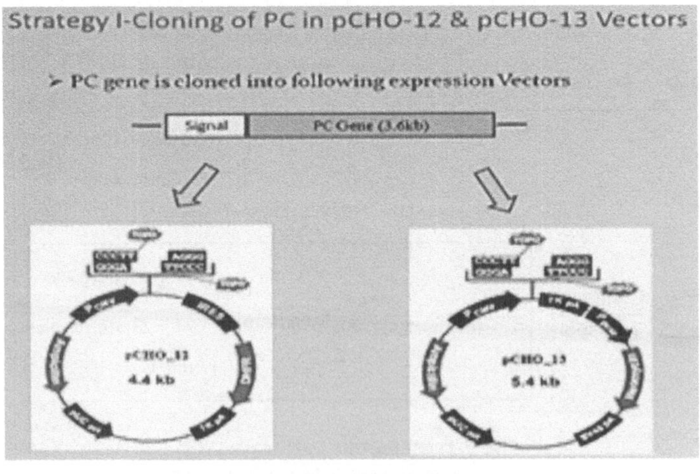

Fig. 9.9: Cloning of PC
(Source: based on review of literature, 2018)

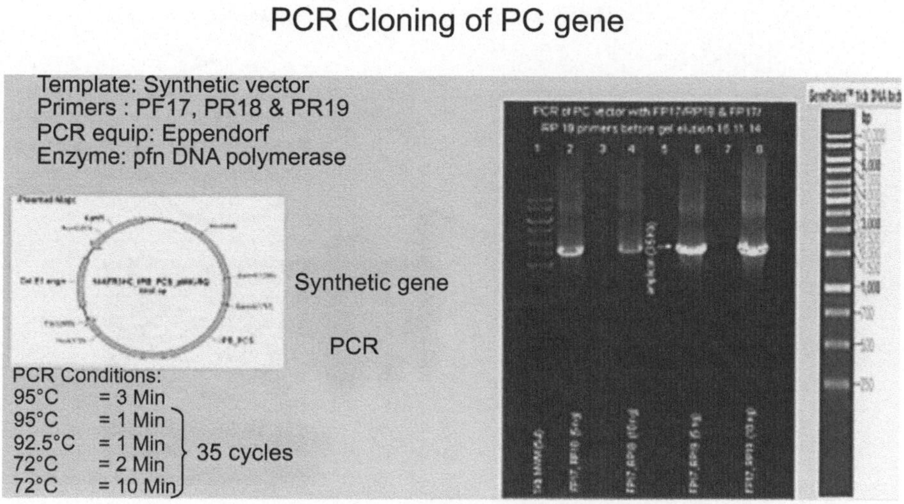

Fig. 9.10: PCR cloning of PC gene
(Source: based on review of literature, 2018)

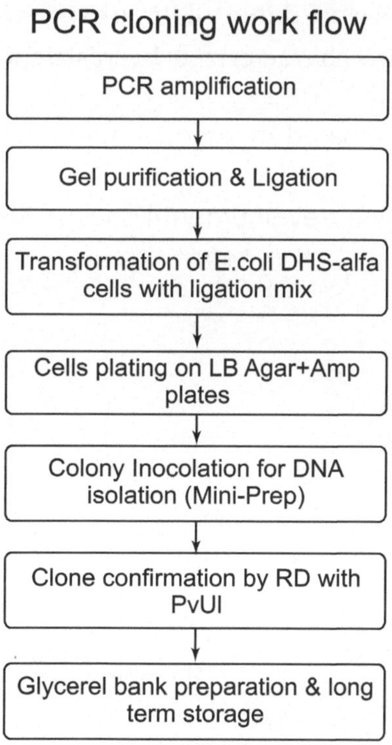

Fig. 9.11: PCR cloning working flow
(Source: based on review of literature, 2018)

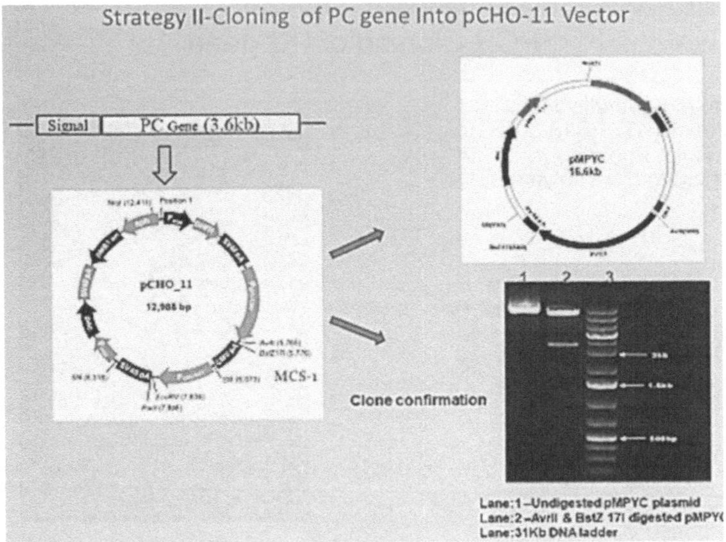

Fig. 9.12: Cloning of PC gene into pCHO-11 Vector
(Source: based on review of literature, 2018)

- The PC gene was cloned into all three expression vectors, successfully
- The vectors were characterized by restriction digestion and DNA sequencing
- Plasmid DNA prepared in large amount for Linear Transfection into CHO cells

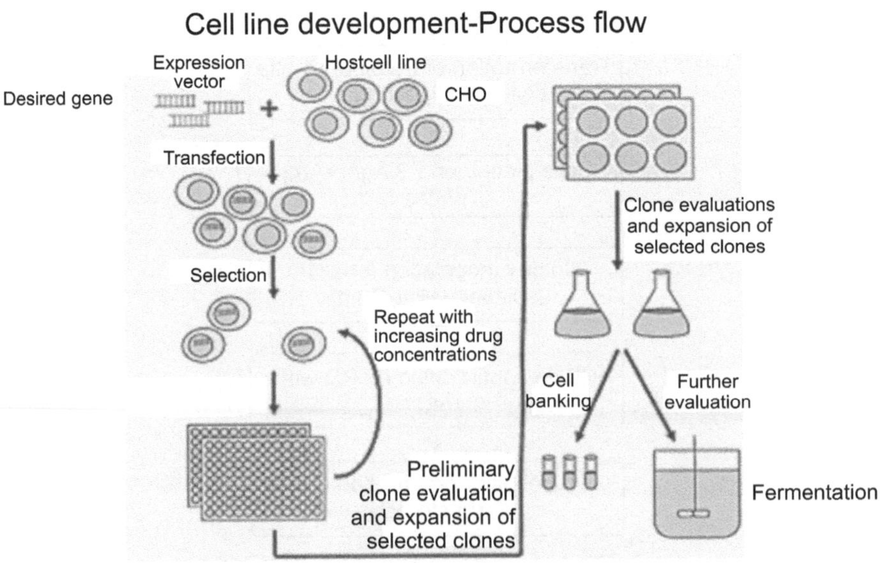

Fig. 9.13: Cell line development- Process Flow
(Source: based on review of literature, 2018)

PC Transfection-Methodology

- Cell Line/Host : CHO-S cell line (Invitrogen)
- Vector Construct : pCHO12_PC & pCHO13_PC
- Method : Neon Electroporation
- Transfection Condition : 1500V/3P/10mS
- Transfection Media: CD-Forti-CHO + 8mM Glut. in T flasks

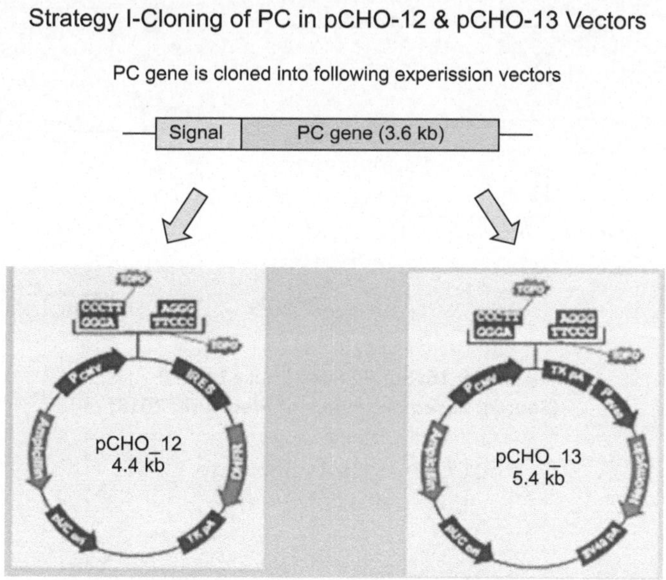

Fig. 9.14: Cloning of PC in pCHO-12 &pCHO-13 Vector
(Source: based on review of literature, 2018)

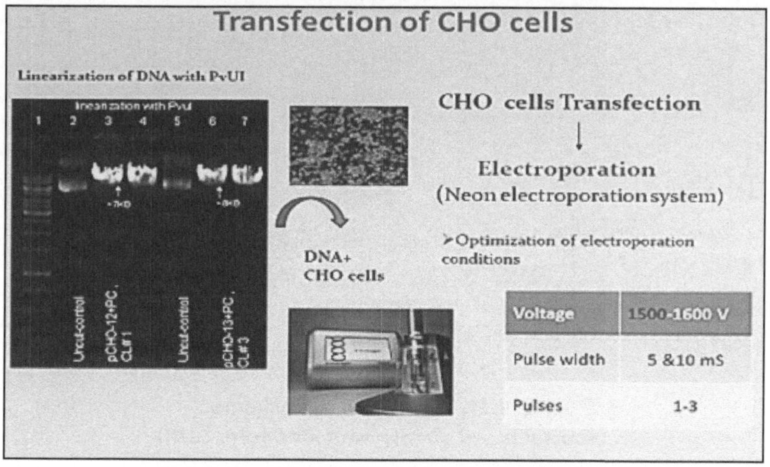

Fig. 9.15: Transfection of CHO cell
(Source: based on review of literature, 2018)

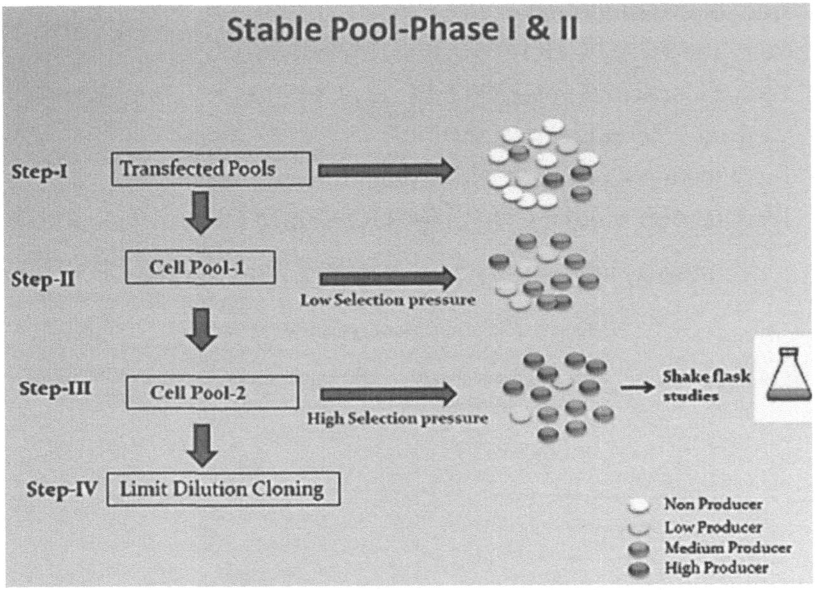

Fig. 9.16: Stable Pool-Phase I and II
(Source: based on review of literature, 2018)

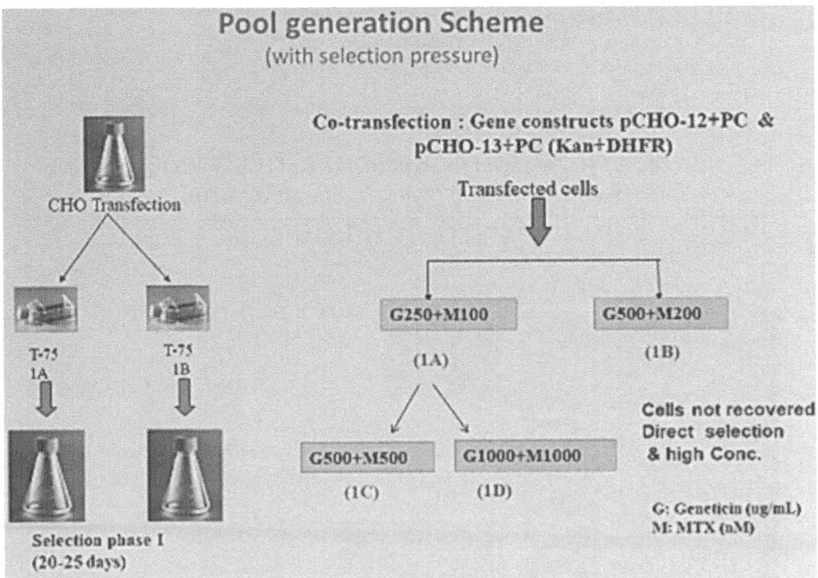

Fig. 9.17: Pool generation scheme
(Source: based on review of literature, 2018)

- No significant PC expression (ELISA) in the cell pool even at higher concentration of the selection pressures

- The vector and host combination didn't work well for PC expression
- To evaluate the protein expression, the second strategy pCHO11Vector with CHO-S cell line is attempted

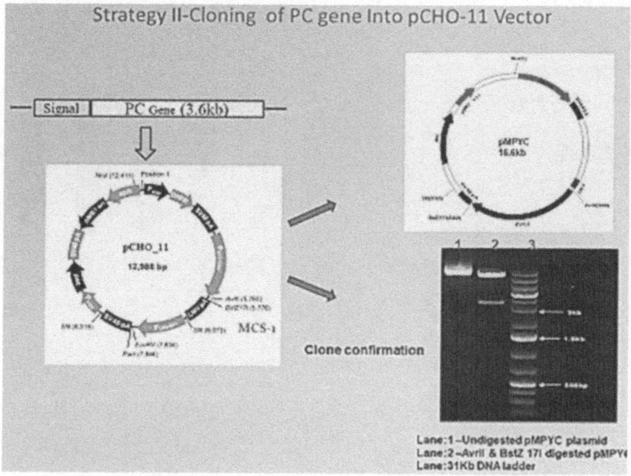

Fig. 9.18: Cloning of PC gene into pCHO-11 Vector
(Source: based on review of literature, 2018)

PC Transfection-Methodology

- Cell Line/Host : CHO-S cell line (Invitrogen)
- Vector Construct : pMPYC-CHO, Clone# 3
- Method : Neon Electroporation
- Transfection Condition : 1500V/3P/10mS
- Transfection Media: CD-Forti-CHO + 8mM Glut. in T flasks

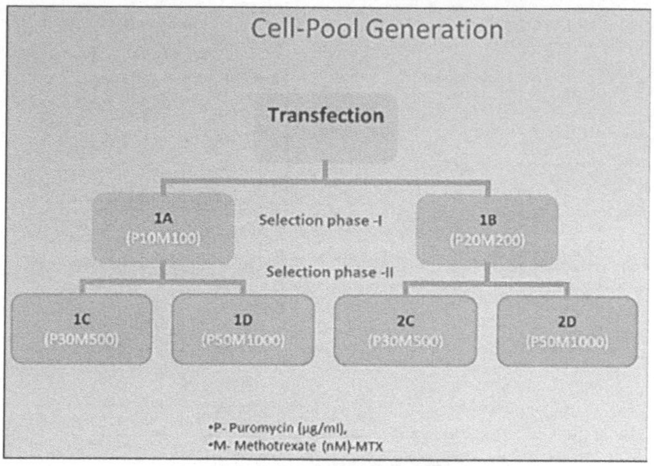

Fig. 9.19: Cell pool generation
(Source: Based on review of literature, 2018)

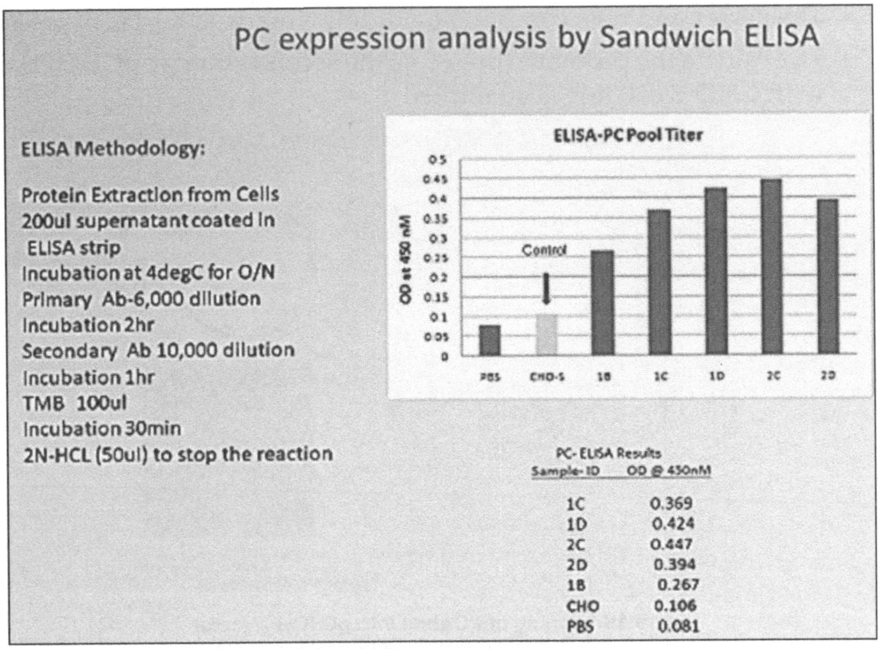

Fig. 9.20: PC expression analysis
(Source: based on review of literature, 2018)

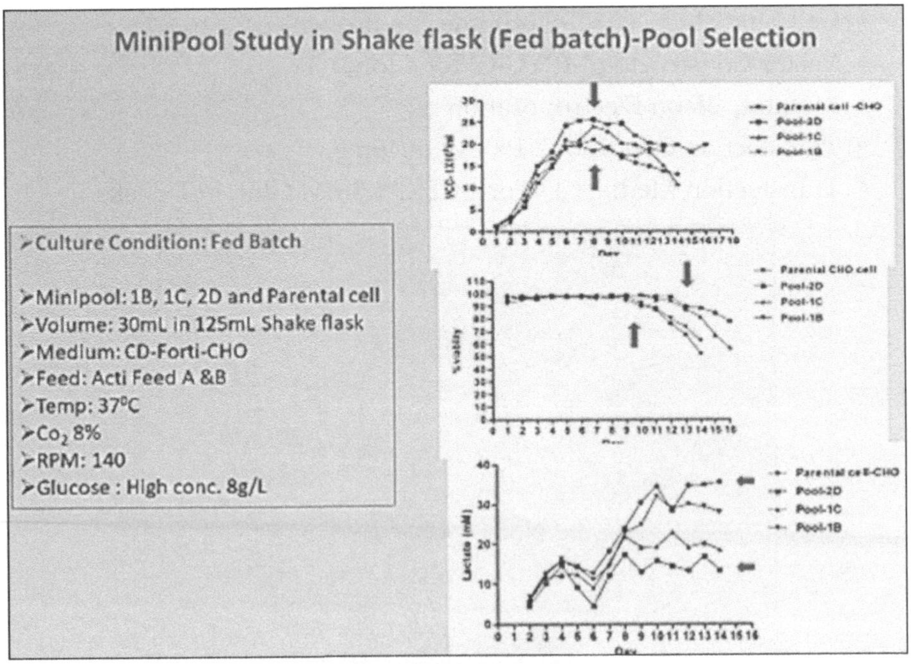

Fig. 9.21: Pool selection
(Source: based onreview of literature, 2018)

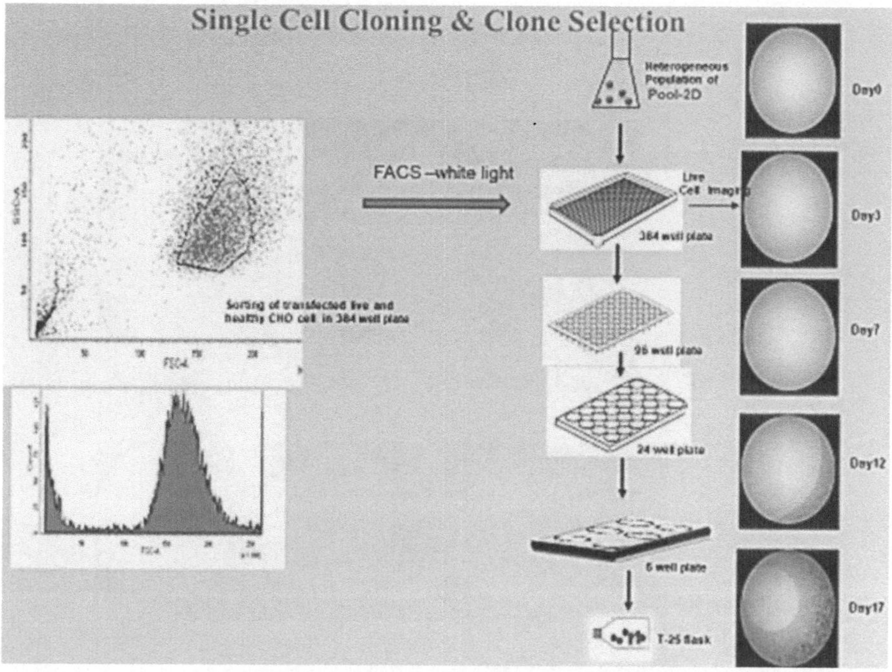

Fig. 9.22: Single cell cloning and clone selection (Source: based on review of literature, 2018)

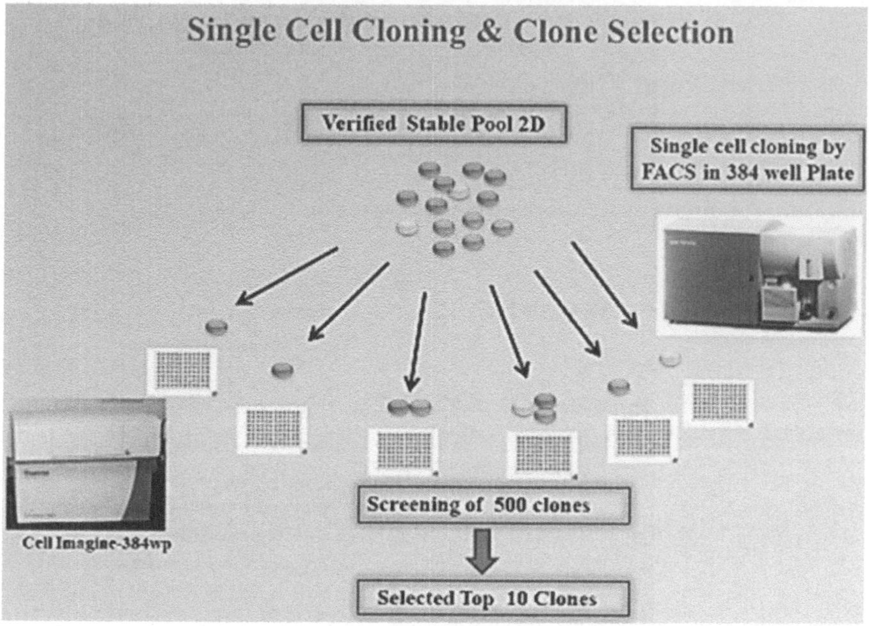

Fig. 9.23: Single cell cloning and clone selection (Source: based on review of literature, 2018)

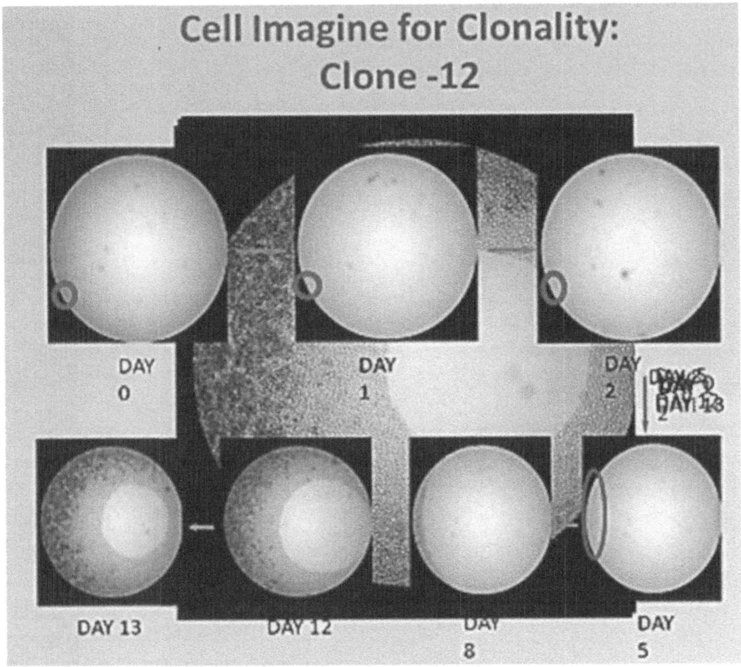

Fig. 9.24: Cell imagine
(Source: based on review of literature, 2018)

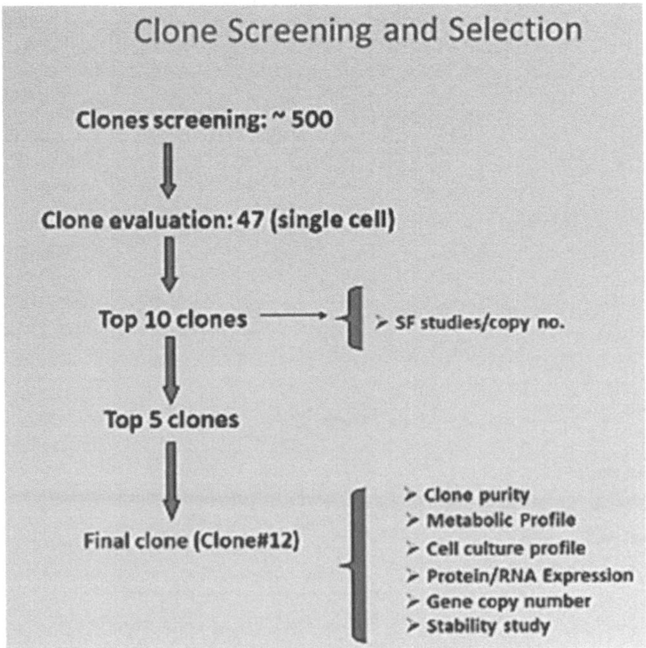

Fig. 9.25: Clone screening
(Source: based on review of literature, 2018)

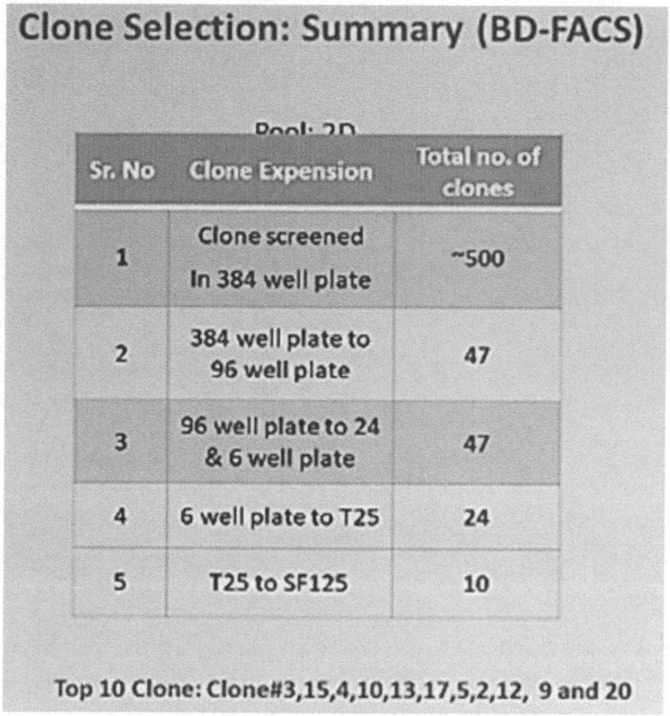

Clone Selection: Summary (BD-FACS)

Pool: 2D

Sr. No	Clone Expension	Total no. of clones
1	Clone screened In 384 well plate	~500
2	384 well plate to 96 well plate	47
3	96 well plate to 24 & 6 well plate	47
4	6 well plate to T25	24
5	T25 to SF125	10

Top 10 Clone: Clone#3,15,4,10,13,17,5,2,12, 9 and 20

Fig. 9.26: Clone selection summary
(Source; based on review of literature, 2018)

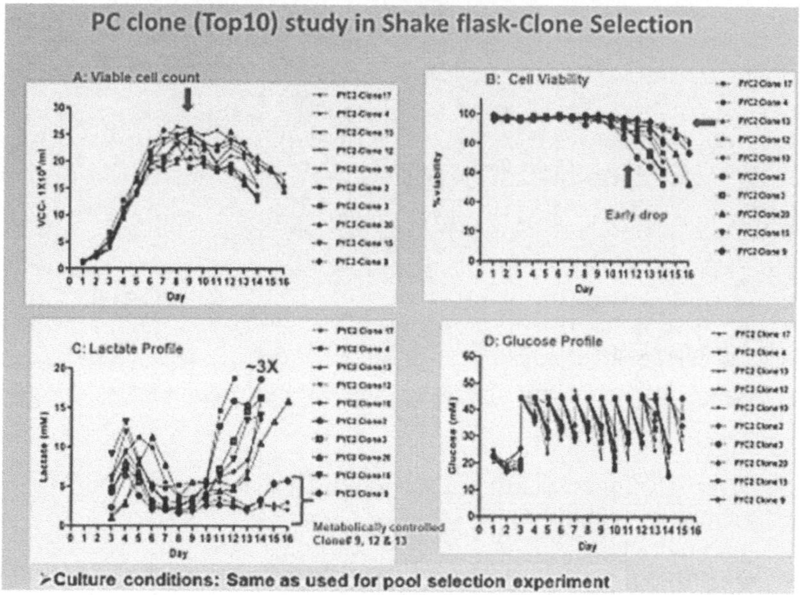

Fig. 9.27: PC clone study
(Source: based on review of literature, 2018)

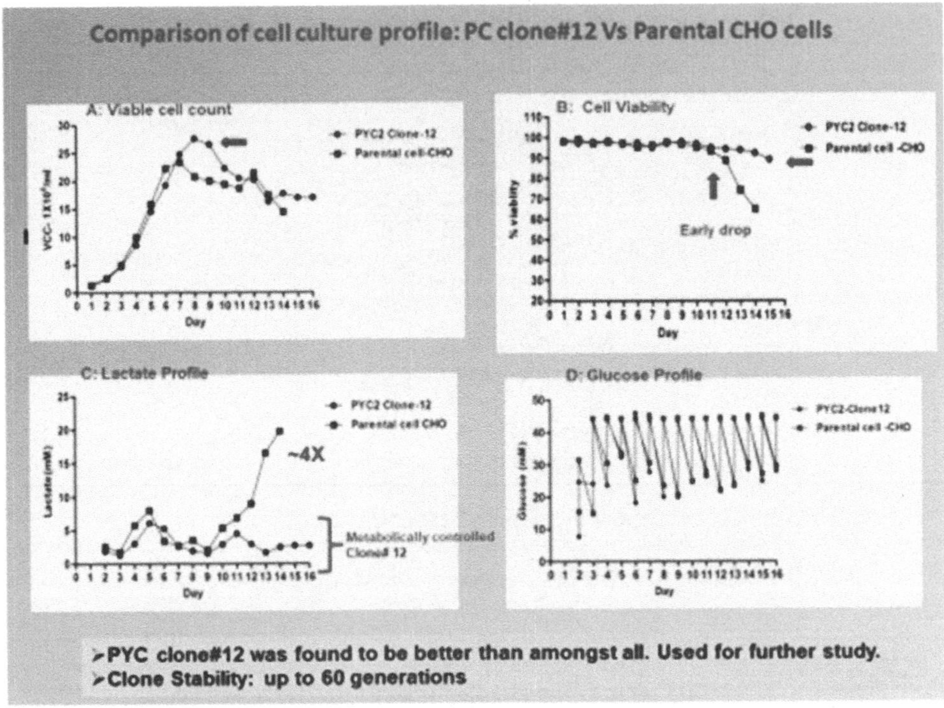

Fig. 9.28: Comparison of cell culture profile
(Source: based on review of literature, 2018)

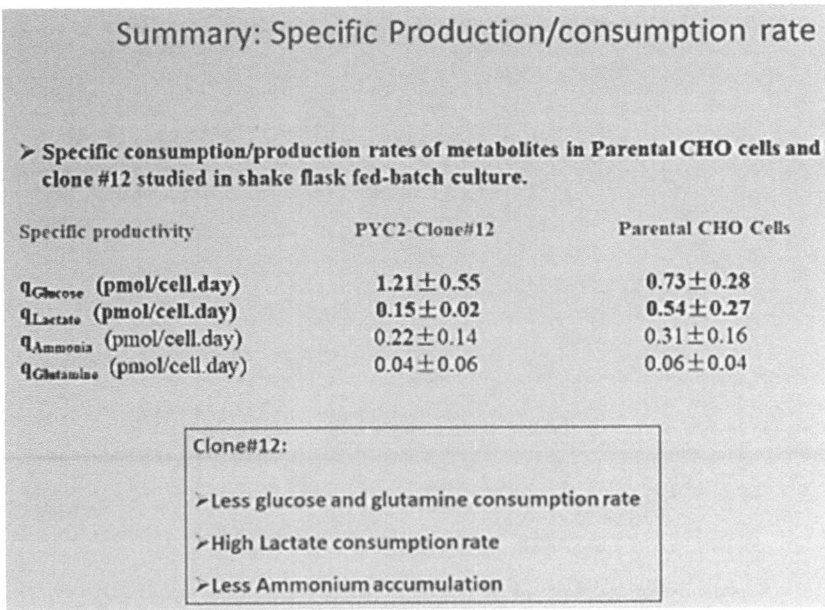

Fig. 9.29: Summary for specific rate and specific production
(Source: based on review of literature, 2018)

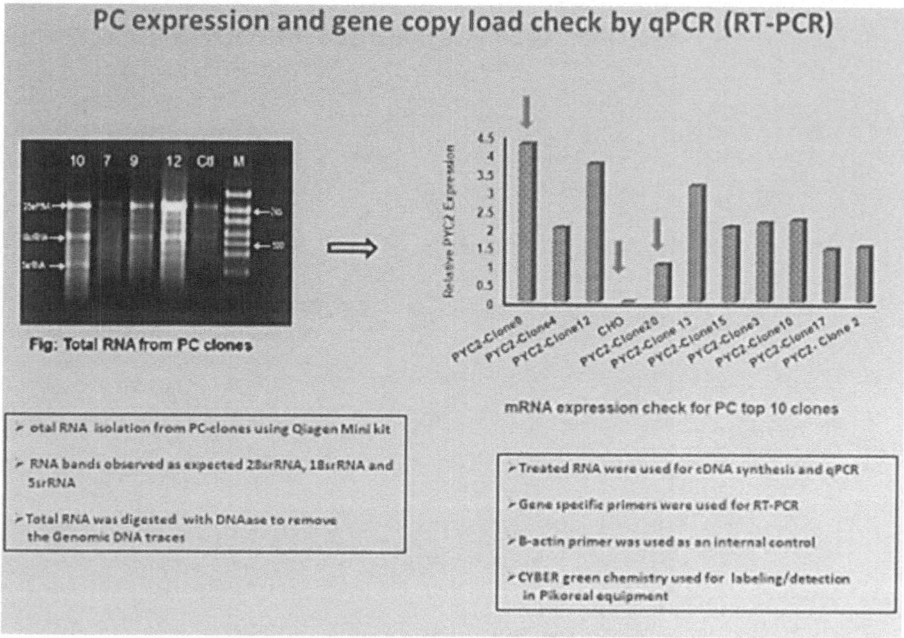

Fig. 9.30: PC expression and gene copy load (Source: based on review of literature, 2018)

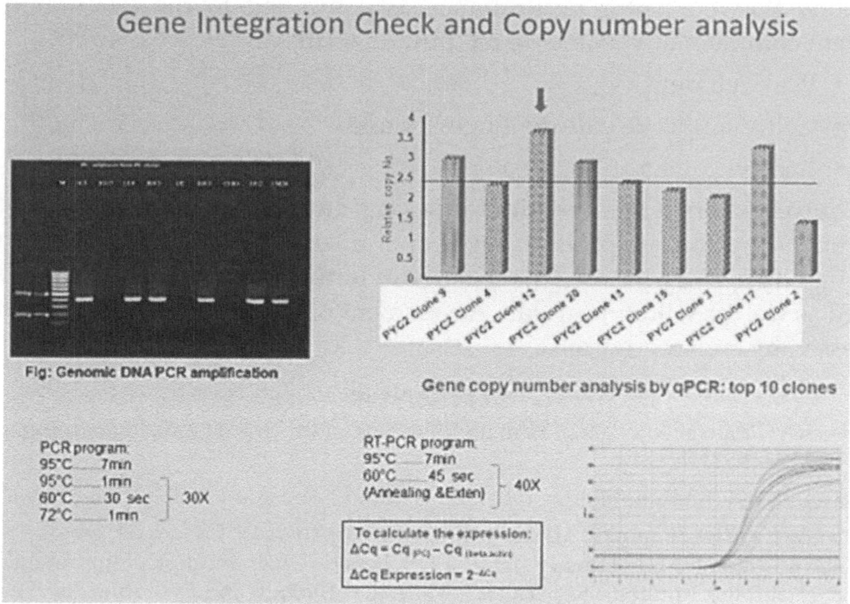

Fig. 9.31: Gene integration check (Source: based on review of literature, 2018)

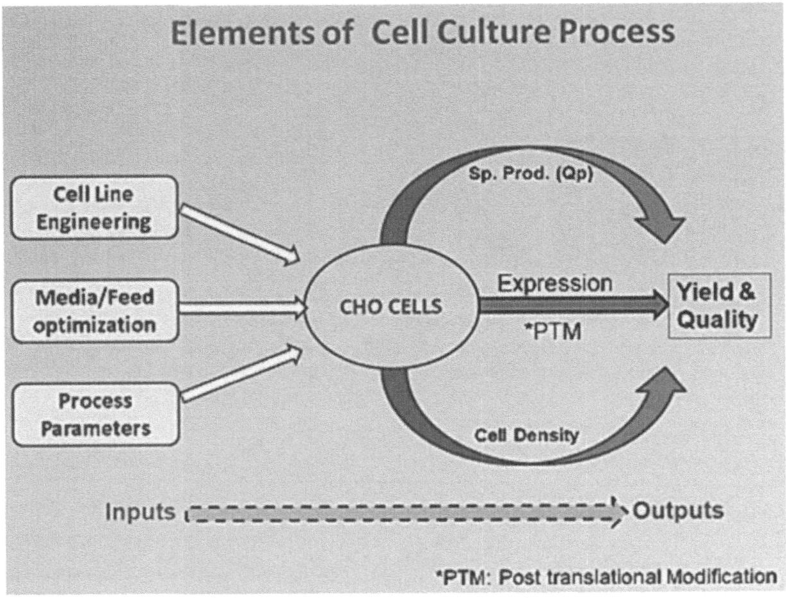

Fig. 9.32: Elements of cell culture
(Source: based on review of literature, 2018)

CONCLUSION

PC clone showed better performance as compared to the Parental cell in different commercially available medium in terms of:

- Peak cell density
- Cell Viability & culture longevity and
- Lactate consumption profile

Co-expression of therapeutic monoclonal antibody in engineered PC-CHO cells for an optimized process, and comparison of metabolic behavior**(Cell growth, Glucose, Lactate, Glutamine, Ammonium, Amino acids etc.)** of engineered as well as wild type strain. Assessment of the product yield and quality expressed by engineered cells.

REFERENCES

Rhoades RA, Pflanzer RG (2002). Human Physiology (4th ed.). Thomson Learning. p. 584. ISBN 978-0-534-42174-8.

Janeway C (2001). Immunobiology (5th ed.). Garland Publishing. ISBN 978-0-8153-3642-6.

Litman GW, Rast JP, Shamblott MJ, Haire RN, Hulst M, Roess W, Litman RT, Hinds-Frey KR, Zilch A, Amemiya CT (January 1993). "Phylogenetic Diversification of Immunoglobulin Genes and the Antibody Repertoire". Molecular Biology and Evolution. **10** (1): 60–72. doi:10.1093/oxfordjournals.molbev.a040000. PMID 8450761.

Maverakis E, Kim K, Shimoda M, Gershwin ME, Patel F, Wilken R, Raychaudhuri S, Ruhaak LR, Lebrilla CB (February 2015). "Glycans in the Immune System and The Altered Glycan

Theory of Autoimmunity: a Critical Review". Journal of Autoimmunity. **57** (6): 1–13. doi:10.1016/j.jaut.2014.12.002. PMC 4340844/. PMID 25578468.

Pier GB, Lyczak JB, Wetzler LM (2004). Immunology, Infection and Immunity. ASM Press. ISBN 978-1-55581-246-1.

Borghesi L, Milcarek C (2006). "From B Cell To Plasma Cell: Regulation of V(D)J Recombination and Antibody Secretion". Immunologic Research. **36** (1–3): 27–32. doi:10.1385/IR:36:1:27. PMID 17337763.

Parker DC (1993). "T cell-dependent B cell Activation". Annual Review of Immunology. **11** (1): 331–60. doi:10.1146/annurev.iy.11.040193.001555. PMID 8476565.

Market E, Papavasiliou FN (October 2003). "V(D)J Recombination and the Evolution of the Adaptive Immune System". PLoS Biology. **1** (1): E16. doi:10.1371/journal.pbio.0000016. PMC 212695/. PMID 14551913.

Williams CM, Galli SJ (May 2000). "The Diverse Potential Effector and Immunoregulatory Roles of Mast Cells in Allergic Disease". The Journal of Allergy and Clinical Immunology. **105**(5): 847–59. doi:10.1067/mai.2000.106485. PMID 10808163.

Diaz M, Casali P (April 2002). "Somatic Immunoglobulin Hypermutation". Current Opinion in Immunology. **14** (2): 235–40. doi:10.1016/S0952-7915(02)00327-8. PMC 4621002/. PMID 11869898.

Maxwell Myer W (2004). Greer JG, Foerster J, Lukens JN, Rodgers GM, Paraskevas F, eds. Wintrobe's Clinical Hematology (11 ed.). Hagerstown, MD: Lippincott Williams & Wilkins. pp. 453–456. ISBN 978-0-7817-3650-3.

Tolar P, Sohn HW, Pierce SK (February 2008). "Viewing the Antigen-Induced Initiation of B-cell Activation in Living Cells". Immunological Reviews. **221** (1): 64–76. doi:10.1111/j.1600-065X.2008.00583.x. PMID 18275475.

Woof JM, Burton DR (February 2004). "Human antibody-Fc receptor interactions illuminated by crystal structures". Nature Reviews. Immunology. **4** (2): 89–99. doi:10.1038/nri1266. PMID 15040582.

Underdown BJ, Schiff JM (1986). "Immunoglobulin A: Strategic Defense Initiative at the Mucosal Surface". Annual Review of Immunology. **4** (1): 389–417. doi:10.1146/annurev.iy.04.040186.002133. PMID 3518747.

Geisberger R, Lamers M, Achatz G (August 2006). "The riddle of the Dual Expression of IgM and IgD". Immunology. **118** (4): 429–37. doi:10.1111/j.1365-2567.2006.02386.x. PMC 1782314/. PMID 16895553.

Chen K, Xu W, Wilson M, He B, Miller NW, Bengtén E, Edholm ES, Santini PA, Rath P, Chiu A, Cattalini M, Litzman J, B Bussel J, Huang B, Meini A, Riesbeck K, Cunningham-Rundles C, Plebani A, Cerutti A (August 2009). "Immunoglobulin D enhances Immune Surveillance by Activating Antimicrobial, Proinflammatory and B Cell-stimulating Programs in Basophils". Nature Immunology. **10** (8): 889–98. doi:10.1038/ni.1748. PMC 2785232/. PMID 19561614.

Goding JW (1978). Allotypes of IgM and IgD Receptors in the Mouse: a Probe for Lymphocyte Differentiation. Contemporary Topics in Immunobiology. **8**. pp. 203–43. doi:10.1007/978-1-4684-0922-2_7. ISBN 978-1-4684-0924-6. PMID 357078.

Lundqvist ML, Middleton DL, Radford C, Warr GW, Magor KE (2006). "Immunoglobulins of the Non-galliform Birds: Antibody Expression and Repertoire in the Duck". Developmental and Comparative Immunology. **30** (1–2): 93–100. doi:10.1016/j.dci.2005.06.019. PMC 1317265/. PMID 16150486.

Berstein RM, Schluter SF, Shen S, Marchalonis JJ (April 1996). "A New High Molecular Weight Immunoglobulin Class from the Carcharhine Shark: Implications for the Properties of the Primordial Immunoglobulin". Proceedings of the National Academy of Sciences of the United States of America. **93** (8): 3289–93. doi:10.1073/pnas.93.8.3289. PMC 39599/. PMID 8622930.

Reth M. "Matching Cellular Dimensions with Molecular Sizes" (PDF).

Mattu TS, Pleass RJ, Willis AC, Kilian M, Wormald MR, Lellouch AC, Rudd PM, Woof JM, Dwek RA (January 1998). "The Glycosylation and Structure of Human Serum IgA1, Fab, and Fc Regions and the Role of N-glycosylation on Fcá Receptor Interactions". The Journal of Biological Chemistry. **273** (4): 2260–72. doi:10.1074/jbc.273.4.2260. PMID 9442070.

Roux KH (October 1999). "Immunoglobulin Structure and Function as Revealed by Electron Microscopy". International Archives of Allergy and Immunology. **120** (2): 85–99. doi:10.1159/000024226. PMID 10545762.

Barclay AN (August 2003). "Membrane Proteins with Immunoglobulin-like Domains—A Master Superfamily of Interaction Molecules". Seminars in Immunology. **15** (4): 215–23. doi:10.1016/S1044-5323(03) 00047-2. PMID 14690046.

Putnam FW, Liu YS, Low TL (April 1979). "Primary Structure of a Human IgA1 Immunoglobulin. IV. Streptococcal IgA1 Protease, Digestion, Fab and Fc fragments, and the Complete Amino Acid Sequence of the Alpha 1 heavy chain". The Journal of Biological Chemistry. **254** (8): 2865–74. PMID 107164.

Al-Lazikani B, Lesk AM, Chothia C (November 1997). "Standard Conformations for the Canonical Structures of Immunoglobulins". Journal of Molecular Biology. **273** (4): 927–48. doi:10.1006/jmbi.1997.1354. PMID 9367782.

North B, Lehmann A, Dunbrack RL (February 2011). "A New Clustering of Antibody CDR Loop Conformations". Journal of Molecular Biology. **406** (2): 228–56. doi:10.1016/j.jmb.2010.10.030. PMC 3065967/. PMID 21035459.

Nikoloudis D, Pitts JE, Saldanha JW (2014). "A Complete, Multi-level Conformational Clustering of Antibody Complementarity-determining Regions". PeerJ. **2** (e456): e456. doi:10.7717/peerj.456. PMC 4103072/. PMID 25071986.

Heyman B (December 1996). "Complement and Fc-receptors in Regulation of the Antibody Response". Immunology Letters. **54** (2–3): 195–9. doi:10.1016/S0165-2478(96)02672-7. PMID 9052877.

Ravetch JV, Bolland S (2001). "IgG Fc receptors". Annual Review of Immunology. **19**(1): 275–90. doi:10.1146/annurev.immunol.19.1.275. PMID 11244038.

Rus H, Cudrici C, Niculescu F (2005). "The Role of the Complement System in Innate Immunity". Immunologic Research. **33** (2): 103–12. doi:10.1385/IR:33:2:103. PMID 16234578.

Racaniello, Vincent (6 October 2009). "Natural Antibody Protects against Viral Infection". Virology Blog. Archived from the Original on 18 November 2010. Retrieved 22 January2010.

Milland J, Sandrin MS (December 2006). "ABO Blood Group and Related Antigens, Natural Antibodies and Transplantation". Tissue Antigens. **68** (6): 459–66. doi:10.1111/j.1399-0039.2006.00721.x. PMID 17176435.

Mian IS, Bradwell AR, Olson AJ (January 1991). "Structure, Function and Properties of Antibody Binding sites". Journal of Molecular Biology. **217** (1): 133–51. doi:10.1016/0022-2836(91)90617-F. PMID 1988675.

Fanning LJ, Connor AM, Wu GE (April 1996). "Development of the Immunoglobulin Repertoire". Clinical Immunology and Immunopathology. **79** (1): 1–14. doi:10.1006/clin.1996.0044. PMID 8612345.

Jump up to:[a] [b] Nemazee D (October 2006). "Receptor Editing in Lymphocyte Development and Central Tolerance". Nature Reviews. Immunology. **6** (10): 728–40. doi:10.1038/nri1939. PMID 16998507.

Peter Parham. "The Immune System. 2nd ed. Garland Science: New York, 2005. pg. 47–62

Mraz M, Dolezalova D, Plevova K, StanoKozubik K, Mayerova V, Cerna K, Musilova K, Tichy B, Pavlova S, Borsky M, Verner J, Doubek M, Brychtova Y, Trbusek M, Hampl A, Mayer J, Pospisilova S (March 2012). "MicroRNA-650 Expression is Influenced by Immunoglobulin Gene Rearrangement and Affects the Biology of Chronic Lymphocytic Leukemia". Blood. **119** (9): 2110–3. doi:10.1182/blood-2011-11-394874. PMID 22234685.

Bergman Y, Cedar H (October 2004). "A Stepwise Epigenetic Process Controls Immunoglobulin Allelic Exclusion". Nature Reviews. Immunology. **4** (10): 753–61. doi:10.1038/nri1458. PMID 15459667.

Honjo T, Habu S (1985). "Origin of Immune Diversity: Genetic Variation and Selection". Annual Review of Biochemistry. **54** (1): 803–30. doi:10.1146/annurev.bi.54.070185.004103. PMID 3927822.

Or-Guil M, Wittenbrink N, Weiser AA, Schuchhardt J (April 2007). "Recirculation of Germinal Center B Cells: A Multilevel Selection Strategy for Antibody Maturation". Immunological Reviews. **216**: 130–41. doi:10.1111/j.1600-065X.2007.00507.x. PMID 17367339.

Neuberger MS, Ehrenstein MR, Rada C, Sale J, Batista FD, Williams G, Milstein C (March 2000). "Memory in the B-cell Compartment: Antibody Affinity Maturation". Philosophical Transactions of the Royal Society of London. Series B, Biological Sciences. **355** (1395): 357–60. doi:10.1098/rstb.2000.0573. PMC 1692737/. PMID 10794054.

Stavnezer J, Amemiya CT (August 2004). "Evolution of Isotype Switching". Seminars in Immunology. **16** (4): 257–75. doi:10.1016/j.smim.2004.08.005. PMID 15522624.

Durandy A (August 2003). "Activation-induced Cytidine Deaminase: A Dual Role in Class-switch Recombination and Somatic Hypermutation". European Journal of Immunology. **33** (8): 2069–73. doi:10.1002/eji.200324133. PMID 12884279.

Casali P, Zan H (November 2004). "Class Switching and Myc Translocation: How does DNA break?". Nature Immunology. **5** (11): 1101–3. doi:10.1038/ni1104-1101. PMC 4625794/. PMID 15496946.

Lieber MR, Yu K, Raghavan SC (September 2006). "Roles of Nonhomologous DNA End Joining, V(D)J Recombination, and Class Switch Recombination in Chromosomal Translocations". DNA Repair. **5** (9–10): 1234–45. doi:10.1016/j.dnarep.2006.05.013. PMID 16793349.

Shoenfeld Y, Meroni P, Gershwin ME (2007). Autoantibodie. Amsterdam; Boston: Elsevier. ISBN 978-0-444-52763-9.

Spiess C, Zhai Q, Carter PJ (October 2015). "Alternative Molecular Formats and Therapeutic Applications for Bispecific Antibodies". Molecular Immunology. **67** (2 Pt A): 95–106. doi:10.1016/j.molimm.2015.01.003. PMID 25637431.

Farlex dictionary > Polyvalent Citing: The American Heritage Medical Dictionary. 2004

Gunasekaran K, Pentony M, Shen M, Garrett L, Forte C, Woodward A, Ng SB, Born T, Retter M, Manchulenko K, Sweet H, Foltz IN, Wittekind M, Yan W (June 2010). "Enhancing Antibody Fc Heterodimer Formation Through Electrostatic Steering Effects: Applications to Bispecific Molecules and Monovalent IgG". The Journal of Biological Chemistry. **285** (25): 19637–46. doi:10.1074/jbc.M110.117382. PMC 2885242/. PMID 20400508.

Muller KM (1998). "The First Constant Domain (CH1 and CL) of an Antibody used as Heterodimerization Domain for Bispecific Miniantibodies". FEBS Letters. **422** (2): 259–264. doi:10.1016/s0014-5793(98)00021-0.

Gao C, Mao S, Lo CH, Wirsching P, Lerner RA, Janda KD (May 1999). "Making artificial antibodies: a Format for Phage Display of Combinatorial Heterodimeric Arrays". Proceedings of the National Academy of Sciences of the United States of America. **96** (11): 6025–30. doi:10.1073/pnas.96.11.6025. PMC 26829/. PMID 10339535.

"Animated Depictions of how Antibodies are Used in ELISA Assays". Cellular Technology Ltd.—Europe. Archived from the Original on 18 November 2010. Retrieved 8 May 2007.

"Animated Depictions of how Antibodies are Used in ELISPOT Assays". Cellular Technology Ltd.—Europe. Archived from the Original on 18 November 2010. Retrieved 8 May 2007.

Stern P (2006). "Current Possibilities of Turbidimetry and Nephelometry" (PDF). KlinBiochemMetab. 14 (3): 146–151. Archived from the Original (PDF) on 18 November 2010.

Dean L (2005). "Chapter 4: Hemolytic Disease of the Newborn". Blood Groups and Red Cell Antigens. NCBI Bethesda (MD): National Library of Medicine (US),.

Rodriguez EA, Wang Y, Crisp JL, Vera DR, Tsien RY, Ting R (May 2016). "New Dioxaborolane Chemistry Enables [(18)F]-Positron-Emitting, Fluorescent [(18)F]-Multimodality Biomolecule Generation from the Solid Phase". Bioconjugate Chemistry. 27(5): 1390-1399. doi:10.1021/acs.bioconjchem.6b00164. PMC 4916912/. PMID 27064381.

INDEX